PARACHUTE TO BERLIN

PARACHUTE
TO BERLIN

LOWELL BENNETT

Foreword by his son
ALAN BENNETT

CASEMATE
Philadelphia & Oxford

Published in the United States of America and Great Britain in 2023 by
CASEMATE PUBLISHERS
1950 Lawrence Road, Havertown, PA 19083, USA
and
The Old Music Hall, 106–108 Cowley Road, Oxford OX4 1JE, UK

Parachute to Berlin by Lowell Bennett first published by The Vanguard Press, New York, 1945.
Copyright © 2023 Alan Bennett

Paperback Edition: ISBN 978-1-63624-316-0
Digital Edition: ISBN 978-1-63624-317-7

A CIP record for this book is available from the British Library

Printed and bound in the United Kingdom by CPI Group (UK) Ltd, Croydon, CR0 4YY
Typeset in India by DiTech Publishing Services

For a complete list of Casemate titles, please contact:

CASEMATE PUBLISHERS (US)
Telephone (610) 853-9131
Fax (610) 853-9146
Email: casemate@casematepublishers.com
www.casematepublishers.com

CASEMATE PUBLISHERS (UK)
Telephone (0)1226 734350
Email: casemate-uk@casematepublishers.co.uk
www.casematepublishers.co.uk

*Cover images: Berlin, 1945 (Bundesarchiv, B 145 Bild-P054320 / Weinrother, Carl / CC-BY-SA
3.0); Lancaster bomber (Cpl Phil Major ABIPP/MOD).*

Acknowledgements

My heartfelt thanks to Thorsten Perl who put me on track to bring back into circulation my
father's book and who supplied me with countless photos and background information for the
present reprint and the French-language translation which will be coming out simultaneously.

Alan Bennett

Contents

Lowell Bennett.

Foreword

Lowell Bennett, the author of this book, was my father. His first-hand account of what it was like to be under Allied bombs in Nazi Germany is a unique achievement. Many books and articles have been written about experiences in German-occupied parts of Europe during World War II by Resistance fighters, undercover agents and the such. But no news story such as this could possibly have come out directly from inside the Reich.

In February 1943, US war correspondent Robert Perkins Post died when his bomber was shot down over Germany. Thereafter, the US government banned American newsmen from flying with USAAF bombers. On 3 December of the same year Lowell, then aged 23, flew with an RAF Avro-Lancaster, with a 20-year-old Scot as chief pilot and a six-man crew of young men of roughly the same age. The raid was compliant with RAF Marshal Arthur Harris' policy of total bombing of Germany every night that weather permitted.

This was by no means Lowell's first experience of war. In October 1942 International News Service had sent him on assignment to North Africa to cover the Allied battle of Tunisia. This he reported in a book published by the New York Vanguard Press in May 1943, *Assignment to Nowhere*.

Lowell was born in 1920 in Kansas City, Missouri. He left home and college in 1939 to seek adventure, picked potatoes in Missouri, cotton in Texas and fruit in California, traveled in or on top of empty box-cars, worked for a while as a ranch-hand in Wyoming, became a seaman and went to Panama and Australia on tankers. He worked as a waiter in New South Wales and a sheep herder in Queensland.

When war broke out in Europe, Lowell tried to join the Kermit Roosevelt International Brigade for Finland, but the Russo-Finnish war was over before he got there. He tried unsuccessfully to enlist in the Foreign Legion, was turned down because of his US citizenship but was accepted in the American Volunteer Ambulance Corps. After the armistice in 1940, he was able to go to London where he worked as an ambulance driver in de Gaulle's Free French Army and where he met my Scots mother, Enid Elizabeth Walker, then aged 20.

★★★

The Dunkirk evacuation in 1940 highlighted the numerical deficiencies of the RAF. When the Luftwaffe bombed Rotterdam in May, the RAF began daylight raids against Nazi Germany, which retaliated in July with bombing various British towns, then escalated to the Blitz terror bombing on major UK cities in September. Over a period of nine months, known as the Battle of Britain, an estimated 23,000 British civilians died—including 1,200 civilians in Coventry—and 32,000 were wounded by German bombs.

At the start of the RAF war against Germany, Bomber Command pilots were specifically instructed to avoid attacking civilian targets. Daylight bombing proved such a high risk to flying personnel it was abandoned in favor of night raids. This resulted in a much higher ratio of civilian deaths and injuries, euphemistically known today as "collateral casualties."

Over the next three years Britain's air fleet made huge technological gains, enabling the Avro-Lancaster bombers to fly over greater distances, carrying up to 5 tons of bombs on each plane.

During the war the RAF would drop close to a million tons of bombs over Germany. The USAAF, which actively engaged in 1942, dropped a further 623,000 tons.

Over the duration of the war the RAF lost 57,000 aircrew killed in combat. Most were young men with university degrees, as required for the highly sophisticated technical skills required for flying the planes.

According to the West German government in October 1956 there were 635,000 civilian deaths during the air war in Germany and the annexed territories, 500,000 killed by strategic bombing and 135,000 from air raids in the 1945 flight and evacuations on the Eastern Front.

Allied air raids over France killed 60,000 civilians, including an attack with incendiary bombs by 347 RAF bombers on the French coastal city of Royan on January 4 and 5, 1945, that killed over 400 civilians and 47 Germans with no destruction of military facilities.

In February 1942, RAF Marshal Sir Arthur Harris was appointed Commander in Chief of Bomber Command. Known at the time as "Bomber Harris," he favored the controversial policy of "area bombing" over "precision targeting," which resulted in a far higher number of civilian casualties, precisely what my father denounces in his book. Arthur Harris received Churchill's support, but he obtained no official recognition on retirement in 1946, to the anger of many RAF personnel who had fought under his orders and who felt betrayed.

The controversy has not abated today. One view argues that blanket bombing of Germany hit public morale and support for the Reich and slowed down essential industrial production whilst diverting manpower for clean-up purposes that could otherwise have been used in combat. Another opinion is that the Allied strategic bombing helped maintain pressure on the Reich in the West with the powerful Soviet resistance in the East. This view is supported by the statement by Albert Speer, Hitler's Minister of Armaments and War Production, that Allied bombs had caused severe damage to the German economy.

In this book my father strongly disputes both of these claims, on the basis of his first-hand experience. Distinguished English historian Sir Max Hastings was later to level the same accusations against the Harris policy in his 1979 book *Bomber Command*.

★★★

Lowell's disappearance on 3 December 1943 was widely reported in the US press, including the *New York Times*, the *Washington Post*, *Stars and Stripes*, the *American Legion Magazine*, the *Milwaukee Sentinel*, the *New York Daily Mirror*, the *New York Herald Tribune*, and unexpectedly the *Bombay Chronicle*.

He had gained a degree of peer recognition with his account of the Tunisian campaign, and his romantic courtship of my young Scots mother and her unshakeable faith in his return had touched the heart of the public, as did the announcement that he was still alive and had managed to sneak out a preliminary report to US news media.

Likewise, the news of Lowell's return to the US to join the family, including his second-born David, was reported in the American news media. When Lowell flew to Berlin I was two and brother David as yet unborn.

The 1945 publication of *Parachute to Berlin* by Vanguard Press in New York was largely well received by media reviewers such as *Foreign Affairs,* and the *Infantry Journal*, who praised the vividness of his narrative and his critical scrutiny of official policies of strategic bombing.

Two important individuals in the book, Ian Bolton, the captain of the Lancaster bomber, and the German officer Josef Borner (a pseudonym used by my father to protect his identity), who took Lowell on the German tour, kept in touch with my father after the war. Ian Bolton's daughter Fiona tells me her father suffered from PTSD, as did so many of the young men who were fortunate enough to come back alive after those terrible years. The three men remained friends until the end of their lives.

THE OFFICE OF CENSORSHIP
WASHINGTON 25

May 25, 1944.

Mr. Ernest O. Hauser,
Hotel Irving,
26 Gramercy Park,
East 20th Street,
New York, N. Y.

Dear Mr. Hauser:

Our Press Division has reviewed the attached manuscript of an article about Lowell Bennett and we find no reason to object to any part of it. It is most interesting and I feel sure will tell the enemy nothing he does not already know.

Thank you for your thoughtfulness.

Sincerely yours,

Byron Price,
Director.

Ian Bolton with his crewmates.

Ian Bolton, chief pilot of the Lancaster bomber.

The Bennett family were only briefly reunited after Lowell's release—the caption to this newspaper photograph, dating from July 1945, explains that Lowell was seeing his wife and two young sons safely aboard a ship traveling from Paris to New York.

David, Lowell, and Alan Bennett.

After the war, Lowell covered the Nuremberg trials as a journalist, then joined the US State Department as a Foreign Service Officer. He served as a diplomat in seven posts, including Germany, France, the United States, Iran, Pakistan, India and Switzerland.

In 1951 he wrote *Berlin Bastion*, a first-hand account of the Soviet Blockade of Berlin in 1948–49, when Soviet forces blockaded rail, road, and water access to Allied-controlled areas of Berlin. The Western Allies responded with a massive airlift to come to West Berlin's aid.

He died in 1997 in his country home in France, where he had chosen to live the rest of his life after retirement in 1973.

Alan Bennett, August 2022

To Elizabeth, my wife,
who waited and had faith

CHAPTER I

Assignment Over Germany

It began in much the same way as had any other wartime assignment. This time it was to be a ride in a British bomber to watch Berlin burn during one of the big night attacks. In the mechanics of arranging the trip there was little to differentiate it from any one of a score of other similar stories. But this time there was one important personal difference: a strong, persistent premonition that it would be a one-way trip.

Giant night attacks against the German capital had been in progress almost nightly for the past fortnight. Air Chief Marshal, Sir Arthur Harris, the RAF's Bomber Commander, planned to eradicate and obliterate the city as completely as his bombers had already destroyed Hamburg, Germany's first port.

Already, apart from earlier, lighter raids during the first three years of the war, some ten thousand tons of explosive and incendiary hell had avalanched down on Berlin. Intelligence and neutral press reports agreed that the devastation was widespread. As much as a quarter of the city was gone.

This would not be the last raid on the city; many more would be necessary to complete the destruction deemed vital to an Allied victory in Europe. But this time four correspondents would fly with the bombers to witness the execution and effect of one such attack.

Edward Murrow, who had broadcast the blitz against London three years earlier, was to represent the American broadcasting companies. He would fly with the commander of one Lancaster squadron. Walter King and Norman Stockton, both veteran Australian war correspondents, would fly with the commanders of two RAF heavy-bomber squadrons. And I was to fly in a Lancaster of a fourth squadron, to represent the American press.

On a late November afternoon, 1943, we four reporters were summoned to the British Air Ministry in London and offered, in the words of a Wing Commander, "an opportunity to see a big raid against Berlin in fairly clear weather." "If you accept," he cautioned in tones overlaid with solemnity, "you'll have to accept the risk which, at the moment, is the highest for any target in Germany. You'll have to take the chance of being shot down and having no story at all. On the other hand, in a Berlin blitz, you'll have a good big story if you do come back.

"The Germans know we are out to destroy their capital," he added with a furtive, confidential air. "And we know they know it. But the old man [Sir Arthur Harris] is determined to finish the job. So there you are—do you want to go?"

In addition to the two Australians and two Americans, there was a fifth man who had requested the mission. He was a captain in the Free Norwegian Army, a big man of about forty, with florid, Scandinavian features which tightened and hardened suddenly as he said, "I go to Berlin, too." Something in the way he said it showed his choice was for a very personal reason: he wanted to see the Germans hurt. Officially, he would represent the Free Norwegian Press in Britain, but it was obvious that his personal reason far outweighed the professional one.

The Wing Commander noted our names and next of kin, then announced that we would take a train the next day to the various air bases from which we would fly. We walked out of the closely guarded Air Ministry to return briefly to the routine of London reporting. With me went that irresistible premonition: it was going to be a one-way ride.

Psychologists have decried premonitions as primitive and unreasonable. Perhaps they are. But this one was so persistent and sufficiently strong that I wrote a letter to my wife, opening: "When you receive this, I shall be walking home through Germany. ... Please do not be perturbed by the report, 'missing in action.' ..." to be mailed to New Jersey when I should not return from the raid.

The train ride north from London onto the flat, village-studded Midlands of England was as dull and uneventful as had been many such rides to air bases to write stories about the fliers and their work. I might study the faces of fellow passengers, when they were not studying mine, or the "U.S. War Correspondent" patch on my uniform sleeve.

One could stare at the faded, peacetime advertisements still on the carriage walls, somehow a melancholy reminder that there was, after all, something to life other than war. Or one might look out of the train window into a dirty November fog, and be reminded by it of the drabness of war and the obscurity of its issues.

Lincoln station was warlike too, with the seemingly aimless rush of uniformed travelers along its bleak platforms. But it was a brief picture, for the RAF awaited us, and all the reporters were mysteriously bundled off in a car to the base where we would await the launching of the attack we would accompany.

And thus began a six-day wait, a delay until Bomber Command ordered another mammoth night raid against Berlin. The weather for the last attack had not been good. Six hundred Lancasters and Halifaxes, after a seven-hour, danger-fraught offensive against the German capital, had returned to find their home bases blanketed with an impenetrable fog.

Fortunately, other airfields in the northeast of Britain had been clear, so the planes were able to land. But their fuel was low, the men were tired, and the emergency landing fields new to them. Losses that night in landing had exceeded those in the actual attack.

Such disasters had to be controlled, such losses kept to a minimum. Harris seemed anxious to prove to the doubters that he could force Germany's surrender with a series of such slashing attacks against its capital. He wanted his bomber fleet to operate as frequently and in as great force as possible. But even with the best equipment and the best spirit in the world, the men could not fly when the weather was too strongly against them. So this time the RAF waited.

Twice, on the twenty-ninth and thirtieth of November, heavy night attacks were planned, then "scrubbed" because of the weather. The first would have been directed against Munich, birthplace of Nazism, and a target notable chiefly at that time for its almost complete lack of industrial war objectives. At the briefing for that raid it was obvious that the city was being attacked almost exclusively for morale purposes. And, since the aim of night bombing was as much to demoralize populations as to hamper industrial production, the fact that the target was a sizeable city and a stronghold of the Nazi Party was considered justification for the attack.

The second mission was prepared for the city of Leipzig, the book publishing center of Europe, and would have involved a feint by nearly five hundred bombers to within fifteen miles of Berlin, before they swung south to deluge their cargoes on sleeping Leipzig.

One aspect of both attacks was that they were intended to throw off the German Night Fighter defences, to encourage the Luftwaffe to believe the onslaught against their capital had ended temporarily. With the diversion attacks it was hoped to force the enemy to disperse his night-fighter squadrons away from the Berlin area where they had been concentrated. Thus, theoretically, the next attack against the capital might be proportionally lighter in cost.

But neither of the diversion raids was carried out. Last-minute warning of bad weather ahead forced their cancellation.

The air crews had been briefed, the planes fueled and bombed up. The tension in the airfield messes and lounges had been there, and the expectancy and the waiting. But the attacks had been "scrubbed."

The RAF, like its brother-force, the Eighth American Air Force in Britain, had—over a period of long months of battle and losses—developed a philosophy perhaps unique to fighting men whose life expectancy is reckoned not in years but in weeks. The constant turnover of new crews to replace battle casualties, the ever present uncertainty, the youthful fatalism—these brought on a cordiality and a comradeship one might ascribe to condemned men living together, and accepting a close intimacy before their ultimate and collective end.

Especially in the RAF, the time had long since passed when much conversation was devoted to discussions of death which clutched, in its myriad and awful forms, at these fresh-faced fliers of Britain. To the outsider, their attitude seemed at first one of adolescent indifference to a subject which they could not fully understand. But it was not that.

Death had become a routine corollary to their business; and they ignored it as they ignored the deadliness of their bomber cargoes.

But when a major night attack was being prepared, the tension rose steadily. It was felt in the air crews' lounge; you noted that the bar ("beer alley" they called it) was deserted and that very few of the men were smoking. Each wanted to ensure that he would be in the best possible condition for the coming night's work.

There was little morbidness or despondency. That phase had ended long ago. But letters were being written home and several boys slumped in easy chairs, staring moodily out of the windows, thinking about the coming mission, wondering and conjecturing what their personal experience would be this time.

Then, when the attack was canceled, it was as the snapping of a taut band. Everyone had been keyed up, had spent hours thinking about the job, had prepared himself for it—and now it was canceled. Now there was no attempt to curtain emotions with solitude or letter writing, and the boys bought beer and cursed the weatherman for not having known sooner.

For a reporter, an amateur at the profession of aerial bombing, the tension and the expectancy were naturally at a higher pitch. Six days elapsed before the Berlin attack was carried out, and there was little to do during that time. I listened to the endless tales of furlough orgies, of "odd types," who had been and gone in the squadron, of strange incidents in Germany's disputed sky—they had told all the stories before but the introduction as "reporter" invited repeat performances and I learned, in fragments, the history and deeds of Number Fifty Squadron of the Royal Air Force.

The pilot who was to ferry me to Berlin was Flight Lieutenant Ian D. Bolton, a twenty-year-old Scotsman, veteran of twenty-nine missions over Europe. His age was incongruous with his skill, for he commanded one third of the Lancaster squadron of twenty-four of Britain's heaviest bombers. His crew, with the exception of one Scots-Canadian who was the "mid-upper gunner," all hailed from Scotland.

If they resented the fact that they would carry an operationally useless load on their next mission to Berlin, they showed it not at all. The crew had been together for nearly an entire "tour" (thirty combat flights) of missions and they were rated the best on the airfield. But Bolton, an unusually matured man for his years, threw another light on the business of being a good airman over Germany at this stage of the war.

"It's really just a matter of luck," he explained, "and so far we have been lucky. These Lancasters are the best the RAF has; they'll take a lot of punishment. Some pilots have actually lost two engines [out of four] over the target and gotten home all right.

"You just have to calculate that the Germans are going to shoot down from five to ten per cent of every bomber force we send against Berlin. They throw flak up all over the sky. They can usually get a couple of hundred night fighters up, cooperating with as many searchlights. If they get you—well, you're unlucky; you're one of the five to ten per cent. If you get through, bomb, and get back home all right—well, then you're one of the ninety to ninety-five per cent."

Word was circulated amazingly quickly the day an attack was planned. Even the identity of the target became common knowledge on the airfield many hours before take-off. The ground crews who fueled and bombed up the planes, for example, guess by the number of gallons of gas and the weight of bombs they stored in the aircraft just about where it would be going that night.

They knew that an attack launched against the industrial Ruhr would mean some thirteen thousand pounds of bombs and about fifteen hundred gallons of fuel. And they knew that an attack against Berlin would require about ten thousand pounds of bombs and over eighteen hundred gallons of fuel. The more distant the target, obviously, the lighter the bomb load and the greater the fuel load. And, from long experience at preparing raids against most of Germany's big cities, guesswork for the ground crewmen had become an almost precise science.

Briefing for the Berlin attack on December 2, 1943—the gathering together of the airmen a few hours before departure for instructions—was at 1330 hours, which indicated an early start. Aircraft captains collected in what resembled a small schoolroom in the "operations building" on the edge of the airfield.

They sat at desks—ten of them, for the squadron was contributing ten Lancasters that night—with their charts and note-books spread out before them. At the head of the room, which made it resemble even more a geography class at school, there was a large map of England and Northwest Europe and a black-board, chalked sharply with pertinent data on the coming mission.

First to speak was the civilian weatherman, a lean, thin-jowled Northcountryman who seemed, if anything, slightly bored with the whole business and more than a little dubious of the value of his information. He announced in a stingy, rasping voice that the temperature would be between thirty-three and fifty-nine degrees below zero Fahrenheit at twenty thousand feet over the target. He said there would be two weather "fronts" that would have to be crossed, one before leaving the English coast and the second over Germany.

But he could not be sure what the weather would be like over Berlin, for it was changing rapidly. It might be reasonably cloudy and so reasonably safe. Or it might be completely clear, which would help the accuracy of the bombing but would also help the capital's defenses. We should have to take "potluck" with the weather, he concluded, scooping up his share of the charts and leaving the room.

Next to speak was the Squadron Commander, Robert MacFarlane, a twenty-nine-year-old Scot and veteran of more than sixty raids against Germany. His job was to detail the raid's mechanics.

Six hundred and sixty-one aircraft would participate, all four-engined Lancasters and Halifaxes, plus a number of Mosquitoes in the Path Finder Force (which led the attack and dropped "target indicators" for the oncoming armada). Another small force of Mosquitoes would launch a "spoof attack" southeast of Berlin to draw off some of the defenses.

Total bomb load would be nearly twenty-five hundred tons, the heaviest raid of the war against Berlin. MacFarlane, with the clarity and precision of a good business executive, emphasized that the attack would be against new areas of the German capital, areas so far almost untouched by air bombardment.

He warned that the Germans were known to be concentrating their night fighters and mobile anti-aircraft weapons around Berlin and that it would be no easy job to fight through, bomb, and fight back home again.

The route, as he traced it, led out over the North Sea, crossing the European coast over Holland, and thence swinging directly toward Berlin, along an often-used route via Hanover. After bombing, the route home led northeast, north, then a straight line back to the base.

"This is the most important target of the war, chaps," he concluded. "Go in there and bomb hell out of them. Make everything count—then bring yourselves and your planes home again safely. Keep your eyes open for fighters. Watch for those flares they drop to light up your route. Good luck to you all."

Then followed the mass briefing, the captain of each plane sitting at a table with his crew of six aides, explaining in detail to them what he had learned at the master briefing. Each crewman had his special interest: the navigator, the route; the bomb aimer, the color and type of target indicator; the gunners listened closely to the information about night-fighter defenses.

At 1500 hours came the special pre-mission meal, including those wartime rarities (for England): a real egg, accompanied by real bacon, and fresh milk. Although RAF flying personnel normally did not fare much better than their families in civilian life, before each mission they were provided with a special meal which, in a small way, compensated for the forthcoming tension and danger of the trip.

To this reporter, most of whose meals had been of the civilian variety in London, the egg was a real treat. But, with the meal and thoughts of the mission to come, came a return of the hunch: it was going to be a one-way trip. So I ate hastily and returned to the lounge to type a story for the next morning's newspapers: "This is being written in case I don't return to make a more complete report of tonight's RAF attack against Berlin. It is based on information obtained at our preflight briefing. ..."

We were to fly in the third wave to bomb the target at 2010 hours. Two waves of Halifaxes were to bomb before us and two waves of Lancasters were to follow. The entire attack was intended to be packed into twelve minutes—the most concentrated heavy-scale air raid of the entire war.

Each wave (including over one hundred bombers) was allotted exactly four minutes in which to complete the bombing and get clear of the target. And it was up to the pilot and navigator of each individual bomber to ensure that the bombing schedule was met.

A few minutes after 1530 hours trucks picked up the air crews and took them to the dispersal areas where the giant, black Avro Lancasters were parked. Around each plane bustled a three- or four-man ground crew making final inspections.

We stopped by the operations office where parachutes were procured, the kind that snapped onto two hooks on a chest harness. An inflatable life preserver ("Mae West" to the air force because of its breastwork) was added. Next, each flier was issued an "escape kit," a small waterproof parcel containing European currency, emergency concentrated food tablets, maps, compass, steel file, and other items possibly useful in the event of a forced landing inside Europe.

I also carried an American Army musette bag, in which were a carton of cigarettes, a notebook and pencils, a hundred rounds of .45-caliber ammunition for the gun I had in a shoulder holster, heavy winter underwear, and toilet articles. The premonition that I would not *fly* back from Berlin had been strong enough that I wanted to ensure I had supplies to help ease the anticipated walk home.

Admittedly, the armament contravened unwritten international rules controlling Allied war correspondents, for we were not authorized to carry arms. But our German counterpart was considered by his government to be first a combatant, and only second a reporter. So I felt some justification, and, most important, was determined to try at least to get back home with the story.

Loaded down with parachute, life belt, musette bag, and heavy, wool-lined trench coat, I struggled back out to the truck. An RAF ground-crew officer stopped me.

"You'll probably be cold wearing those light shoes. Why not borrow my flying boots?" he suggested. The idea was a good one; the flying boots seemed warm and comfortable. And the stories of frostbitten airmen, coupled with the weatherman's prediction of a forty below zero temperature, made the offer easily acceptable.

"Just one thing, though," he added as I pulled on the foot-wear. "Of course you'll come back all right. But, if you don't mind, would you sign for the boots in case anything happens to them—then I can draw another pair." The premonition came back sharply as I signed a chit.

The heavily dressed and harnessed crewmen climbed into the truck and a two-minute drive around the concrete perimeter track brought us to the bomber, squatting enormously on the parking strip. The bombs and fuel were safely stored and everything was ready.

With the bomb aimer, I inspected the bomb bay, a gaping twenty-foot by six-foot opening in the plane's belly, in which had been packed more than five tons of explosives and incendiaries.

The main bomb ("cookie" it was called in RAF understatement, and "blockbuster" by the Germans who knew its effect) was four thousand pounds of high explosive concentrated in a metal canister that resembled a steam boiler, eight feet by three feet in diameter. Curiously, the can which enclosed the tight-packed explosive was slightly rusty, but, imagining the deadliness of its contents, that made no difference.

Around it were tightly packed nearly a thousand four- and thirty-pound incendiary bombs. RAF Bomber Command, through the hard test of three years' experience, had discovered the best method of destroying a city was to burn it down, not to knock it down. The Germans themselves had helped prove that during their great Christmas attack against the City of London in 1940, when, in a single raid, they wrought more damage and destruction through fire than bad any tan previous attacks with demolition bombs.

Hamburg had been the first real test of the fire policy for the RAF. The city had been divided into four quarters and each night one quarter had been systematically gutted by a cataclysm of fire bombs. Now Berlin—and eventually every major city in Germany—was to be "Hamburged."

We were carrying to Berlin, then, a two-ton explosive bomb and slightly more than three tons of incendiaries. The bomb aimer, a nineteen-year-old, rosy-cheeked, enthusiastic youngster, explained that the bombs were all released by a master switch which he operated in the forward compartment.

"They don't all go down at once", he said. "There is a timing device—an intervalometer—which releases them in the correct order. The cookie goes down first to blow the roofs off, then the incendiaries go down to burn up the houses. Or, the incendiaries go down first to start the fires, then the cookie goes down to spread them about."

We followed one another into the bomber, climbing up a short ladder and entering a hatchway in the side. The gunners crawled to their turrets, one in the plane's tail turret (where he operated four 30 machine guns) and the other into an elevated turret above the plane's center (where he handled two 30 machine-guns). The radioman squeezed into his narrow compartment; the bomb aimer edged forward and down into the plane's nose. The pilot lifted himself into his seat and the engineer went to work immediately on the formidable array of instruments and machinery which mazed the bomber's inside.

Bolton, the pilot, ranked as captain; the others were all flight sergeants. One gunner was aged twenty-two, and he was the oldest of the crew. This team of seven airmen, every one of whom might still have been in school had there been no war, was preparing to ferry more than five tons of destruction to the capital of Nazi Germany. They were to fly a bomber which had cost hundreds of thousands of dollars and weeks of highly skilled labor to construct. In their youthful hands had been placed an instrument of death unimaginable in its capacity a few years previous.

For twenty minutes before take-off, the four engines were warmed, each idling, with a full-toned, reassuring rumble. The reaction of each instrument was tested. Then the bomb bay doors were closed, as the pilot threw a switch beside his seat, and we were ready to go.

At exactly 1630 hours the ground brakes were released, the chocks jerked away by the ground mechanics. We moved slowly out from the parking strip onto the perimeter track which led to the main runway.

Along the track, from half-hidden dispersal areas all over the airfield, other Lancasters trundled slowly out in single file toward the end of the broad runway.

"Take-off is always the worst moment for the pilot," Bolton had explained. "You think of all those bombs crammed in the belly and what an awful mess it would make if you crashed or turned over instead of lifting off the runway. It's something of a worry. Once you're in the air, you feel much safer."

Our bomber was eighth in line; seven Lancasters wheeled into position, their engines opened to full throttle, and began rolling down the long concrete strip, increasing speed until, almost imperceptibly, they were off the runway and flying.

Finally it was our turn. At the side of the strip stood some fifty ground crewmen who watched and waved to us. With them was the Squadron Commander, the Airfield Commander and Air Vice Marshal Cochrane, who commanded an entire section of the RAF Bomber Force. They waved and made the "V" sign. Then came the signal from the control tower, and Bolton throttled the engines to a higher-pitched roar, released the brakes, and the plane began to roll forward.

Slowly at first, then gathering speed, faster, faster, faster, the ground flooding past on each side at nearly a hundred miles an hour, suddenly a slight lift then a bump as we settled back, then another lift—we were airborne rushing from the earth like some broad-winged bird up toward a dying winter sun.

We were aloft, rising into the cathedral of the sky, Berlin-bound for the strangest and most terrible form of battle man had yet devised. We were to witness and participate in the destruction of a city from front-line seats, four miles above it.

I watched the ground recede for a moment as we climbed, then twisted around and looked back down on the airfield. "Take a good look, you won't be back for many months," I recall thinking to myself. The premonition was still there, annoying and impertinent, but there as a subtle, mocking reminder.

CHAPTER 2

Parachute to Berlin

The Midlands of England, jigsawed with farms and occasional villages whose chimneys vented swirling jets of dark smoke, spread out before us as we wheeled and climbed for altitude. Roads and streams wandered ribbon-like across the flat-chested earth below. Above was a darkening void of the unknown; below, the familiar, friendly bosom of man's home before he sprouted metal wings to lift him into that unknown.

Everywhere around us were Lancasters, huge black birds, majestic and heavy-laden, climbing steadily. The hand on our altimeter indicated five hundred feet, a thousand feet, then recorded a gradual increase as we gained height during the next half hour.

As we climbed, our horizon lowered and a red sun seemed to rise with us. Twilight dimmed and shadowed the earth below. Hundreds of bombers were rising about us, but we could now see only a few, for a crepuscular haze and a cloud-brushed winter sky deceased visibility quickly. The engines chanted a solemn, steady quartet of harnessed mechanical might, two bulky cowlings protruding from each sleek wing. The crew members settled to their work.

England stretched out beneath us, a soft-toned panorama of nature, quilted with the changes wrought by men. Shadowy, miniature villages huddled together, thin dark lines of railroads and highways streaked across the earth, cement-splashed patches that were airfields: roost of the armada rising about us.

Our route led eastward, above the North Sea, crossing the English coast somewhere above East Anglia, then swinging south-ward toward Holland.

A sharp lookout had to be maintained for the scores of planes above, below, and on all sides of us. Although we could see aircraft only when they were within two or three hundred feet of us, for it was now quite dark and clouds were thickening into banks of rain-bloated fog, we knew there were over six hundred bombers converging into one mighty stream—all aimed the same way and all at about the same altitude.

We reached twenty thousand feet altitude before crossing the Continental coast. We would bomb from a slightly greater height, but our present altitude was sufficient to keep us above the range of light and medium flak we should encounter before the target.

The first enemy reaction was met just off the Dutch coast after two hours of eventless flying. Ahead, flak spattered and flecked the now dark sky, scintillant red and rose lights bursting into evanescent brilliance far ahead. They seemed quite impotent, impersonal—nothing to be feared. Clusters of flashes sparkled, exploding into momentary life but they were always ahead or well off to the side. Bolton announced that they came from flak ships off the coast or from coastal batteries with which the Germans sought to make new crews nervous and unsure.

We climbed to twenty-one thousand five hundred feet, through and above a heavy, wet "front" of cloud. It was not the safest operation, flying through thick cloud banks, for the stream of planes constantly narrowed as the hundreds of bombers funneled into the cubic road to Berlin.

Driving rain splashed and streaked the windshield, reducing visibility still further. An urgent tinkling on some electrical instrument warned us whenever we approached too near another machine, and the pilot swerved slightly to leave the other plane's orbit. Occasionally we were caught in the "propwash" of a bomber immediately ahead, and our Lancaster lurched and heaved, but each time Bolton's firm hand brought us back onto even keel.

Our air speed remained constant at about one hundred and sixty miles per hour (neatly two hundred and thirty m.p.h. ground speed, considering a tail wind and instrument correction), and the navigator called brief alterations in direction every few minutes over the intercommunication system. The flight engineer made occasional changes in the fuel mixture and frequent inspections of the instrument panels, but there was little that required mechanical attention.

We were in dangerous airs now, crowded with our companion bombers and enemy night fighters, and the lookout was intensified. From my position just behind the engineer and just forward of the navigator, I was able to see out both sides of the pilot's compartment, forward through the bomb aimer's chamber and back into the tail of the plane. A phosphorescent glow from the instrument panel and the fiery exhaust from each engine was the only light.

But there was no excitement—only the steady, sonorous pounding of four mighty engines drawing us through the night. We might have been alone, for no other plane was visible. I ate some of the concentrated food provided for a "mission meal," lifting my oxygen mask briefly, took occasional pictures of the moonlight gleaming all too brilliantly on our wings, watched the pilot silently, self-assuredly gripping the truck-sized wheel. There was nothing to this vaunted bombing of Germany! Where was the aerial hell that supposedly accompanied each raid? Where were the bombers going down in flames, the columns and walls of flak the airmen described? It was peaceful, almost dull. Premonitions were assuredly nonsense.

Suddenly, ahead in the star-broken darkness, dashes sputtered indistinctly and spasmodically. We were nearing our target. Off to both sides, flak clawed at the sky, tearing and puncturing it with sharp, explosive bursts.

The weather was far too good; as the weatherman had warned, It was very light. A third of the moon reflected brightly off our wings, and all the stars in creation had come out to witness the coming battle and to roof the arena over Berlin.

It was strange how quickly the situation had changed from monotony to swift action. For three and a half hours, we had been cleaving our way toward the target almost without incident. There had been little flak and no fighter interference as far as our bomber was concerned. Three and a half hours of what would have been, for me, sheer boredom, except that it had the novelty of being a first time, and that compensated for the sleep-inviting pulsation of the four roaring engines.

Bolton had been almost apologetic for the quietness of the missions so far. "That's nothing. … Wait until we get to the Big City," he had said when I asked about the anti-aircraft over the Dutch coast.

When we passed above and to the north of Hanover, where hundreds of searchlights were aimed straight up, motionless, illuminating the thick cloud layer beneath us into a solid white blanket, he had explained; "That's so we are silhouetted against the light, and the night fighters above can see us. ..." Neither explanation had been particularly frightening; both had offered promise of exciting action to come.

And now, with a sense-shocking abruptness, we were beginning to have all the excitement that could be desired. As we approached the Big City, the flak became sharper, clearer, and much more personal. It burst thickly around us, sometimes only a few hundred feet distant, above and below. In what seemed a very few minutes we were approaching the edge of the city.

Here, from the outer ring of defenses, heavy blots of fight checkered crimson in the sky, scores of ghostly searchlights swept and fingered across the backdrop of night, and fighter flares hung everywhere—a surrealist display, lighting the world to an unnatural day.

Not far ahead, the Path Finders had already arrived and dropped the target indicator, a chandelier-like cluster of red and green flares. Beneath and all around it chains of dull red tracer, eighty-eight millimeter flak, climbed and arched upward as the Germans sought to shoot down our aerial target.

That was our bombing target—bombs aimed at it would tumble down in a terrible avalanche on a residential section of south-east Berlin—and it hung beacon-like, centered in an inferno of flashing flames and explosions. Each moment brought us nearer it and each moment the tension increased. The flak engulfed our horizon, competing, it seemed, with the stars above in number and with a gargantuan Fourth of July celebration in technicolored brilliance.

Explosions from light guns flecked and ruptured the sky below us; heavier bursts rent the air around us. But there was no noise above the steady, vibrant pounding of the engines. Somehow it was reminiscent of the silent film, when the wildest action might have been in progress, but there was no accompanying noise.

I was not frightened; I was far too impressed for any other emotion to register. The display ahead, and now behind and on both sides—for we were coming in over the city—was spectacular without comparison with any previous experience. Eight hundred flak guns and over two hundred searchlights were concentrated in the Berlin area, we had been told at the briefing.

But here it seemed as if every weapon in creation had joined in that awesome and fantastic jubilee of light and color. Ahead, it seemed now almost a solid wall of explosions, and the target indicator, dropping slowly, was framed by a curtain of hundreds of flashing explosions.

Below, fires had already been started—blood-red patches splashing and heaving in a Dantean hell on earth. I counted five areas that were glowing and trembling, cadmium crimson enshrouded by billowing masses of flame-lit smoke. Elsewhere, other fires—which the Germans had set to bait the bombers away from the city—shone, isolated and obviously false.

Suddenly, not far ahead, a bomber was directly hit. A tremendous explosion, though inaudible to us, rocked the sky. Flaming fragments tumbled and drifted downward like crimsoned autumn leaves, all that remained of a bomber and its seven-man crew. It seemed certain their bomb load had been exploded by a direct hit.

Almost immediately there was another explosion and a searing gash of light. Another bomber had been hit, and it swirled earthward like an immense firebrand. We watched it strike the ground with a yawning, gushing explosion and its fiery incendiaries spew out about it in a solid ring.

This was now a tremendous battle. Night-fighter flares hung everywhere as if suspended, and—with the searchlights and flak—lit the sky into a fantastic arena for twentieth-century struggle. The moon still shone with a shameful brilliance, and the stars looked down on the greater light below.

Veritable lanes of phosphor-white flares, joining almost like the skeet lights of crossroads, hung everywhere. The night-fighter squadrons were ensuring plenty of light for their deadly work.

"Fighter climbing ahead on starboard," one of our gunners called. We watched the green navigation lights of an enemy plane, swinging slowly upward in our direction.

Bolton twisted our plane in violent evasive action, first one way then another, corkscrewing to reduce the chance of successful enemy attack. But trouble was tracking us down from the rear. The gunners had just signaled two more night fighters, closing in from astern, and the metallic stutter of our own machine guns rattled over the intercom. Those fresh-faced kids had gone to work; we were almost to the target, and it was their job to keep the fighters away until we bombed.

But suddenly jets and bursts of light flashed past us. We were on the "bomb run;" the bomb bay doors would be opened in a moment and out five tons of death would go down into Berlin. A fighter had closed on us. Bolton pushed the wheel forward and we turned into a twisting dive to avoid the tracer-guided cannon shells from a night fighter.

Flak walls were dead ahead; the fighter was coming in fast from astern. I held on tightly to avoid being thrown to the roof as we dived.

Bolton was a magnificent flier, throwing the heavy-laden Lancaster around like a toy to shake off the fighters. Every crew member was peering out into the melee of light and action that was the night, following the fighters and firing short, clattering bursts. Curt, clear warnings from gunners to Pilot told of flak concentrations and two other fighters which seemed to be coming in nearer and nearer.

Corkscrewing and diving had shaken off the first interceptor. But the two new fighters were approaching, one diving from the rear, the other climbing from the side. We were trapped.

Disaster struck with a terrifying abruptness.

Our world burst into an inferno of flame. The plane shuddered, then heaved and rocked violently. A long burst of cannon fire had slashed into our right wing and both engines had exploded into a furious fire.

We could see the metal twisting, melting, and tearing away from the wing with the intensity of the heat. Flaming strips of fabric flashed past. A solid panel of fire blocked vision on our right side. Despite all the preflight Premonition, the realization that we were lost—on fire and going down over Berlin, six hundred miles inside Germany—was panic-striking.

But the pilot's controlled, even voice, "Feather [cut off] star-board engines," brought momentary sanity. The engineer leaned forward, switching off both right-wing engines to put out the fires. It might still be possible to get home on the two left-wing engines. But it proved hopeless.

The intercom still echoed the chatter of our machine guns. Our crew still fought. The pilot reached down to the emergency bomb jettison handle. It had been smashed. "Unable to jettison," he called.

A roar drowned even the noise of our two remaining engines and of the fire. One of the fighters was near to us, closing for the kill, his target a flaming beacon. Cannon fire smashed into the bomb aimer's compartment, missing his head by inches, disintegrating his instrument panel.

The fire had spread to the wing fuel tanks and flames enveloped us, a whitish red sheet which swamped and covered the entire right side of the plane. Its heat penetrated the cabin in a wave of furnace-hot breath. Searchlights swung into us and coned the stricken bomber with blinding brilliance.

In frenzied urgency I reached down, snatched up my parachute, and buckled it to the chest hooks without awaiting instructions. I knew without being an airman that this Lancaster would never carry us home. The camera, with which I had been photographing the flak and the wing fire, I jammed hastily into a pocket.

"Okay, boys, bail out. Sorry," came Bolton's amazingly unhurried words over the intercom. The other men struggled to fasten their parachutes, while he fought to keep the plane level. It was surging and bucking like a wild horse, and for a moment, I watched the splendor of man battling with shattered machinery, fighting to keep us out of a fatal spin.

There was no time for reflection, for analysis. Hours of preflight expectation were crowded into split seconds of emotionless action. Panic, the first reaction, was replaced by cold, trained instinct. Every man on the crew had a job; mine was to keep out of their way. This great bomber, with five tons of instantaneous oblivion packed into its belly, was a flaming coffin. It would become—within the next few seconds—an aerial pyre for its eight passengers, unless we could leave immediately.

"Hurry, boys, can't hold it much longer," the pilot urged, still with cool restraint.

Ahead, the bomb aimer unlocked the emergency hatch and kicked it free. A torrent of cyclonic wind rushed through the pitching plane, like a flood of stabbing ice water. The engineer was having trouble buckling on his parachute. I was debating mentally whether to take off the oxygen mask and risk fainting in the thin air, four miles up, or let it be torn off as I jumped.

Events in our shattered world were crowding each other with unprecedented speed. Bewildered, shaken, my thoughts raced through a confusion of ideas and reactions. Most impelling was, "This is a helluva way to get a story."

But the blinding searchlights, the coruscating panorama of flak everywhere, the plane shaking and shuddering as if it would tear itself apart, and the sight of Bolton fighting desperately, silently, to hold it in the air until we could bail out—these created a frantic urgency that required no rationalization.

I glanced at the starboard wing. It was melting away. Both engines had torn loose. Large sections, glare-red with fire were breaking off and flashing backward. It seemed a miracle we were still flying.

"Bye, skipper. Good luck," called the young bomb aimer as he plunged out of the hatch. Then the engineer, still struggling with his parachute, followed, paused a moment over the escape door, then dropped forward out of sight.

I heaved myself forward, weighted down with parachute life belt, musette bag, and trench coat, and fell over the steps leading into the bomb aimer's compartment. My borrowed flying boots both came off. But there was not the slightest desire to stop to collect them. For all five senses there was only one sensation and one command: "Get out of this plane alive." I tore off the oxygen mask.

Behind me, bumping a little with his head for he was in a hurry too, was the navigator. Following him was the wireless operator.

The gunners would leave through another hatch. When everyone had cleared, the pilot would try to get out of his seat, then dive out after us before the plane exploded or began to tailspin. Already, it was lurching and plunging wildly, despite his efforts to hold it. Any moment the fuel tanks or bombs might explode the thirty-ton plane into sudden nothingness.

I crouched by the hatchway with a wild wind pounding my face, thinking suddenly and quite coldly, "Should've doubled my insurance. This is no good for a family man," grabbed at the parachute's rip cord, and hunched forward through the opening.

One sock caught in a metal strip, torn loose by the wind, and ripped noiselessly and unimportantly. The back of my coat caught too and ripped. The musette bag swept up with the rush of wind and caught around my throat.

We were four miles up, over twenty thousand feet above the center of Berlin, in that vast, unearthly void. Below, just as I jumped, I could see the fires and the flak, the flares and the searchlights. It was a kaleidoscopic nightmare.

CHAPTER 3

Unexpected Visitor

It was cold, that was the first reaction—biting, numbing cold. I had pulled the rip cord almost immediately, which was quite wrong at such an altitude. We had parachuted tight over the target area, and the flak was vomiting lustily into the sky, choking the air with a crimson cordon of death. I should have fallen two or three miles before opening the parachute so as to clear the barrage and reach warmer air.

Almost immediately there was a back-twisting jerk and I thought my arms and legs would be torn away. I glanced up to see a white sheet billowing out reassuringly above, and at the same time saw the flak and flame framing a fantastic background, With already-frozen fingers, I could not untwist the musette-bag strap which had caught around my throat. When I did succeed in moving it, the strap snapped into my mouth and cut my lip. But the blood froze immediately, at least one blessing.

At that point there was a sort of lifting of the eyebrows, an idiotic thing to do coming down over Berlin, but that's what happened. I said aloud, "You wanted a big story. Well, here it is. Goddamnit."

Flak spangled the blackness around me. My ears rang with the concussion of explosion and with the change of air density. My lungs ached for oxygen in the bitterly cold, thin air and my head whirred with the wildness of this nightmare.

There was an annoying, biting realization—even in all this madness—of my own appalling insignificance: dangling up there, impotent in that vastness, alone and helpless against the jagged streaks of light which filled the icy void. A man-made sheet of silk, and a woman-made man suspended and swinging beneath it—an animal intrusion, an atomic impertinence in this infinite wilderness of the unearthly.

And there was a thought of the fulfilment of the pre-mission premonition. In the musette bag was all the equipment I needed to get away if I should land safely. I laughed to myself at the morbid foresight. I found it hard to believe that the shadow of suspicion had become the terrible substance of reality: it was a one-way flight to Berlin.

Practical thoughts, too, chased through a bewildered brain. A young British wife, only recently arrived in the strange newness of America, and a two-year-old son were hardly baggage for such adventures.

A creaking, straining sound from above came to my ears. The parachute shrouds were weakening under my weight; the thought dispersed any academic analysis of a personal catastrophe. Every few seconds came that sound, as of the taut strands of rope parting under strain. But now a numbing albeit tardy, fatalism intervened. I had already lived a few minutes longer, it seemed, than fate had planned, so what came next mattered little.

Beneath me, as much as I could see with the strap cutting into my mouth and throat, the fires spread larger and clearer. I was coming down right into the target area and a new fear, that I would drop into one of the fires, rushed through my brain, elbowing out all other thoughts.

A burning plane screamed past below, so close there was a momentary rush of hot wind on the bootless feet. A nearby shell-burst rocked the parachute and for a frantic moment I thought it had been pierced. Then, in the space of a few short gasps for breath, I counted three stricken bombers, careening like flaming meteors toward the ground. A gust of wind caught the parachute and I twirled and spun as helplessly as an untended marionette.

The wild panorama of battle and death, the crazed symphony of bombs and planes and guns—it was fantastic. The tumultuous jigsaw of color and sound, of consuming fear and bewilderment and wonder—an experience defying description.

The descent was desperately slow and deathly cold. Fifteen or twenty minutes had elapsed since I had left the plane; it seemed eternal hours. I felt myself drifting away from the city and the fires. My eardrums were now so swollen inward with the air pressure, I could no longer hear the planes and guns clearly. Deep anger began to replace fear and excitement.

A lone searchlight swung onto me, its glaring whiteness eating through closed eyelids. I waited a moment for it to swing away, and when this did not happen, was overwhelmed with fury. I reached into my coat, unsnapped the shoulder holster, and pulled out the automatic. Without thinking I aimed it down the search-light and pulled the trigger several times in rapid succession. Then fear closed in again. "That's not good politics," I thought, replacing the revolver and waiting breathlessly for machine-gun bullets in reply. Nothing came, and after a moment the search-light moved off through the sky.

Suddenly, off to the side and below, there was a glint of light, sparkling and reflecting on water. I tugged desperately at the shrouds on one side of the chute, to veer off landwards, but to no avail, for the lines were ice-coated and stiff.

Almost immediately I struck, smashing through thick reeds, plunging waist deep into mud and chest deep into water. Its frigidity brought quick sanity. I twisted the release apparatus on the chute harness, punched it, and felt the sail fall loose and drift away. Then I seized the life preserver and tote down the handle which automatically inflated it.

I was down safely. Worst damage, as far as I could make out, was a badly cut lip, two scratches on an ankle from flak or plane fragments, and awfully cold arms and legs.

The trench coat, with a heavy woolen lining absorbed the water like a dry sponge and its weight multiplied. I tried to pull my legs out of the mud, clutching at the reeds, and I managed to take two or three steps, sinking back each time, thigh deep in its viscosity.

I attempted to climb onto what seemed more solid ground at the base of a particularly thick clump of reeds, but with each step I sank back into the mud as deeply as before. Several times I slipped and fell into the water, staying afloat thanks only to the life belt.

The coat and musette bag were becoming heavier all the time. I was dully aware of a terrible coldness throughout my body. The exertion of each step was a tremendous physical effort. I had managed to take only about twelve steps, and had no idea if I was going in the right direction.

My watch had recorded 8:35 after I landed, and by 10:30 I had covered less than twenty feet from the harness, behind which stretched the parachute, limp, deflated, ghostly white.

I could feel my legs freezing in the mud and water; my fingers were already numb and helpless. I knew I would have to reach dry land soon or freeze in the black solitude of this lake. But with the best intentions and the most desperate efforts, self-exorting and shouting and cursing, it was no use. I was freezing faster than I could move.

I tried tearing down the reeds, to make a platform on which I might climb to orient myself. But to uproot the ten-foot rushes was a first-class impossibility. I thought, again quite irrelevantly, of a cradled Moses in the bulrushes on the Nile remembering idly that an Egyptian princess had saved him. And anyone who would be searching for people to save from the mud and reeds this night would be as mad as the amateur airman who was struggling without progress in an endless morass.

Someone was alive and about that night, however. Toward midnight I heard voices not far away. I shouted in English, French, Spanish—and remembered those languages were of no use here. "Komm hier. Help. Goddamnit, get me out of here." But the German was too limited and my voice too weak.

Sometime later, I had reached the stage where it no longer mattered if I were saved. Blood can be kept warm with determination and anger and desire for only so long. After that the cold of December air and water won out, and it was a losing battle to shout and struggle. I could no longer move either leg, my arms were leaden; I felt ineffably weary.

The bombardment was long since over. The sky had grown completely dark except for a red reflection in one direction, and the water no longer mirrored the vivid hues of explosions and fires as when I had first landed.

Then came more voices in the distance: men's voices, faint and unclear. I found strength enough to shout again: "Come out here and get me, please. Ist kalt hier... Komm hier, bitte." After a moment the voices became more excited, then stopped. I wondered what was to come next: survival only to be lynched? I remembered the automatic ... other men had reached England after parachuting over Europe ... I would hold up these Germans, take their shoes, seize a vehicle ...

I believe now that I was half-mad then. I recall no coherence in my thoughts nor any full appreciation of my position.

The voices were shouting back to me. I heard the washing of water against wood, the creaking sound of oars, and the rhythmic breathing of men as they pulled on the oars. I tried to tell them I couldn't move a nerve let alone a muscle—then laughed and announced I was an American and if they were rescuing me only so I could have the lead in a lynching party they might as well leave now because I wouldn't play. Four hours in the water had brought waves of semi-hysteria.

It was an eternal half-hour before they reached me. They pushed their way through the reeds with a long pole, finally came within reaching distance and shoved the pole out to me. I grasped the end of it. As they pulled, my numbed hands slid off. They tried again. I twisted my arms around the pole, getting the end of it under an armpit. But that was futile too.

So they pushed their way another few feet nearer, laboriously, for the reeds were thick and stubborn, and then one of them reached out and took hold of my arms. He was a big man, I could see that even in the dark, but he could not budge me. His comrade, who had been balancing the boat by standing in the other end, came forward, and each took an arm.

They both heaved together—ridiculously, I was reminded of the Paimpol fishermen dragging in their nets—and I was in the boat: the night's catch.

One of them stood me up, supported me for a moment, scrutinized me, and said, "*Ja, Amerikaner,*" as if in confirmation of what I had already announced from the water. The other moved to the forward end of the boat, and in so doing tipped it slightly. It was enough. I lost my balance and, board-stiff with cold, fell flat on my face in the shallow mud and water in the bottom of the boat.

The second man pulled me to my feet again, then seemed to think better of it and sat me down on a wooden board seat. While the other maneuvered us out of the reeds, he knelt and rubbed my legs. Poling out of the reeds took long minutes. First one man worked the pole while the other rubbed my legs—then they changed places. I could not help thinking how decent of them it was to do that for me. It was annoying to feel that I should have to hold them up to escape.

Finally, we broke free from the reeds, out onto clear water, clear moon and starlight, and I saw we were on a fair-sized lake. Some feeling was coming back into my legs and arms, and morale was returning.

After a while we approached a blurred, darkened shore. The man who had been rubbing me straightened as our boat scraped on the rocky beach. He moved forward, leaving me momentarily alone. I slid my hand, still half-numb with cold, through the unbuttoned trench coat and tunic, and drew out the automatic. It felt enormously heavy and unwieldy as I dropped my hand to my side.

The man who had been rowing stopped and drew the oars into the boat. The other leapt ashore and with a quick motion pulled the boat a third out of the water. The rower took my arm and helped me ashore, the other climbing back into the boat to collect the oars. Now or never, I thought. We had taken a few steps up the beach. My legs were not steady, but I felt I could stand on them alone.

I shook the man's hand from my arm, swung away from him and turned to face both of them. The other was scooping up the oars in the boat, and looked up at the noise. In the bright third-moon, I could see their faces and felt sure they could see the gun which I pointed and waved at them, motioning the one on shore back toward the boat. He hesitated.

"*In dem boot*," I ordered, as softly as possible, in case there should be others neat by, and pointed the gun toward the row-boat. Both men looked stupidly surprised. I honestly felt very badly about it. They had been kind to me, much kinder than I would have been to them under opposite conditions.

"Look men," I had to say it in English, but I had to excuse myself somehow. "I don't want to hurt you. But I'm not a soldier. *Ich bin nichts Soldat*. The government doesn't pay my salary if I get caught. I'm a reporter, *ein Korrespondent*. So I've got to get back home. Climb in the boat and row back out." I felt very foolish, having said all that, but it was some redemption of conscience. And there was no precedent for this kind of thing; events and reactions had to take an untrained course.

The man on shore stepped back into the boat, and I silently thanked him for making it so easy. The other man stood stock-still, balancing the two oars and looking more than somewhat confused. Neither of them made any move to sit down and row.

Then I made the mistake. I had been standing in water. It had not been important, for it was only ankle deep, but I felt my shoe-less feet becoming numb again. I moved sideways out of the muddy hollow, still facing the boat, toward what seemed slightly higher ground. The second step was into a hole. My right foot sank at least six inches and I fell sideways, the gun spilling out of my hand as I clutched for something to keep me on my feet.

I didn't see him, but I felt him coming, one of the men from the boat. He hit me in the back with his shoulder like a football tackler and I thought my leg was broken. The air went out of me as into a vacuum. I struggled to get clear, to twist out from under him, but even as I tried I knew it was hopeless.

My clothes weighed enormously. And the brief demand of energy to stand alone had taken all my remaining strength. I almost wriggled free, getting one arm around his neck and tightening as much as I could, then suddenly trying to break away. and get to my feet. But his weight, and that of the sodden clothes, was too much.

Then, just as abruptly, he was off me and I was alone on the ground, panting as if I had been wrestling for hours. I wondered, coldly, quite unconcernedly, if they would shoot me. I looked up to see the other man, holding my gun and pointing it at me, motioning me to get up.

One of them slipped his arm under mine, leading me along a stony, rising path toward a cottage some hundred yards from the lake's edge; the other, who still gripped the uncocked gun purposefully in this bewildering melodrama, followed a short distance behind. I was now too weak to be angry at myself. The only emotion I felt was one of complete resignation and an obtruding perplexity that these men had not yet hurt me for the idiotic escape attempt.

The cottage was a small one, a workingman's home, and furnished accordingly. I was led into the kitchen, stripped of my trench coat, tunic, and trousers. One man heated a basin of water on the coal stove while the other filled another tub with cold water and motioned me to soak my feet. Then he took a half-loaf of brown bread from a wooden cupboard and cut several thick slices, smearing margarine and a heavy layer of liverwurst on each. To my surprise, the bread was for me. And, from the heated water, they made coffee which was also for the unexpected visitor. The actions were quick, decisive; they seemed not at all interested in the personality of their prisoner, only in his immediate physical needs.

Both bread and coffee were ersatz. But after the experience of four hours in a lake, both were eminently acceptable. No fine brewed coffee has since been as welcome even though this drink seared a dangling, badly cut lower lip.

With the food, the light, and the decreasing numbness of brain and extremities, sanity returned slowly. I looked about the room and at these two strangers who had saved me.

One was an *Unteroffizier*, a corporal in the German Army, a pleasant, sallow young man of innocuous enough appearance. The other was older, harder. He could not have been the father, for the types were too different. He was a lumberman, I found out later.

I gestured toward the musette bag (I had already found that a torn lip did not improve my mediocre German) where two hundred American cigarettes should still have been dry under their much-advertised cellophane wrapping. But the entire contents had literally melted—paper, tobacco, wrapping—during the long immersion. The lumberman, however, guessed my desire and offered a tasteless German cigarette from a cardboard package in his pocket.

That gesture brought on this reporter's first major bribe attempt. "How would you like a thousand dollars and a letter of introduction to Mrs. Roosevelt?" I asked the lumberman. He understood, after several minutes of hybrid German-English, and wanted to know how that was to be earned.

"You supply a car, fuel, a map, and my gun—and give me back my trousers," I added, thinking suddenly to myself that this was better than Hollywood, if only I wasn't so damn cold.

Both men laughed, shook their heads "no," and the gesture was ended. I guess I hadn't really expected it to work anyway. Then came hypochondria—I will surely get pneumonia and die. Or if I don't, I shall never again be warm, I thought to myself with perturbing dispassion.

About an hour later, a woman neighbor came in to see the prisoner (who was consuming brown bread, liverwurst, and dung-filled cigarettes). She spoke a reasonable English and brought a tremendous dictionary to help the conservation. In the hours before daylight, in a cottage kitchen by a lake outside Berlin, we talked of the war. Not many hours previously I had been on an airfield in Britain.

The woman, healthy and not unattractive was about forty years old. Her husband was a sergeant, commanding a rifle unit on the Eastern Front, and she had not seen him for seventeen months. A few days previously she had been evacuated from Berlin with her remaining child, a twelve-year-old daughter. The other, a seven-year-old son, she said, had been killed during an RAF raid on the capital in August.

She brought a blanket with her, in which she wrapped me. When she noticed my badly torn sock, she magically produced a darning needle and some wool. In five minutes the sock was as new. In a halting confusion of German and English, we attempted a discussion of the war. We compared food rations; we spoke of the air raids. Of the second subject, I remember she said quite emphatically and with a hitherto unnoticed vitality "They are hard. But we will never capitulate."

Toward daylight, two sergeants arrived from a nearby search-light battery. The lumberman had telephoned to announce his prisoner during my conversation with the woman.

One of the newcomers carried a submachine gun, the other a revolver. Both were impressively military. The revolver bearer, a rough, hard-looking man of about thirty-five, stared closely at me and announced that his wife was in a nearby hospital with two broken ribs from the last RAF attack against Berlin. What did I think of that?

What the hell could I think? First of all, I was too cold to think. And if I was doing any mental work, it was about my own seemingly pathetic condition—about a wife and son and the absence of a bank account—and not about some comic-opera sergeant's rib-less wife. What did I think about broken ribs? Too bad, that's all. I drove an ambulance during the blitz on London, and picked up a lot of good people whose bomb-authored injury was far more severe than broken ribs. War is obviously hell. But his wife's ribs were hardly my concern.

Those things, however, must not be told to an armed German sergeant, when your marrow imitates an icicle, and you're wrapped in a blanket with no pants. So I tried to register deep sympathy and asked the woman to translate, "It's a difficult war."

That must have been the right attitude, for he offered me another of those tasteless, but warming, cigarettes. Then we marched off, the prisoner in carpet slippers borrowed from the lumberman, toward the searchlight battery.

Walking along, through the sharp, sobering morning air, in half-dried clothing and with half-warmed legs, I attempted to analyze the situation. It defied comprehension. I was amazed at the way I had become in the space of a parachute jump, an extreme introvert and egotist. Everything was happening to me: this whole farragotic circus, the German uniforms, the woman and her dictionary, the bomber and the flak and the lake. It was all background for my entrance and my act; and what a hell of an act.

The morning was beautiful: pine trees, silvered with frost and rooted beneath virgin snow, sentineled our route along a climbing path. There was no war in the crisp invigoration of the air, nor in the white-mantled fields stretching away on either side. The only war here was in the sergeants and in myself.

I stumbled along slowly and awkwardly, for the slippers were too large and my feet sore from the hard ground. The revolvered sergeant led the way, solemn, unhurried. And the tommy-gun bearer brought up the rear by a few paces. I was neatly sandwiched between them and to attempt an escape was assuredly futile.

At the searchlight battery, a youthful, dapper lieutenant awaited us, and I observed that the sergeants treated him with a respect akin to reverence.

"How do you do? You speak German? your papers, please," he asked politely, but a bit confusingly.

"Feel like hell, thank you. German's pretty poor. Sergeants have my papers," I answered, trying to sound friendly, both because he seemed a decent sort and because such an attitude is inherently politic for a prisoner.

While he checked through my identity folders, I sat by a large open fireplace in wandering meditation. A few minutes later an orderly knocked, pushed open the door, offered a starched "Heil, Hitler" salute, and ushered in—Ian Bolton, my pilot. This was a real surprise. I had seen the wing of our plane tearing away as I had bailed out and had doubted seriously that the pilot would escape alive.

Now, he walked into the room looking just as neat and composed as he had on the airfield in England. We greeted each other as reunited brothers. Young Bolton, however manly and dignified under such circumstances, had none of the oft-accompanying reserve. The German lieutenant, learning that we knew each other, announced that we might talk together while he recorded our identities and capture.

We talked of the mission "B for Bolty" had half completed, and its pilot detailed his version of our personal disaster over Berlin.

"Just after you and the rest of the crew got out," he explained, "the old plane fell off into a straight dive. The controls were useless; I believe they had been shot away. I crawled out of my seat and down into the nose just as the starboard wing tore loose.

"Something fell on me and I was pinned against the hatch. Then there was an explosion and I was hit on the head. Next thing I knew I was dropping out into the darkness. I remember vaguely pulling the rip cord.

"When the parachute opened, I remember nothing more until I noticed trees below me. Then a crashing noise and a very abrupt stop. I swung against the tree trunk, loosened my harness, and slid and fell to the ground.

"At the same time there was a terrible roar. It seemed to fill the whole world. I saw a flaming aircraft coming down—straight for me, it seemed. It struck a few hundred feet away with a terrific crash, sending debris far over my head. I rolled over and watched it for a moment in the distance. I felt pretty badly about it, as I lay there on my side watching it: a bright burning circle that was our bomber's funeral pyre.

"Then there is another blank. Later on I got up—it was bitter cold—and started walking. I kept going through the woods until I came to a track. There were some buildings ahead so I tried to skirt them, passing through what I thought to be two clumps of bushes, They were really two piles of sandbags.

"Suddenly a shadow detached itself from the darkness and I saw a gun glinting. I was on a flak site and a sentry challenged me. Then another blank space—civilians coming to stare, and swear—journey in a car, a hard bed, and a few hours' sleep. Then another car ride with German guards. That's it; here I am. What's next?"

In fairness to Bolton, I must report that his account was much less the recital it appears. He talked in a low voice, breaking off frequently and trying to remember. He interrupted the story with self-questions of what had happened to his boys, the six other airmen in the plane. He was obviously heavily weighed down with the responsibility of their charge. And he was still shocked by the blow on the head, still dazed and unsure.

The German officer had coffee and brown bread brought in, and we ate as starved men. Other RAF flyers were brought into the miniature headquarters during the morning. The first was a small, bony Scotsman with a fiercely dirty face and a broken kneecap who had to be supported as he hopped painfully along. He had been the bomb aimer of another Lancaster and, as far as he knew, was the sole survivor. His grief was genuine, and it had nothing to do with the broken kneecap. For he had been married only two days before the fatal mission to Berlin. What was his lassie thinking now?

Other airmen were escorted to the room, to sit in a semicircle around the fire, each enveloped in his own personal bewilderment, his ideas of escape, his half-dazed post mortem of the mission which had brought him here.

None of us talked much. What conversation there was came in sporadic bursts. Each tried hard to be brave and nonchalant and unruffled, although his own disaster filled his consciousness. The RAF boys, with a self-disciplined British background, held themselves well. One Canadian boy, however, represented another reaction to the situation. He was also the sole survivor from his plane, and cursed abruptly and violently every few moments, as if to show he was as unbeaten as when he had been in England a few hours previously.

"These goddamn krauts," he said once, "they're really in a worse jam than us. Christ, I'd rather be a prisoner here now than be a German when the war is over. The Russians and the French and the Polacks, they'll be on our side. We'll be all right. But these poor bloody Heinies—what a bellyful of trouble they'll have."

CHAPTER 4

To Solitary Confinement

Berlin was an unimaginable shambles, beyond comparison with the London of 1943. We passed through the center of the city in a truck, nine of us prisoners with four German guards. Our escorts were not anxious to have us witness the havoc we had helped to cause in their capital, and they dropped the tattered canvas shades. But it was an ancient vehicle and the canvas had a crack for every eye.

Curiously, the guards watched us looking out at their shattered city as we passed through it. Not one word was said during the entire ride.

Until then I would not have been able to comprehend such destruction on so massive a scale. Wrecked villages I had seen in France and Africa, torn by artillery fire, rubbled and barren from dive-bombing and strafing. London had sections of gutted and gaping ruins, block-square fields of smashed debris where buildings had stood. But here was a city that had been killed, hammered and pulverized, burned out and blown up with a completeness defying description.

We did not tour the city. The object of the drive was certainly not to exhibit to us what we, and others before us, had done to the German capital. We were being driven from the searchlight battery to the main airfield, *Tempelhof*, and so took a course along the *Ost-West Achse*, along *Unter den Linden* and into its south-east corner. But in that drive we saw very few doors left in the remaining buildings—and not one whole glass window.

The bulk of the damage seemed to have been caused by fire, as the RAF's Bomber Command had planned. Block after block, as we drove along, contained only shells of buildings, scorched black and half-molten with the heat of tremendous fires which had devoured them. Occasionally, there were evidences of the terrible "blockbuster," and here, ten-story apartment houses were telescoped into ten feet of rubble.

Householders and shopkeepers in the less damaged areas were sweeping a harvest of glass off the streets and into neat piles along the gutters. Everywhere squads of khaki-clad Russian prisoners of war struggled to clear the wreckage. For every fifty prisoners there was a German guard, but these seemed hardly necessary for the workmen appeared strangely enthusiastic about their task.

Todt workers (of the German labor corps) were also to be seen in profusion. These men too were uniformed in khaki and worked, much as the Russians, to clear debris from the sidewalks, load trucks with removable salvage, tear down partly destroyed buildings, and return what was left of the city to a semblance of orderliness.

Other than the two groups of workers, very little civilian interest seemed focused on the awesome wreckage. Berliners hurried along the streets, some carrying suitcases and boxes, possibly containing their last worldly possessions. Others moved along much the same as people on business in New York or in London.

It was late afternoon when we arrived at the airdrome, and the sky was thickening with heavy, driving masses of rain clouds. "Looks like another good night for a raid," commented one over-garrulous young flyer who was perturbing the rest of us by his frequent comments on Germany's unhappy situation.

In the administration building our names were listed by efficient, somewhat officious *Luftwaffe* clerical sergeants and *Luftwaffettes* (as they became known to us). Here we surrendered our watches, pens, papers, and other personal belongings to a lieutenant.

"You get everything back—later," he explained in laborious English, but eager to assure us that we would be well treated.

The ceremony lasted half an hour. Then we were marched to a row of cells in another building, and each locked into a tiny room. It was solitary confinement, and the reaction was an overwhelming sense of hopelessness, friendlessness, and weariness. My cell contained a small radiator, a slightly sloping wooden table with a wooden box at one end which was to serve as bed and pillow, and a three-legged stool.

The room itself, by repeated pace-measurement, was nine feet long and four feet wide. At one end, and just below the ceiling, was a tiny window, locked and barred on its outside. Someone had scratched a few "V's" on the walls; there were a few wisps of straw on the floor and a loose plank in the "bed." That was all; other than that, the room was colorless, barren, lifeless.

Two or three hours after our arrival the door was unlocked and a plate of thick barley soup was passed in by an armed guard. The tasteless, gluey substance was, by virtue of its being the first substantial food for more than twenty-four hours, perfectly delicious. The plate was collected a few minutes later by the same guard.

After that, and until late into the night, there was no further interruption, no noise. The *cafard* of solitary confinement set in with a will. Singing and whistling were no time-passers; the noise rattled off the walls and only re-emphasized the personal misery of such solitude.

I picked a sliver of wood from the loose bed plank and cleaned my fingernails, carefully, slowly. When they were clean, I scratched them on the floor and began the process again. After a while the game lost its interest. I tried reciting all the poetry I knew, then the Gettysburg Address and some of the Rubaiyat. I tried contemplating and planning an escape. But the barred window and heavy door quickly redirected those thoughts.

Sometime during the night a guard swung open the door and the prisoners were led from each cell into an anteroom. Here we were told we would be taken to a camp, but just as we were started out the door to a waiting truck, the air-raid sirens mourned their dirge.

They sounded just as had the sirens in London. It was almost humorous to hear them. "Go through every goddamn *Luftwaffe* raid on London," I thought, "then come to Berlin and be bombed by the goddamn RAF."

The guards were hurried and jittery. They led us into a deep shelter beneath the building and they were impatient with our wounded, who could not move fast enough. We were led, single file, through a maze of rooms, past hundreds of scowling, anxious German faces, to a small chamber at one end. It was far too small for our number, but the door was shut and bolted behind us.

After a little while we could hear the indistinct coughing of the guns, and soon the hollow thumping of bombs. But our most serious problem was lack of air. It became hot and damp, and the oxygen was going quickly from the low-ceilinged cell. Everyone was perspiring and breathing in short gasps.

Finally, a red-faced Australian gunner banged on the door and, when it was opened a crack by the guard, called out, "No air, mate. Leave the bloody thing open a bit. No air."

The guard peered at the airman, seemed desirous of striking him, then turned away and left the door open a few inches. The air did not worsen, though it hardly improved.

Sometime later we heard the thin wailing of sirens again.

The guards returned and we filed back out of the shelter to the administration quarters. Instead of the truck, this time an ancient bus awaited us and, without further ado, we were driven for several hours along an *Autobahn* to another depot. Toward morning we arrived and were each placed in solitary confinement again.

About noon we were allowed the luxury of being together in a large room. One new addition to our group was a husky, heavily bearded Canadian pilot who said he had been "on the loose for eight days."

"I landed okay in a field," he declared. "I figured I'd walk north to one of the Baltic ports and stow away to Sweden. During the daytime I hid in woods or in ditches. I covered myself over with branches but it was too cold to sleep.

"About six each night I started walking. I stayed away from the roads and used my little compass to head north and northwest. It was hard going; I had to climb fences, and I fell down pretty often in the dark. That used up my strength fast.

"Sometimes I was so cold I almost decided to give myself up. I'd run a little to keep warm, then I'd have to sit down because f was so tired, The only food I had was a package of Horlick's tablets, and I sucked one of those every few hours. In the mornings, I always looked for a barn or a shed to hide in, and to keep out of the wind. But they were always locked. These bastards lock up everything. Where's one good thing, though, you don't have to worry about dogs. Heinie dogs bark all the time. So when they bark at you it's nothing unusual. It doesn't mean somebody's coming out with a gun.

"How'd I get caught? You guys really did it. I was about fifty miles north of Berlin by my map. I could see your raid from there—the whole sky was lit up red and the flak was going up like fireworks. But every time there's a raid, the search parties are out looking for us. And I didn't have sense enough to stay hidden for a couple of days. Or I was just too cold; and it was getting pretty damn lonely keeping away from people.

"I was just starting out in the evening—the night after your raid—and I walked smack into some old grandpa with a *Landwehr* patch on his sleeve. I could have socked him and run, but I was too tired. We both looked at each other. Then he said, 'British?' And I said, 'That's right, bud.'

"He was an old guy, maybe seventy-five, and he sure got excited. He whipped out a pocket knife opened it, and pointed it at me. I could have taken it away from him like a lollipop from a kid. But I was awfully tired and the old guy was so funny I wanted to laugh. And the whole war was too goddamn bloody crazy. So we walked to the police station and they drove me here. Tomorrow I'll probably be sorry I didn't sock the old man and run like hell. Prison camp is an awful waste of time they say. And these Krauts captured my brother in that commando raid on Dieppe—it'll be tough on the old lady to have both of us over here. But, Christ, I was tired."

He was a big, well-built boy, the Canadian flier. He looked too big for his dirty uniform. There was a rough, youthful majesty in his clear eyes and his scrubby beard and the way he talked. For eight days he had lived like an animal. He had starved himself and pushed himself and fought himself to keep from surrendering. His talent, that sturdy, manly enthusiasm for freedom, and the friendly honesty that spoke more clearly for him than he himself—it will be useful when the war ends and we may start to build a healthier world.

One other new arrival, a thin, slight lad from New Zealand, had been tail gunner in a Lancaster trapped by fighters soon after leaving the target. The night fighters had attacked from below, invulnerable from the bomber's defending machine guns.

"I didn't see it until it had gone past," said the New Zealander. "But then I got in a short burst at the second fighter. Our kite was all over the sky. Something had been hit, I knew, because the plane shuddered just before I saw the fighters. I called out 'Everything okay, skipper?' over the intercom … and there was no answer. I tried it again. And no answer. The kite was flopping about almost completely out of control.

"Then I got worried. I thought the intercom had been cut, or the skipper killed. I happened to look back and, oh my God, there was no kite—just stars. The fighters had cut us in two and I was in the tail end, alone. I thought I was a goner. The bit I was in was the back half and it must have been falling with the tail at the bottom, because I distinctly remember seeing stars and black sky when I looked back.

"I started to crawl out of the turret to get out. But I couldn't move because the tail, or what was left of it, was flopping all over the sky and I was pinned to my turret. There was a helluva wind.

"The next thing I knew I was out in the sky alone. Something must have happened to blow me out, or I fell. But I don't remember crawling out, and I don't remember buckling on my parachute.

"I came down in a forest and landed in a tree. My leg was smashed up against something and I remember hollering for somebody to come and cut me down. After a while a man and a woman came and got me, took me to their house, and put me to bed. Next morning the police were there and they brought me in a truck, with two other chaps, to a hospital where I was bandaged. I'll never know how I got that chute on."

That typified, in a way, a good many stories of the airmen. Few of them knew all the details of their misadventure. On the other hand, there were a few fliers who had landed almost as if they had leapt off a wall in practice jumping, had buried their parachutes, lit cigarettes, rested awhile, then started walking—and bumped into alert civilians or the search parties.

Toward evening we were packed off in two trucks and driven into Berlin again. We pulled up in front of the *Anhalter Bahnhof*, one of the city's major stations. With us were seven guards—one guard for every four prisoners—and each was armed with an efficient-looking machine gun and a shoulder bandolier of extra ammunition.

While we stood in a loose group at the back of one truck, as the wounded were helped down and brought from the other truck, a crowd of citizens began to collect in a half-circle around us. There were housewives, with their laden shopping baskets and one with an armful of bawling baby; there were boys, dirty-faced little urchins who stopped their street playing for a moment to watch the strange procession; and there were old men, who watched us as they might watch any other street spectacle.

And we were a spectacle! With myself as an exception, everyone wore the blue battledress which was RAF flying uniform. But many of the jackets were torn; all were by now unpressed and dirty. Every one of us had at least two days' beard. Most of the boys still had on their flying boots; I was still clad in carpet slippers. A third of us were wrapped in bandages, many standing on one leg and leaning an arm around a companion's shoulder for support. We must have looked slightly deranged, like Dead End kids, and like the air gangsters Dr. Goebbels had been describing to his readers—all at the same time.

But one of the English sergeants said something as the crowd thickened into a sizable group of sullen, curious, curious spectators. He said something that made me think suddenly of Elgar's *Pomp and Circumstance*, and of the glorious renascence of national self-consciousness four years of desperate struggle had brought to Britain. I had been watching the British boys more than the crowd. I wanted to see their reaction to the crowd. I noticed the sergeant looking around. He said, suddenly, without any apparent fore-thought:

"Chaps. Remember we're soldiers. We're British."

And everyone straightened a little: the British, the Australians, the Canadians … and the American. Such a gesture meant nothing to the crowd, for it was busy inspecting our uniforms, our fares, our boots, our wounded, but the sergeant had suddenly remembered something about his nation and about his people's tradition, And at least one non-British witness was proud of him for it.

The guards formed us into a column, four abreast, and we marched into the station. "Marched" is the wrong word, for two-thirds of us carried the other third and after the first few steps were well spread out. In the station, up the long sweep of stairs and onto the train platform we straggled, the guards hovering about us, their tommy guns slung but within easy reach should any one of the unwounded try to leave in another direction.

I helped carry a pilot officer whose legs had been badly crushed by a crash-landing outside the city. It was hot, tiring work, with the crowds pushing through our group. But I remember looking around the station as we climbed the stairs. It reminded me of Grand Central in New York, of Victoria in London, St. Nazaire in Paris—there were the same thousands of hurried travelers, the same seeming confusion.

But there was something more than that. This station looked entirely too much like New York and London and Paris. It was absolutely undamaged. It was one of the most important rail terminals in all Europe. And to recall the destruction outside and to witness the peacetime conditions within brought a sudden unanswerable question: "Why had we bombed an obscure corner of residential Berlin and left this target untouched?"

Our train was half an hour late in leaving. We climbed into a French *troisième classe* coach and arranged ourselves as best we could in the unlighted, unheated carriage. Our destination, admitted one guard after several questionings, was Frankfort on the Main in the southwest of Germany, where we would be interrogated before going to a permanent camp.

At halts along the route, Red Cross girls offered coffee and biscuits from the stations. Our guards, anxious to keep us quiet—and perhaps appreciating our position—helped by unbuckling their canteens and having them filled with the ersatz liquid they described as coffee. To see this ceremony authored an idea for escape. Attention was entirely directed on the station-side windows while we were halted. So far, no escape attempt had been made from the train; we were all too tired, too bewildered.

The toilets were at each end of the coach, and every time a prisoner wanted to visit one, he was escorted there and back by a guard. But on the last occasion, I had simply announced to the guard with whom I was trying to talk (in execrable German) that I was going to the toilet. He had waved "all right," and I had gone off and come back by myself.

I decided to capitalize upon his unsoldierliness. As I felt the train beginning to slow down and pull into the next station, I announced another need to visit the urinal. The guard waved another "all right" and reached for his canteen for more coffee when we should stop.

I felt my way through the pitch-black passage between the rows of seats filled with sprawling, half-sleeping airmen, and pushed open the toilet door. Inside, I buckled my belt more tightly, then waited a moment as we pulled into the station and I heard the voices of the prisoners and guards calling to the girl.

Through the half-opened door, I saw them all crowding at the windows, just as we had at the previous station. The coach was dimly lit, from the reflection of the station lights, but it was still dark at my end. I twisted out of the door, opened the communicating gate to the next coach and slipped through, closing it behind me as softly as possible. I walked quickly along the passage of what must have been a German second-class carriage, for a narrow alley flanked compartments on the left.

Two men stood in the middle of the passage and I said pardon in French as I squeezed past them, for I could not think of the word for "excuse me" in German. There was a sudden surge of fright that they had noticed the bright tunic buttons and "U.S." insignia on my uniform and had realized that something was wrong. But they did not follow me.

At the end of the coach I saw several people grouped around the exit, either coming or going. I did not dare risk trying to get through them and out of the train. So I turned left into the lavatory, shutting the door quickly behind me.

The window was bolted, but I wrenched it loose with a hurried desperation. I saw right away that it was too small for escape. But I tried anyway. I stood on the toilet seat, facing inward, and got my head out through the window. But it was a first-rate impossibility to go further.

I was struggling there and my mind was racing through a jumble of alternatives, when I felt a hard knob press deeply into my stomach. Someone said something in German, but I don't know what it was. I believe I jumped a foot. I slipped down out of the window, off the toilet seat, and stood on the floor facing the guard with whom I had last been talking. He held his tommy gun, its muzzle buried hard in my stomach, and noisily, obviously cranked a shell into the barrel.

I lifted my arms over my head and wondered, half-frantically, if he would shoot anyway. We were within two feet of each other, crowded in that narrow compartment, with a dim, blue light. The train creaked and started moving. I thought of hitting him or spinning him around and choking him. But I knew it would be suicide, and that knowledge saved me for he could have fired the gun with a twitch of his finger.

He reached behind him and opened the door, then stepped quickly out and beckoned to me. I walked out slowly, feeling terribly foolish, terribly frustrated. He motioned to me to walk back to our coach, ahead of him, and to put my arms down.

As we walked he said something which I believe meant: "I saw you leave the toilet. You must not try to escape. You will freeze in this weather. And if you get away you might be killed . ..."

And I ground my teeth together, angrier than I had ever been before, thinking, "You bastard, what are you being nice to me for? If I caught you trying to escape I'd probably kick your teeth out. Skip the advice and the condescension. Next time there will be no recapture. Next time I'll write you from London and tell you to watch our parade down *Unter den Linden* after the Unconditional Surrender."

The remainder of the trip, another three hours, was quiet. The guards spoke with none of us. And weariness brought on sleep despite the hard seats and cramped quarters. There was no more interest in coffee or cigarettes. The reaction of the past two days' events was setting in, and everyone was exhausted with fatigue. Moreover, it was after four in the morning. The guards took turns napping too. But now they diligently counted heads after each station stop.

At Frankfort we were bundled out of the train and into a local one. At that hour of the morning just before daylight, it was at its coldest.

We were joined by two other airmen who wore light cotton shirts and khaki battledress. They had been shot down in a Beaufighter on patrol over the Adriatic Sea. They had been captured after five days of wandering around searching for the ephemeral guerillas. But the German occupation forces of Albania had found them first. In clothing made for the Mediterranean climate they were chattering cold.

The second train ride, also in a blacked out third-class coach, lasted only half an hour, and we alighted at a small station called *Oberursel*. Another long flight of stairs, deeply painful for the wounded, and we were out again in the frigid pre-dawn air. The first hints of gray light were beginning to streak the sky.

Again forming in fours, we marched (and again not marching, but fumbling and stumbling along) to a trolley-car stop! For at least half an hour we waited there, shaking with the cold. During the entire time a guard stood beside me, but even without that there would have been no thought of escape. None of the boys talked; no one had anything to say, or could or wanted to say anything if he had.

Finally, a three-carriage trolley car rattled up the hill from the quiet gloom below and we climbed aboard. The civilian passengers were moved to another of the coaches and we sat down in the lighted interior.

This was ridiculous. It was the most humorous yet. It was perhaps six-thirty in the morning. We were twenty-nine prisoners of war and seven guards with seven gleaming tommy guns, riding a streetcar on the outskirts of Frankfort, Germany, on our way to prison,

The advertisements in the car boasted German hair tonics, German toothpastes, German stockings. And the *Nichtraucher*, no smoking sign. And the conductor debating with the chief guard whether or not he should collect fares from us.

Fares from us; German streetcar; prison camp; Frankfort, Germany; hair tonics; flak and searchlights over Berlin. Women with dictionaries whose children get killed in air raids and sergeants with tommy guns whose wives get broken ribs. And pilot Bolton sitting by a fireplace like a story-book Britisher, neat and self-assured despite being blown out of an exploding bomber. It was all too fantastic.

The imagination played a wild symphony, and the knees beat a rhythm for it with the cold. Eyes swam with the sheer idiocy and tragic hilarity of the whole panorama, today's, yesterday's, and guesswork as to what would be tomorrow's.

It was pure, out-of-this-world madness. It was like a movie or a book. Only it wasn't. Because you can put down a book or walk out of a movie. And here you were one of the chief actors in this crazed play.

It was only seventy-two hours old, this episode, this personal melodrama. But the vortex of sudden change, of emotional and physical antithesis into which we had been flung, or had flung ourselves when we jumped from our planes, this confused, exotic lunacy was overpowering and uncontrollable.

CHAPTER 5

Questions and Answers

Solitary confinement is a severe test. Philosophers and imbeciles would fare much better in such an environment than the ordinary human who relies heavily upon others for diversion. I must admit that, while I survived, I was not happy in the closet-sized cell where I resided for five days at the interrogation center near Oberursel.

Purpose of the solitude was to "soften up" the prisoners, to loosen their tongues so that, when questioned, they would more easily divulge their nation's secrets to its enemy. As far as most airmen were concerned, however, there was a kick-back to the plan. Rough treatment proved angering rather than tongue-loosening.

My cell, measuring seven feet by four, contained a paillasse and a straw pillow, a small radiator, a bench, and a switch on the wall with which to call the guard. I spent five days in the room, trying hopelessly to devise a means of escape, trying to pass the time thinking, singing, sleeping. I will not describe my emotions except to say that, for me, solitary confinement was a mental torture which no physical torment could exceed.

Fliers were prepared for this treatment. Allied intelligence officers cautioned them not to weaken despite confinement in the tiny cells, not to talk when taken out to be interrogated. But, as a civilian passenger, I had never enjoyed the experience of being told what would happen if I were shot down.

Finally, I was led out of the chamber down the hall of the low barracks, past the long rows of identical cages, out into another small building which was the interrogation center. There I met *Luftwaffe* Lieutenant Joseph Borner, Stuka pilot of seventy-eight bombing missions, who was to question me. He had been a salesman for several years in England and America, I was to learn, and so spoke good English.

I was later to hear from shot-down fliers of the "wily Hun" and his schemes to force prisoners to divulge information. "Watch out for the wine and women they will offer you," was the Air Force advice. "Tell them nothing but your name, rank, and serial number. Don't argue with them or try to fool them. *Don't talk.*"

But, unfortunately, Borner had no wine and no women to satisfy this prisoner's hopeful anticipation. As I walked into his office (closely followed by a bulky guard), he rose from his chair, extended his hand and said, "How do you do, Mr. Bennett? We have been wondering when we would see you again."

That was an awful moment. I had been captured in France as an ambulance driver in 1940, I had gotten away and enlisted in De Gaulle's Free French Army. Members of this force were considered *franc tireurs*, guerrillas, who were not protected by the international agreements governing prisoners. Despite the overdose of rest during the past five days, I suddenly felt very weak and afraid. Perhaps, despite my present noncombatant status, the Germans would still consider me a *franc tireurs*.

"Do sit down. Here, have a cigarette" was his dubiously reassuring next statement. (This is where the euphemism begins, I thought, the saccharine cordiality—until I talk, then I'll be shot.)

I braced myself in a chair, lit my first cigarette in a week, glanced around the room half expecting to see a microphone protruding somewhere and waited.

"So you wanted to see the RAF bomb Berlin? What do you think of it?"

"Interesting." (Must watch what I say, I thought; mustn't tell them anything.)

"Well, let's see. You flew from Skellingthorpe in 'B' of number fifty squadron of Bomber Command. Bolton was your pilot. He's a good boy; we've been waiting a long time for him." (Got to keep from registering emotion; don't say anything; don't think anything.)

"You know, the BBC said three of you correspondents were lost the other night. You are the fortunate one. The other two were killed. That Norwegian chap and Stockton, the Australian, neither of them got out of their bombers. They were both killed, yes, you're the lucky one."

"What happens now? What about repatriation as a noncombatant?" I had to say something, so I fell into the routine, rehearsed in the cell for five days. "Am I not eligible for exchange?"

"Perhaps," he mused. "We'll have to look into that. But for the moment, how about having 'tea' with me?"

"Thank you. I would, very much." (This is it. This is the charming prelude to the big shakedown. I'll be damned if you learn anything from me, you soft-voiced ape.)

But Borner was not an ape. He was a handsome man of about thirty-five, wearing the Iron Cross First and Second class on his immaculate uniform, quiet-spoken, and an affable host. I gorged bread, liverwurst and jams, swallowed several cups of coffee, and smoked a dozen of his cigarettes at "tea."

The conversation was concerned solely with subjects non-military. We discovered that our homes in Britain had been near each other, in the northwest corner of London, and most of the talk was of peacetime trips into the tourist corners of France and England. I was not so good a guest as Borner was host: I suspected doped coffee, doped cigarettes, microphones in the jam bowl, in the chandelier, in the telephone. And I was not very clever at concealing my wariness.

"My last guest was young John Winant, son of your ambassador in England. He was a very pleasant boy. He's working with the Red Cross now at Frankfort." That was the type of conversation, and it was not until a guard had cleared the table that Borner turned to more serious subjects.

"You know," he said, "our job is to identify you, to make sure no spies nor saboteurs are dropped out of the bombers. Now if you will answer some of the questions I have here, you will identify yourself completely and we will start work on the repatriation question.

"First of all, what do you know about the Path Finder technique?

"What do you know about 'Grapefruit'?

"What can you tell me about the new Ninth Air Force?"

After each question, Borner evidenced only a mild disappointment that the answers were negative shrugs. "I am a reporter and the army tells us none of their secrets," I insisted (which was not entirely true. In England I had heard of the "H-S" technique of the Path Finder Force, of wing-to-wing formation and flying bomb tactic, known in code as Grapefruit, and of the Ninth Air Force then being developed to supply tactical air cover for the coming invasion of France).

"Well, then, I'll tell you a few things you probably don't know." He dug into a stack of files, producing a large folder. "Would you like to hear something about your air forces?

"Our defenses have brought down an average of thirteen per cent of all American bombers sent over Germany, and an average of seven per cent of all British planes. Seventy-two per cent of the American airmen get out of their planes alive; only twenty-seven per cent of the British are so fortunate. Sixty per cent of the surviving Americans are wounded or hurt; forty-four per cent of the British are injured. About one third of one per cent of your fliers manage to evade us and to get back to England, usually through the Underground and Spain, but this figure is dropping steadily because our occupation force are cleaning out the Underground systems.

"You say you don't know how many planes there are in Britain. I'll tell you: the Eighth American Air Force has 1,250 Fortresses and Liberators, and this figure is planned to be doubled within the next seven months. RAF Bomber Command has 1,750 planes, and 175 of these are the two-engined Mosquitoes."

I thought he might well be inventing these figures. "What do you know about the individual American bomber groups?" I asked.

"Let's take the ninety-first Bomb Group under Colonel Stanley T. Wray," he answered, turning to another file. He read the date of its arrival in England, the names of its Squadron Commanders, location of its base, the chronology of its operations. "Wray has lost sixty-one bombers to date. That makes his group the hardest hit of them all." I recognized and tried to keep from being visibly surprised by the accuracy of his information. It was quite clear he was volunteering all of these facts only to encourage me to add to them.

"Where do you get all this information? From the shot-down fliers?"

"Oh, there are agents on both sides. Your 'most secret' and 'highly confidential' documents in England are in our hands a few hours after their publication. I have the blueprints of your new jet-propelled fighters. You know, probably more people in Germany know your secrets than people in England or America."

"Do you think you can stop the invasion with all this information?"

"That is going to be a ticklish question," he said more seriously. "You know, a lot of men on Eisenhower's staff don't believe it will work. It is going to be like a show that is being presented for the first time. You've had your rehearsals—Africa, Sicily, Italy—but no one knows how the real performance will come out. We surely cannot stop you with information alone. But, by knowing the facts in advance, we can make it terribly expensive for you, and we can make the American people realize the cost of the war is more than the victory is worth."

I was beginning to become angry, which was not the correct attitude. I wanted to hear everything he had to say. This was an interview such as I had never before had, and I was still confident the moment would come when I would be able to get away and back to England.

But the interview was at an end. Borner glanced at his watch, remembered an appointment, and announced that I would come back in the morning. "You correspondents don't really belong here," he added. "I shall have to telephone Berlin and see what is to be done with you."

The next morning, after a wearying night's battle with the Nazi variety of bedbugs, I was taken for a walk through a beautiful forest in the Taunus Mountains north of Frankfort. Borner told of his experiences at Crete, Stalingrad, and Tunisia.

I had written a book after the battle of Africa explaining in part why a shoestring offensive against Tunis had failed immediately after the initial invasion of Algeria. Borner, who had flown a Stuka against the same positions where I had once sheltered in foxholes, declared the reason Tunis was not captured by the Allies in that first surge forward was simply because of overcaution on our part.

"We had a few batteries of .88s, one battalion of medium tanks, and four companies of infantry," he explained. "There was no reason why you shouldn't have smashed right through—you got within twelve kilometers of the city and we were expecting it, we were ready to evacuate. But you overestimated us—you've been doing that all through the war—so we were able to reinforce and it took you six months and a mountain of equipment to get us out."

We walked for two hours through the forest, and I marveled at the giant trees veiled with frost and the twisting paths along which children, completely oblivious to the war, played their winter games. Solemn couples walked along, hand in hand, and they were less insensible to the war, but seemed to be trying hard to forget it.

It would have been easy to forget the battle in the lovely serenity of the woods. There was no war here, in truth. The singing streams chasing down into the valley below, the majestic dignity of the pines. ...

But overhead was the almost continuous roar of fighter engines, for the Forts were attacking another German target and the enemy defenses were in action. And I had on the uniform of an American officer and I was a prisoner.

Afterwards, we visited a small hospital used for Allied airmen who were wounded. In its beautiful surroundings, the buildings seemed guarded only by the towering trees which circumscribed it. We talked with a few of the prisoners. One, to my surprise, was Colonel Loren McCollom, whom I had last seen a few weeks earlier on the airfield in England where he commanded a Group of P-47 Thunderbolts. We both feigned non-recognition, but it was a shock to see his head and wrists swathed in layers of bandages. He had been burned when his fighter was hit by flak over France and had barely escaped with his life.

Another of the prisoners was a British Medical Corps captain who had been captured a few weeks earlier on the Dodecanese island of Cos when the Germans overran it. For sixteen days, with hundreds of other prisoners, he had been transported in an open cattle train through Greece, the Balkans, and southern Germany.

"In Athens," he said, "we were marched through the center of the city by the Germans. Probably they wanted to impress the Greeks. There were a few Britishers and several hundred Italians in a long column. But the Greeks made it seem like a victory parade. They came out and cheered, made the V-sign, and booed our German guards. The Germans didn't seem to mind, though.

"The peasants always waved to us as we passed through their country on the train. Only in Bulgaria did we encounter any hostility. … There, they obviously preferred the Jerries." We left after a cup of Red Cross coffee, which tasted wonderfully familiar and luxurious after its German imitation, and an American cigarette which brought with its fumes a hint of self-pity that we should be in such a position that even a single cigarette was so rare a delight.

Returning to the interrogation center, Borner talked about America. What he said might have been skillfully prepared propaganda, but I have always remembered his words and now—eighteen months and many experiences later—they still hold the same importance.

"You in America," he began, "you can have almost any kind of government. Your country is so rich by natural endowment, and your people have such an energy by heritage that no government could completely ruin you. For even with the great waste under the New Deal and during this war, your earth yields such wealth that there is always enough left to feed your population.

"And while you were able to burn corn, kill pigs, and allow fruit to rot on the trees because the selling price was too low, we in Europe had to have the strictest economy to keep our people alive. Haven't you noticed how every home in Germany has its own garden, how every hectare of our soil is cultivated to the fullest?

"You don't like our government, you hate our leaders. I know the way you feel, I receive your magazines through Lisbon and you say you are fighting against dictatorship and oppression. Have you never thought that we cannot afford the luxury of waste, and waste is the partner of democracy?

"You are fighting us because we are trying to unify Europe under a single head, under Germany and can you blame us for feeling that Germany, by location and by the qualities of our people, is best fitted to lead Europe? There will never be real peace or economic well-being on this continent if it is to remain broken up into small nations. Their very entities make for friction; the expenses of their defenses and competition make for waste. We cannot afford disunity.

"Even if we Germans lose this war, and I have thought of that possibility, unity *must* come to Europe. It *will* come, through the Russians, the British, or through you Americans, or there will never be anything here but war and chaos. We are fighting to establish *our* authority and *our* unity. We believe we are best qualified and we shall never stop fighting for that unity …"

I heard the answers to his questions come surging into my consciousness: your unity is rooted in fear, in the suppression of disagreement by concentration camps, in the ballyhooed fantasy of a super-race. But however much I might find to combat his view, I could not help but be deeply impressed by his solemnity and apparent sincerity. This man knew what he was fighting for. He would not surrender easily.

The next afternoon, I was brought again to the lieutenant's office.

"We are going to Berlin," he announced as I entered.

"There are some people there who want to see you. We will leave tonight by train."

That evening he brought me a pair of Red Cross boots and we rode—on the same streetcar which had brought me to the camp—to Frankfort. Outside the main station Borner paused and put down his suitcase.

"Take a good look around," he suggested. "What you can see in the dark is Frankfort. In a few days, or perhaps weeks, you may hear that it has been destroyed. For in a single night your bombers can sweep away all of this with their fire-bombs," and he pointed out and named several of the buildings that walled the main square.

(Two months later, giant Eighth Air Force raids destroyed more than half of the city. Twenty months later, General Eisenhower was to establish his headquarters among its ruins to enforce a peace on conquered Germany.)

I thought of a story, current in England at the time, which quoted an alleged German air communiqué: "RAF terrorbombers attacked Germany last night. By our flak and fighter defenses, twenty-five of them were shot down. One of our cities is missing." And suddenly, in the quiet and cold of the night air, I felt it was a very unfunny joke.

Our train was sixty-five minutes late: it had come from Paris and had been delayed en route by British intruder planes patrolling France, according to our conductor. I was pleasantly surprised when Borner produced tickets for a double sleeper compartment, for I had expected to repeat the uncomfortable Berlin–Frankfort trip of a week previous. Behind our coach, I noticed, was a French carriage and behind that, an Italian one.

Almost as soon as the train got under way, I was in bed and asleep, for the invigorating air of the Taunus had been tiring and, most important, this was the closest to a real bed I had seen in a week. I wanted to lie awake and to plan the next escape attempt but fatigue came over me in a heavy, deadening wave.

The train ride was fast and smooth. At eight the next morning I awakened to watch the flat country west of Berlin sweep past from the corridor window. By eleven we were entering the suburbs of Berlin, then moving more slowly into the city itself.

Bomb damage was at first scattered, but it increased in concentration and in totality as we drew nearer the center of the city. Germans standing in the train corridor watched the passing destruction without visible emotion. For the last few minutes before we reached the station, damage along the left side of the track was stupendous. Almost everything was destroyed or burned out. We passed through several marshalling yards and there seemed no shortage of rolling stock, nor serious damage to the warehouses and depots.

The *Potsdamer* station was roofless, and parts of its walls were missing, evidently from bomb blast, but it was crowded and busy. A young woman and a chauffeur-guard met us and we were driven to an office building near the *Wilhelmstrasse*. I found my thoughts in a turmoil: see everything you can; this is a good story, I felt. But watch out for what's coming next.

I had expected a Hollywood-type Gestapo grilling and I was almost disappointed. A Dr. Steiner met us, led us to his office, and bade us make ourselves comfortable. Again, with the background of too many movies,

I wondered where the inevitable microphone was hidden. Steiner asked if there was anything I needed.

"A haircut, a meal, and some cigarettes," I answered.

And so it was that we were taken to the Esplanade Hotel, a few blocks distant, and I received a haircut in the center of Berlin in the middle of the war. The barber, an imported Italian, had not the reserve I had noticed on the part of most Germans toward the incongruous American uniform.

"*Sie sind Amerikaner?*" he asked, looking at me queerly.

"No, Swedish," I answered in French, forgetting momentarily the twin "U.S." insignia staring him in the face from my tunic lapels. In the shop was a German general, several other German officers, and a number of civilians, all awaiting their turn in the barber chairs.

The general, a gawdy, heavily mustached old man, overheard our brief conversation, put down the *Völkischer Beobachter* he was reading, walked over to my chair, squinted at me, at the uniform, then back at me, and turned away. Borner walked with him to an empty corner of the room and evidently explained the situation.

For the general returned to his chair, picked up his newspaper, squinted at me again, and resumed reading.

CHAPTER 6

Nazidom's Guest

It was still all somewhat fantastic, more a dream than reality, this business of finding yourself dumped suddenly and unceremoniously into the capital city of your enemy. There was no precedent for such an experience; reactions had to be intuitive for there was no mundane guidance.

Neutral newspaper correspondents stationed inside Germany had not helped with their colorful dispatches. I had read in England, for example, that armed Gestapomen were to be seen everywhere; that pillboxes faced every street corner to squash ever-brewing revolution; that millions of prisoners and slave workers only awaited a favorable moment to launch a master blow against their oppressors. I had read that civilian morale was upheld at the point of a bayonet; that sabotage was rife; that the anti-Nazi Germans were preparing to embroil the country in violent civil war.

And I was to discover in Germany that not one of these much-publicized reports was true.

The first afternoon, I was interrogated by Dr. Steiner and two of his colleagues (evidently representing the German Foreign Office). The quality of their questions and their prolix redundance soon exposed a flaw in German method.

"What do the people in England think of William Joyce (supposedly American-born Nazi radio propagandist)? What do the British people think of Stalin? What has Rudolf Hess (Nazi number two man who flew to Britain early in the war) told Churchill? How do American troops get along with the British civilians? Will Averill Harriman go to Moscow as ambassador? How is Maisky (Soviet ambassador to London) regarded in England? Are the people of London afraid of the Secret Weapon? When do you think the Invasion will take place? Where?"

These questions and others, repeated over and over again, brought either a noncommittal shrug or, in a few cases, an enigmatical reply. I did offer the speculation—presented as "inside dope"—that the Invasion would never take place. It was all a gigantic bluff, to keep the German general staff busy inventing defenses.

Feeling so good at being alive, and feeling more than a little bemused by the situation, I endeavored to brighten the session with repartee. One little man, whose face mirrored every emotion he experienced, became peeved at my statement that God and Stalin ranked about the same with Londoners.

"Now, Mr. Bennett, you must not joke with us. You *must* answer these questions properly."

"You worry about the questions; I'll worry about the answers," I replied, and the little man's face darkened further.

In fact, after the first few tense minutes—of self-warnings that almost any answer would be valuable to the "wily Hun"—the interrogation became rather entertaining. These men were trained in their work. By Nazi standards they were undoubtedly considered skillful. But, as I and many other prisoners were later to have often re-emphasized to us— German thoroughness and persistence have been seriously misidentified as brilliant craftiness.

At one point I dared interrupt with the question, "Look here, am I going to a prison camp or will you repatriate me?" The answer was a whimsical shrug which left the situation exactly as before.

"Understand you've got quite a city here," I tried next. And that one succeeded. They beamed as happily as any small town chamber of commerce. If there was one facet of the Nazi character more susceptible to flattery than his own appreciation of Germanic might, it was surely his vaunted *Kultur*. The interrogation was quickly ended and I was offered a sightseeing tour around the capital.

We drove, and walked, for four hours through the battered city. The experience of visiting the enemy capital in the midst of war was one that I shall never forget, and one whose details still remain vividly in my memory.

The varied sights of destruction I had glimpsed on the first drive through Berlin were multiplied throughout its entire breadth. Whole sections were reduced to gutted, gaping skeletons and tangled masonry. Some streets were completely blocked with mountainous debris; others were walled only by shells of burned-out buildings.

The famed "Embassy Row" (*Tiergartenstrasse*) had suffered heavily. Only, and oddly enough, the Japanese Consulate and two South American legations had remained undamaged of the sixty diplomatic buildings. But the American Embassy on *Unter den Linden*—now occupied only by the Swiss Legation, said Steiner—was still untouched.

Twisted, blackened trees, stretched grotesquely across one another in a jumbled mess, were all that remained of the *Tiergarten*. Bulldozers and sixty-ton "Tiger" tanks were being used in some areas to clear the wreckage. Other sections were cordoned off and were being dynamited; repair was out of the question.

But streetcars and the subways still operated. Train stations had lost their glass roofs, but they still handled a massive freight. It was a picture of a population fighting hard with every means at hand to prevent desolation from overwhelming them.

Berlin was very spy-conscious. Everywhere, I saw posters warning against *Spions*, advising the populace how to recognize Allied agents, how to deal with them, and, with a typical Nazi touch, adding a serious warning of what would happen to the citizen who failed in this duty to the Fatherland.

Another oft seen poster displayed a shadowy figure of a man in black coat and slouch hat. In white on his back was a large question mark. And underneath were the words: "Beware, the enemy listens."

"Berliners are calling that picture, 'Mussolini in Flight,'" quipped one of my escorts.

The most colorful poster was that of a lecherous, heavy-lipped individual peering out from behind the draped, full-color flags of America, Britain, and Russia. The caption: "The Jew is behind it all."

The Jew in Berlin was particularly conspicuous for his absence.

The very few I observed wore a large, yellow Star of David prominently displayed on an outer garment.

In the *S-Bahn* subway, the escalators were clearly marked, "Use for Jews forbidden." But apart from the decimated Jewish community, Berlin was surely as cosmopolitan as London or New York.

As already noted, thousands of Russian prisoners were to be seen working in the debris. Other parties included Frenchmen, Italians, Poles, Serbians, and Englishmen, each marked on a sleeve with the first letter of his nationality and each group guarded by a sentinel or two.

Occasional Hungarian, Japanese, and Finnish officers were to be seen, envoys or observers from Germany's respective allies. Near the Esplanade, I noticed three Cossack officers, members of the Anti-Bolshevik League which the Germans had recruited among Russian prisoners. All wore furred caps, long thickly lined greatcoats, and three-foot swords swung, as they walked, with heavy dignity.

A few French officers, most of them of the Medical Service, could be seen. Other Frenchmen and a scattering of bereted Spaniards were members of the All-Europe Legion, recruited and shanghaied to serve Hitler on the East Front. These men wore the distinctive skull and crossbones insignia of the Nazi SS.

Traffic in Berlin's wide streets was amazingly light. Most of the roads had not suffered to any measurable extent from the bombings (because the penetrative force of "blockbusters" was not great and because the Nazis knew the best way to return a city to order was to clear its streets). But there seemed a dearth of vehicles, explainable in part by the severe fuel-rationing system and in part by the Nazi credo that soldiers and civilians should endure equal privation.

More than half of those cars to be seen were propelled by some other fuel than gasoline, Most of them mounted large tanks, attached to the roof or rear, containing coal, coke, or wood from which gas-producer equipment, also attached to the car, evolved a combustible fuel.

But a large number of giant trucks were in evidence, many towing two or more trailers. Thus, evidently, did the Germans relieve some of the strain on their heavily taxed rail system. Many of the trucks were likewise propelled by some fuel other than petrol, and the alcoholic aroma they emitted was reminiscent of French North African cities where anything but gasoline had been used to power an automobile.

Many of the remaining buildings were heated by means of crude, homemade stoves, from which a pipe took out the exhaust through the nearest window. A contrary wind would blow the smoke and soot back into the house but that—at a moment when life itself was so precarious—was probably of small importance.

Office buildings in the *Wilhelmstrasse* section, however, had not yet suffered heavily from the bombing, and these were as modern and as well heated as any in America. By contrast to my experience with the illusory and purely sentimental value of English fireplaces, German buildings seemed stuffy.

There was a profusion of military personnel in the city. Even more than London, then the gathering point for fighting men from all the United Nations, Berlin was crowded with troops. And there was a phenomenal quantity of saluting and Heil Hitlering. Officers of the same rank saluted each other and privates saluted corporals.

At each entrance of the so far untouched Reich's Chancellory stood a helmeted and armed guard. Every branch of the German armed forces was represented: the *Wehrmacht, Luftwaffe, Kriegsmarine*, along with the SA (*Schutz-Abwehr*) and SS (*Schutz-Staffel*).

To every officer passing, each snapped noisily and ceremoniously to a starched attention. The SA and SS sentinels invariably gave the Hitler salute, whereas the other guards merely brought their rifles to attention.

One saw many khaki-uniformed SS, SA and *Hitler Jugend* in the streets, With them my expectations, for once at least, were completely fulfilled. Most appeared to be the German counterpart of our Dead End type, sullen, insolent, swaggering. They wore red armbands, emblazoned with a black swastika, and their march was as close to a goose step as to a walk.

The capital's civilian population, outnumbered it seemed by both its own military and by the veritable armies of war prisoners, appeared tired, pale, listless. Berlin had already endured by this time nearly fifteen thousand tons of bombs and the people's mannerisms clearly showed their fatigue and nervousness.

But they were well-dressed, that was an immediate and a lasting impression. Heavy coats, well-lined and collared with fur, were everywhere. The colors were drab browns and blacks but there was no mistaking a warmly dressed people.

And there were many more silk stockings to be seen than I remembered in wartime London. England could boast more cosmetics, but hardly as warmly nor as comfortably dressed a population. The answer was quickly evident: England, isolated, depending upon carefully cargoed convoys from the outside world, had to forego the luxury of good clothes, while Germany—the hub of a new, temporary empire—drew its wants from all Europe.

"We receive shipments of rubber and other scarce materials from Japan by submarine," boasted Steiner. "Your people think you have the Atlantic ports bottled up—but we get in much more than you sink."

Of all my impressions of Berlin, the most startling was to witness the capital's complete barrenness of children. For months before the raids had begun, Nazi authorities had encouraged the evacuation of children, old people, and nonessential women. Total evacuations to date, said Steiner, had totaled nearly two million, about half the population. This gave the city an additionally deserted, sterile appearance.

Queues of shoppers, a familiar sight in England, were also noticeably and remarkably absent. Despite the surrounding destruction, shops seemed well stocked. Only before one florist and one wine store did I see a line of women—never in front of a food shop.

Social life in Berlin had been seriously dampened by the turn of war events, explained my guides. Public dancing all over Germany, as in all occupied countries, had been strongly *verboten* since the beginning of the war. There had been a fortnight of legalized jubilation at the end of the victorious Polish and French campaigns, but since 1941—and the turn of Germany's military fortunes—dancing had been forbidden. Private parties, of course, were unaffected.

The reason underlying this order, explained Borner, was that soldiers battling on distant fronts should not be forced to think of their more fortunate civilian brothers enjoying themselves too gaily at home.

I thought of the difference between a trench-lined sector of the Italian front and the whisky-laden bars in New York and realized the Nazis were one up on us here.

Perhaps similar reasoning had brought about the very heavy penalties for discovered adultery. Two years' imprisonment was the minimum punishment, and in some cases the death penalty lad been invoked for both offenders. How effective such dissuasion was against so basic a pastime, however, remained an open question.

But there was still music, if of an incredibly poor quality. In several *caféhaus* restaurants, and in a few of the remaining hotels, small orchestras were maintained to churn out an interminable violin drivel, more depressing than it was diverting. Most of the musicians, by appearance, should have been content as retired grandfathers, and the others should have remained in the occupied countries whence they had come to entertain nerve-frayed Berliners.

Afternoon coffee gatherings seemed almost the sole social medium. There were still left two opera houses and the *Wintergarten* music hall. A large percentage of the movie houses had been destroyed. A few ice-skating rinks were left. And that was about all.

Berlin was a sober, grim city whose populace was too occupied struggling with the necessities of life to indulge in the luxury of social entertainment which keynoted life in London. Germany's capital was now, in effect, the blitzed London of 1940—but graver, more depressed, lugubrious, and far more heavily bombed.

Yet the city did not *have* to be sober. For here was every brand of wine and liquor known to Europe: Moselle, Rhine, Sauterne, Burgundy, and Hungarian wines were available in all the hotels. French and German champagnes (including Ribbentrop's *Henkel* brand) were obtainable in far greater quantities and far cheaper than in London or New York. Schnapps, the German blanket word for every type of liquor, could be obtained from Finland to Italy. Only American rye and Scottish whisky were evidently in short stock.

Beverages were rationed, as was everything else in Germany. But everyone seemed to consume far more than any ration could allow.

And every host proclaimed loudly and emphatically, at least to this American "guest," that what he drank was "my own allowance ... there is NO black market in Germany."

Hitler jokes were more prevalent in London and in neutral capitals at this time than in humorless Berlin. One current, however, and one which exhibited the weight of German wit, concerned the little man who tried to buy his rations and who found an endless queue outside the shop. He dutifully awaited his turn for a few hours, becoming more and more angry as the time passed. Finally he could stand it no longer.

"I shall kill the man who is responsible for all this, for the bombs and the queues," he exclaimed. He made his way to Hitler's headquarters. And there of course, he found a queue waiting too.

As with Londoners, the people of Berlin had their marvellous bomb-stories to tell: the big one that just missed, the fifty incendiaries that fell on their roof but neglected to burn down the house. And they had some fantastic ideas about the airmen who carried out the bombing.

"Every one of your fliers receives a five hundred dollar bonus for each trip over Germany, isn't that so?" asked one Nazi quite soberly.

"Is it true that your bomber crews are made up from the cells of your prisons all over America?" asked another man's wife. My answer to such questions, and to the more important, more insidious type, was that I was only a reporter—who ought, moreover, to be repatriated—so I knew nothing of the armed forces.

One story, which seemed to be true, concerned the crew of a British bomber which had as mascot a small Spitz dog. The plane was shot down over Berlin during a night attack and the crew forced to bail out. The dog had been fitted with a special oxygen mask and a special small parachute. He too was bailed out.

He landed safely near the city zoo and was picked up after the raid by Countess Waldersee (niece of a famous German general), who adopted him. If any of the crewmen should read this, they know now where to claim their dog.

A great number of wounded soldiers were to be seen in the capital. Crutches and bandages were far more commonplace than they had been in London, blunt testimony to the cost of four years' almost continuous fighting. With the bandages were an amazingly large number of decorations, chiefly Iron Crosses and bestarred service medals.

The traditional German passion for uniforms was surely in evidence here. Almost everyone in the city seemed entitled to military garb. Policemen, conductors, garbage collectors, and a host of minor dignitaries all wore uniforms which, at least to the newly arrived American, seemed remarkably similar to the regular *Wehrmacht* dress.

And there was a glut of swastikaed flags and drapery, of postered ballyhoo for the National Socialist Party, and of gaudy war propaganda. The sharp contrast of billboards with their shrieking colors set against the somber background of ashen rubble was somehow symbolic: it painted a prologue to the death of vaunted, hollow nationalism.

That night there was a heavy British air bombardment of Berlin.

A genuine fear of being in the city during a raid had been gnawing my consciousness since my arrival. I knew the RAF had only begun its terrible work against Germany; I had witnessed the blitz against London three years earlier and knew the British retaliation would be a hundredfold worse. And when the sirens, one after the other, began their haunting, swelling quaver, I trembled with a deeper fright than I had experienced a few nights earlier above the city.

It was early evening. We were walking to the hotel, where evidently I was to spend the night, from the office buildings a few blocks away. Borner and Steiner, well disciplined by previous experience, found a nearby shelter, beneath a small apartment house, and we entered it immediately.

Inside was a normal cellar, converted into an air raid bunker by crossbeams and heavy timber supports for the ceiling. About twenty women sat in groups of two or three huddling together on benches and canvas stools. Three old men and a youthful fire warden, in addition to ourselves, were the only males in the shelter.

On the walls hung axes, shovels, first-aid kits, buckets, and a variety of civilian gas masks. Two small candles provided the room's only light.

A few minutes after we arrived, the flak began firing. Sharp, rapid salvos from a nearby battery echoed loudly through the cellar. Soon the gunfire became an almost solid thunder as batteries all over the city spread a carpet of death over Berlin.

I felt perspiration running down my arms and face. I was breathing in short gasps; my eyes were half closed and my hands tightly clenched. I was terribly conscious of the "U.S." insignia on my uniform—these people will recognize me I thought, and if the bombs don't kill us all, they'll kill me for what my allies are doing to their city.

But no one in the shelter was interested in anything but himself. The women sat hunched over, their heads on their knees, their hands over their ears, holding themselves together—waiting, waiting for the bombs. One woman clutched two tiny children to her breast; one baby squeaked annoyingly and incongruously.

The men stood against the wall, hands at their sides or crossed on their chests, eyes staring straight ahead into the opposite wall. One old man, wearing a last-war helmet, stood stiffly at attention, rigid with fear and anticipation. The young warden paced an open space on the floor, watching the women, listening, waiting.

Then the bombs started. The staccato thunder of the guns was suddenly overwhelmed by an ear-rending avalanche of sheer terror. It was an express train, a waterfall, a drum fire … whistling, swishing, screaming … pounding, erupting, thumping.

"My God, this is a nightmare," I thought frantically as my fingernails dug painlessly into my palms. "This is a nightmare; reality cannot be this terrible."

No words can describe the next twenty minutes. I was there; I shall always remember the incomparable hell. But I know no words to picture it. The London of 1940 paled into nothingness beside it.

I remember the clattering of incendiaries on the roof, on the street outside, the gushing, shuddering explosion of a land mine across the road. I remember one women screaming in a high-pitched, crazed shriek, and falling prostrate across the floor. I remember the candles going out, plaster falling in strips from the ceiling, the door crashing open, and lumber from the floor above blocking the entrance, the air rushing from the room as another bomb smashed into a building on the same block. But I am not capable of picturing the scene, of recapturing the full horror of the sounds and emotions.

After a while the bombs and flak stopped. A deathly lull hung over the dark cellar. Then bells clanged in the street outside; fire trucks raced past and I looked up to see a red panel of flame through the shattered door.

"We can go now," said Steiner. "It is finished." Outside, we saw our building was afire, the top two doors blazing fiercely. No one was interested. It was only one burning building among thousands.

We walked for an hour around the center of Berlin, watching the firemen and the civilians battling the inferno. Here was a conflagration such as I had never seen in London. Whole streets were alight; billowing flames and smoke gushed upward from department stores, buildings, homes. Occasional streets were impassably blocked where the high-explosives had fallen.

Ambulances and fire engines chased through the open streets. Wounded were carted past on stretchers in every direction. Dead were lying in piles along the gutter. "Berlin's garbage trucks will collect the corpses tomorrow when there is time," said Steiner.

Parts of airplanes were scattered through the roads, strips of wings, tails, fuselage. Here a whole engine had half buried itself in the macadam and a few yards distant lay a wheel from some unlucky Lancaster.

Fire-bombs which had fallen uselessly in the open streets patterned out neatly in long rows, each issuing a white-hot flame from its wasted phosphorous.

Before one house, which was being quickly devoured by fire, an old woman sat on a chair, sobbing bitterly above the crackling flames. She had saved two chairs, a suitcase, and a meshed hamper—that remained; the rest was gone.

We returned to the hotel which, surprisingly, had lost no more than most of its windows and a part of the top floor burned out. Inside we swept a harvest of glass from the beds and fell on them exhausted.

Neither Borner nor the corporal-sentinel guarded me well that night. But it did not matter. I was too tired to try to escape.

CHAPTER 7

Wartime Tourist

The next morning, after a several hour discussion with Borner, I was offered a "trip around Germany." The idea was born during an argument over comparative cultures, which subject seemed of supreme interest to all patriotic Germans.

"You people are riding on your grandfathers' laurels," I argued. "Your music and literature has nothing to do with this new fantasy of Nazism. You've been too busy making guns during the past ten years to turn out anything enduring."

"You don't know," answered Borner. "You haven't seen Germany. We have wonderful architecture, fine roads and schools—all built since 1933."

And it developed something like that. Borner was so deeply proud of his country, of the new Germany, that finally he was brought to make an unusual offer.

"After we finish here in Berlin, you know, I must take you back to Dulag and from there you will go to a prison camp. Perhaps later on you will be repatriated, but that will be out of my hands.

"Now, I have an eight-day furlough due me, I might be able to keep you out of the camp for those eight days. I have some friends here and I could get a car and fuel. If you would promise me that you would not try to escape, perhaps we could take a look around Germany. And you may see that we are not so primitive a people as you think."

And so it came to be that I was able to obtain, in the middle of the war, a first-hand picture of conditions inside Germany. A thought might arise with the reader that this was a propaganda tour, that it was all carefully planned and arranged by the Nazis for the first reporter who should parachute to Berlin. I want to state right now my firm personal conviction that it represented exactly what Borner described it—"a look around Germany … you may see we are not so primitive a people as you think."

The thoughts I have come to hold regarding Germany, based in part on observations during that tour, are entirely my own. I was not led to admire nor appreciate the Germans by the experience of seeing them at work in their battered cities. Briefly what I relate here are the observations and reactions of an American reporter who tried to forget neither his allegiance nor his profession.

From a friend in the Berlin city hall, Borner obtained a false identity card for me (which he carried, to ensure I would not back out on a verbal promise not to try to escape). By it, I became "Robert Durand, journalist, born Paris, French citizen. …" He lent me an overcoat which covered my uniform and a felt hat which covered my un-Parisian hair.

We drove out of Berlin through its northwestern suburbs, in a small Mercedes Benz, with Hamburg as our first destination. While still in the capital, we passed the *Funkhaus* (Berlin's BBC) which the RAF had officially claimed destroyed, but which, I noted glumly, was still entirely intact.

The weather was dismal. A slight rain fell cheerlessly and a half-mist enshrouded the landscape. But the prospect of leaving the lifelessness of Berlin and the opportunity of doing some legalized spying was a compensatingly exciting one.

A few miles outside the city we began to pass miniature barracks towns where the bombed-out families had been absorbed.

These wooden camps were set a few hundred yards off the highway and consisted of a score or more of low, single-story barracks quite similar to military cantonments. Each building was entirely of wood, with a brick chimney and glass windows. Counterbalancing the crudeness of such a home was its pleasant rustic appearance and its undoubted safety from the bombs.

Smoke swirled from the chimneys, children played in the open spaces, and women could be seen hanging out the family wash. Each barrack seemed large enough to house perhaps twenty or thirty families and each settlement probably included several thousand inhabitants.

The country outside Berlin was uninterestingly flat. It was cultivated perhaps as intensively as only Japanese lands are developed, every acre bearing some food or providing grazing fields. But a few score miles northwest of the city, rolling hills unfolded, and the wonderful German forests began, the air becoming sharper with a cold tang from the North Sea.

The woods were being tackled by an army of foresters, "to get timber for the new barracks and wood for fuel," explained Borner. A large percentage of the woodcutters I saw were Russian women, their heads bound in traditional white scarves and their working capacity clearly equal to that of Western men.

Occasionally, groups of fifty or a hundred prisoners of war—usually Russians—could be seen working on pipelines or clearing land along the road, each contingent loosely guarded by a German or two. In villages along the way we saw many French prisoners, still in their 1940 uniforms, who worked with the farmers to replace conscriptees.

Traffic on the good road from Berlin to Hamburg was exceptionally light. In the nearly two-hundred-mile drive we passed barely a dozen vehicles, and nearly all of these were trucks whose loads were all directly connected with the war.

We passed through several villages of varying size, most of them sleepy towns with the Old World pastoral architecture, and saw the farmers, apparently indifferent to the war, leading their oxen- and horse-drawn loads of steaming manure to fertilize winter crops.

One cheering sight was that of children in the villages. Here were gathered the youth of Berlin and other bombed cities, and it was pleasant beyond description, after the barrenness of Berlin, to see the happy abandon of youngsters in the streets, laughing and chasing each other.

We reached Harburg and the southern outskirts of Hamburg after a five-hour drive from Berlin. First impressions were that it was a German Pittsburgh, for there were factories everywhere, smoke jutting finger-like into fog-laden skies. Workers' homes seemed to have been built as a second thought, squeezed and trammeled together between the factories. There was little damage here, little evidence of the bombing war in Hamburg's industrial southern suburbs.

But after a short drive we entered the city itself, and there the desolation began. (Hamburg had been attacked four times by the RAF in July–August, 1943, and three times by the Eighth USAAF during the same period. It had suffered many subsequent air attacks, but this series had spelled its death as a city.)

We drove north through the main street to the city's center, and for at least three miles there was not one house standing on either side of the street. I had seen the badly damaged areas of Berlin and the spotted destruction in London, but this was a devastation unimaginable by previous experience.

This was one hundred per cent destruction. It was desolation such as no earthquake, no natural phenomenon could have caused. It was deeply perturbing to witness what a terrible weapon man had invented in the air force and the incendiary bomb.

We drove to the center of the city, which, surprisingly, was not badly damaged. The main railroad station had lost its roof to fire, but the train schedule was operating to all major cities in Europe. There seemed much more life in Hamburg's center than in Berlin, many more shops open, crowded trolley cars and a large number of automobiles on the streets. Many sailors walked the sidewalks, arm in arm with their girls, and the sight was not unlike that of any British or American port city.

Borner drove to the police station and asked for a guide to "show the city to a French journalist whom I am accompanying on a trip around Germany." A Lieutenant Freier joined us and he proved to be an enthusiastic guide who had experienced all the attacks against Hamburg and, as a member of the police force, was well acquainted with their details.

After a few minutes' drive from the center, we reached a street that was barricaded with bricks and timber, with a large notice: "*Eintritt streng verboten.*" A chunky, tommy gun-armed soldier stood at one site to enforce the poster. But Freier passed our car inside by showing his police permit, and we began a tour of the "dead zone" of Hamburg.

These areas had been closed to the public since the raids, for they were absolutely lifeless. One such zone, I measured later on a map at the police station, covered nearly four square miles.

The totality of destruction was appalling. Street after street of dwelling houses was smashed and rubbled, leveled and pulverized into heaps of granulated grayness. Sometimes a broken radiator, a stove, or part of a bathtub poked out of the ruins. One thought of Pompeii, but surely this was worse.

There was no height. Of buildings that had been perhaps five or eight stories tall, there was left nothing more than piles of broken bricks and mortar, twenty feet high, and fused with the adjoining debris of one-floor houses. Everything had been crushed, both by the explosives and by the melting intensity of the fires, and everything had been reduced to meaningless mounds and tangled jungles of mashed, crumbled masonry.

Not one bit of wood or paper or cloth was visible anywhere; the heat had been so great it had burned everything within its rapacious reach. Everything was colorless for, as Freier said, "an ocean of fire" had devoured the entire area.

Our guide explained the phenomenon which occurred during the great raids. "The bombing was so concentrated," he said, "that tremendous fires were started. Their heat, against the cooler air outside the fire areas, created a hurricane as it expanded.

"A terrible wind raced through the city, as the heat from the phos-phorous bombs and the fires expanded, and nothing we could do would halt the flames." Only the natural fire-breaks of lakes, rivers, and treeless parks had averted disaster to the entire city.

In this great dead wilderness, the only sign of life was that of prisoners working in the debris, loading trucks—not with salvage, for there was nothing to salvage from such absolute destruction, but with rubble to be used in the port area.

We saw French, Italian, and Russian war prisoners—and the Italians were the most pathetic in their thin, dirty green cloaks and feather hats—trooping miserably along the streets in long columns. Political prisoners, in striped blue and gray uniforms, were also to be seen. These,

Freier explained, were used to dig bodies from the ruins, for that work was still in progress more than five months after the raids.

In the streets, which had been cut anew from the mountainous ruins, there was no traffic other than the prisoner columns with their picks and shovels and a few dump trucks with rubble. Sometimes the twisted, rusted, almost unrecognizable frames of cars could be seen parked along the curb, still standing where they had been burned out during the fires.

At one point we passed a row of what had been trolley cars, still standing in the middle of a cleared street: Freier told us a story in connection with those burned, twisted wrecks. After one night attack the people came out of their cellars in that street, for it had become too hot inside from the tremendous fires outside. But they could not leave the area for the fires surrounded them, and the heat was becoming more and more intense.

Some two hundred of them climbed into the trolleys which, standing in the middle of the street, were the farthest from the fires and the furnace heat. Finally, the tramways themselves had caught fire.

The next afternoon, when the fires had abated, some two hundred scorched and charred bodies were taken from their streetcar crematoriums.

"Sometimes," added Freier, "we could hear people screaming and crying for help from inside the fire zones. But there was nothing we could do because the wall of flame was too great, even hours after the attack was ended. And our water supply failed under such tremendous bombardments." (I watched his face for emotion as Borner translated, but I saw none.)

There had been no gas and no electricity for three weeks all over Hamburg after the series of raids had ended. Water had been missing in most parts of the city for a fortnight, and the telephone exchange did not resume operation for nearly a month.

We drove down to what had been the main business thoroughfare, the *Hamburgerstrasse*, and everything on both sides was completely obliterated. We stopped at one corner which, because of the unchanging scenery of monstrous rubble, appeared no different from any other part of the street. But Freier pointed to one particularly high pile of debris and explained that it had been Hamburg's biggest department store, *Karstadt* by name, and he told of what had happened there during one of the night attacks.

A big communal shelter underneath the store held six hundred people and, at the height of the attack, the entire area for acres around it was set afire. The shelter became hot and the air thickened with smoke.

The air-raid wardens ordered the shelterers to march out in a column, fearing the fires would spread to the department store and soon there would be no escape. About two hundred people reached the street when the fires attained such a heat that the remaining four hundred became frightened and refused to leave. The first two hundred trooped down the street, despite the great heat, and out of the conflagrated area to safety.

Soon afterwards, a land mine fell through the glass-roofed areaway in the center of *Karstadt*, exploding just in the middle of the store and completely demolishing it. But so far no one in the well-constructed shelter had been injured. A few more decided to try to get away, for it was becoming even hotter inside the packed cellar. These few were the last to leave the shelter alive.

The next afternoon, when the fires had subsided somewhat, the bodies of nearly four hundred people were dug out; every one of them had been asphyxiated from the coke and coal gasses spreading from fires which had caught nearby fuel stocks.

Further along the street we passed a huge cement bunker, at least a hundred feet high, which could shelter up to five thousand people. It was constructed entirely of cement and steel. Although everything around it for at least ten acres was completely leveled, it stood there somehow like a monument on a recent battlefield.

During one raid, our guide explained, three two-ton mines and over forty incendiaries had fallen on the roof, but no one inside had been hurt, for the walls and roof were two meters thick. One heavy bomb had struck a corner and chipped off a sizable piece of cement, baring the steel girders. But that had been the total damage.

But during the raid the fires had become so intense outside, the ventilation system had to be shut off. Nearly five thousand shelterers remained inside for fifteen hours before the fires died down sufficiently to allow them to leave.

Several thousand people were still under the ruins in various parts of the city, Freier said, but there was no attempt to recover most of the bodies for there was more important work to be done, and—because all landmarks had disappeared—their location was chiefly guesswork.

Ninety-five per cent of the fatalities in some areas had been impossible to identify, he added, because their death had come from fire, and the scorched, blackened bodies were hardly recognizable as those of human beings. Twenty thousand people had perished in the four-square mile area where the "ocean of fire" had surged.

Total casualties for the city during the series of attacks, according to the metropolitan police figures, were forty thousand killed, forty-five thousand seriously wounded, and more than twenty thousand lightly wounded.

Such figures are cold, brutally indescriptive. They convey no impression of death in its myriad and terrible forms and the grotesque maiming of human beings through air bombardment. Happily, America has known nothing of air attack in this war. But because of this good fortune, our people have little conception of the tremendous horror of such raids.

At the police station I looked at snapshots taken on the days following the raids. These were not propaganda pictures. When I asked if they had been printed or circulated, Freier said "they are too terrible. Propaganda should not be carried that far."

But I cannot help feeling they should be circulated to all of us, now the war is ended. I have seen the atrocious pictures of concentration camps, and my deep-felt conviction is that those horrors are nothing to the pictures of death from aerial bombardment. I remember, that day in Hamburg, looking at pictures of women who had fallen or thrown themselves across their children for a vain attempt to shield them from the heat, and all had died in that position.

I looked at pictures of streets littered with bodies, charred, chipped, cremated with scorch, lying in impossible positions, with arms and legs stretched out at grotesque angles. I remember what Freier said—"Ninety-five per cent unrecognizable. ... We had to bury them in mass graves outside the city. ..."

I could not think, "These are Germans ... it is all right because they are the enemy." That was impossible. I could think only of London, Berlin, Warsaw, and Moscow. These pictures showed not only Germans.

They represented humanity. They disclosed with a clarity and a horrible exactness just what we did to each other during the war.

The answers were all ready: the Germans began it in Warsaw and in London. By killing their children we are showing them that they must not begin another war. To attack morale is as effective as to attack industry. But these were not adequate answers to the sickening sights I saw that day.

I looked at a large-scale map of the city, on which were marked in different colors the areas where the heaviest bomb concentrations had been in each attack. In the four RAF night raids, about sixty per cent of the city was affected and between eighty and a hundred per cent of that area was absolutely wiped out, chiefly by the hurricane-like fires.

I saw that no more than a dozen RAF bombs had fallen anywhere near the dock or shipbuilding areas on the outskirts of the city. But, despite a high number of misses, the USAAF formations had clearly attempted to bomb military targets. Their heaviest concentrations were in the storage warehouses and dockyards along the rivers Alster and Elbe.

I asked if we could visit the harbor, and Borner telephoned the Blohm & Voss shipbuilding yards to ask permission for himself and a French journalist to visit the works. After another drive, and under the Elbe River through a narrow wooden tunnel, we emerged near the expansive shipyards.

Accompanied by a minor company official, we toured the extensive machine shops, storage sheds, welding and assembly halls. Blohm & Voss, formerly the birthplace of luxury liners, was then devoted almost exclusively to the production of ocean-going submarines.

We passed slipways on which U-boats were being constructed, and I counted sixteen in various stages of completion. Six finished submarines lay anchored in the broad river or tied up at docks. Over the slips, great nets of multicolored camouflage hung on wooden frames. The completed U-boats, said the official, each had their own underwater air-raid shelter into which they were driven at the first sign of an attack.

Twenty per cent of the workers were "imported labor," he said. French, Ukrainian, and Dutch were predominant. Each wore an armband with a distinctive color and the first letter of his nationality. And it was a serious shock to witness the "slave" laborers working with the same enthusiasm as did their German colleagues.

The guide emphasized that the French were the best workers (although this may well have been because I was introduced as a Frenchman) and he insisted that there had never been any evidence of sabotage. The same food rations and accommodations were allocated to foreign workers as to the Germans, he added, and they enjoyed the same wage levels.

He stopped one young Frenchman who was sweeping a tool-shop floor and asked if I would like to speak with him.

"*Cela va bien ici?*" I asked the boy.

"*Oui,*" was his brief answer, though he said it as if he had a toothache. Our guide patted and pinched his cheek for my benefit to prove that he was well fed, which certainly seemed the case, but his treatment of the boy seemed more to resemble that of a man toward his pet dog.

It was eye opening to witness the activity in all the shops and sheds. We visited many sectors of the yards, and my impression everywhere was that here an important contribution was being made to the German war effort. I judged that less than five per cent of the entire area had suffered from air bombing. This is a frank, honest estimate, based on an extensive tour.

It was incredible that the Allies had not yet inflicted more damage on such an important element of the German U-boat production (Blohm & Voss, I was later learn, was the largest submarine-producing company in Germany).

With their Path Finder technique, the RAF had been able to achieve a record concentration and accuracy in the city. Why had they not attacked the shipyards and the workers' barracks near them? Was "revenge" guiding RAF strategy; were men being thrown to their death in German skies and the population of whole cities being wiped out to satisfy some Minister's lust for vengeance?

I recalled the smug pride of RAF officials after the Hamburg attacks. "Wiped out," they said. "That will pay them back for Coventry."

"Wiped out" was true. Most of the city was gone. And the cost to Britain had been tremendous. In bombs (twenty-five thousand explosives and three million five hundred thousand incendiaries) and fuel (over six million gallons of high-test gas) and lives of fliers (over a thousand of the best sons)—plus the incalculable cost of time, training, and planning.

But the dockyards, U-boat slipways, and huge warehouse facilities—except for the spotted damage by USAAF bombs—were still operating all out for a Nazi victory.

And, eighteen months and very many bombings later, when the war was over and won, I read this in a New York newspaper:

"Hamburg will take fifty to seventy-five years to rebuild. ..." Its harbor and dockyards were in full operation nine days after its capture.

CHAPTER 8

Daylight Bombing Commentary

The German cities of Bremen and Münster were not good examples of successful daylight bombing. They had been subjected to the persistent and exclusive attention of our Eighth Air Force for some months when I saw them. In each was clear evidence both of the difficulties of precision bombardment and of the resultant havoc and misery when an attempted attack fails.

We drove from Hamburg to Bremen in the early morning, after a night in a Hamburg hotel, following a long, straight *Reichsautobahn* as good as any American highway. From perhaps ten miles outside Bremen we began to see bomb craters pockmarking and rupturing the planted fields for wide areas along both sides of the road. The American technique of dropping veritable carpets of bombs to blanket military targets was well demonstrated here, But the carpets had fallen in pasture land and plowed fields—and hundreds of varying sized craters had erupted over the earth's bosom like some horrible disease.

We heard later that no fewer than two thousand bomb craters had been counted in the fields surrounding Bremen. Not all the explosives had fallen wastefully outside the city, however.

As we entered Bremen's outskirts, the clusters of bomb craters increased. Many bombs had fallen on the road, which had been repaired with crushed stone—or was in the process of being repaired by parties of French and Russian prisoners, or by units of the *Todt* organization.

We passed beneath a railroad bridge which had been directly hit and saw two of its tracks still being repaired. Gas and water lines, under the streets, had also been damaged at several points and were being restored by gangs of prisoners or civilian contractors. Along the sidewalks at frequent intervals were small, metal, one-man shelters, the first I had seen in such numbers.

In the city's outskirts we had passed many high observation towers, not unlike those built for American forest rangers as lookout posts for fires. But these were equipped with twenty-millimeter cannon or heavy, multiple machine guns, as defense against low-flying bombing or strafing attacks.

Toward the center of Bremen we began to see the eleventh- and twelfth-century Hanseatic homes and buildings, their richly coppered roofs rusted and mildewed with age. In the town's center were grouped, around a main market square, the ornate and intricately designed chambers of commerce, the town hall, churches, and the homes of once-famed merchants.

We were met, for Borner had telephoned ahead from Hamburg, by a newspaperman of the local journal, who took us immediately to a quiet restaurant and a meal of smoked eel, herring, and ice cream—a somewhat incongruous lunch considering the December weather—but it was a "meatless" day. I buried my restraint and decided to be as much a reporter as possible.

Bremen had experienced, up to that time, one hundred and twenty-two air attacks and more than eight hundred alerts. In most German cities, an extra food, wine and tobacco ration was allotted to the population after air raids. But because the state of "alert" was almost a permanent one for Bremen, the extra tobacco ration at least was also a permanent one. Every man received thirty cigarettes extra (to his ration of a hundred and twenty) per month, and every woman fifteen. There was an odd suggestion there that a woman is less affected than her mate by air attack; perhaps it had been worked out on a psychological basis.

Extra food rations after each raid depended upon the attack's intensity, said our host. The bonus varied from one extra day's rations to three extra days.

Despite the great number of raids, claimed by Bremeners to be the largest for any German city, the official casualty figures showed a disproportionately low toll of life. There had been two thousand four hundred killed, four thousand nine hundred wounded.

After lunch we walked through the town and saw something of its damage. Later, we drove to the dock and shipbuilding areas and saw what had happened to the military-target area.

After a comprehensive visit to both sections, I noted the following estimates: damage to town, twenty-five per cent; damage to waterfront, seven and one half per cent. For curiosity's sake, and to settle a quiet suspicion that was always with me, I asked our guide for the official estimate of damage. His answer: thirty per cent of the town destroyed and ten per cent of the dock area. This confirmed, at least, that there was as yet no attempt to conceal the facts from "Robert Durand, French journalist."

"What paper are you with, by the way," asked the German reporter.

"Paris Soir," I hazarded, suddenly wishing I had chosen a smaller, less known one, for he proceeded to name several collaborating editors.

"You know them, of course. How are my confrères in Paris?" he added, as the situation became ticklish and Borner was obviously trying to think of a polite conversation changer.

"Fine, fine. Everybody's fine in Paris," I answered. I had not been in Paris for three and a half years, but that didn't matter now.

It was interesting to note the different aspect the destroyed houses had after a daylight attack employing chiefly explosive bombs, and a city which had been the target for an RAF incendiary attack. Here in Bremen the damage was much less widespread than it had been in Berlin or Hamburg, but it was far more permanent.

Houses had been crumpled and flattened by single explosive bombs, streets torn up, gas and water mains burst, and other public facilities smashed. Fire had gutted most of the destroyed buildings in Berlin, but here high-explosive had done the work. Debris here looked broken and smashed, but it was still distinguishable, whereas after the great fires in Hamburg, nothing was identifiable. Here, colors and paints remained, but restoring a bombed house was out of the question, for the high-explosive was final and irreparable. Fire, on the other hand, frequently left the main structure capable of repair.

We walked through the narrow, winding streets, walled by the tall Hansea buildings—which seemed almost to lean outwards over the road—with their individual and ornate design. There was much more life apparent in Bremen than there had been either in Berlin or Hamburg, for the population's baptism to air attack had been a more gradual one here than in either of the other cities.

We drove to the dock areas, inspecting drydocks and harbor installations along the Weser River. Damage seemed to run between one-fifth and one-quarter of the built-up areas. We passed great grain and wood storage buildings, most of which were intact, and drove past a veritable city of oil storage tanks, entirely covered by vast camouflage netting, propped up on hundred-foot wooden frames.

Occasionally, there were small barrack towns, where the Germans and foreign waterfront workers lived, and most of these were also still intact. From a distance, we saw well-guarded U-boat construction pens, housed in thick cement casemates and evidently invulnerable from all but the heaviest-caliber bomb.

We passed through fields of loading cranes, dockyards, railroad switching areas—and to these there was almost no damage whatsoever. It again brought on the thought, as had the sight of Hamburg's docks, that if the Air Force could find a city and bomb it with reasonable accuracy, surely it could locate and destroy much of these vital installations. The marine works of Bremen covered at least as great an area as the city itself.

Driving back into the town, we passed its civic cemetery, which had been extensively plowed up during one of the daylight attacks when a whole carpet of bombs went askew. According to our guide, the cemetery had to be closed for three weeks while the twice-dead bodies were sorted out and reburied.

That evening, awaiting dinner in a hotel lobby, we experienced a running commentary of an RAF night raid. The city sirens opened their mournful chant just after six o'clock and the lobby quickly emptied as the hotel dwellers hurried to their rooms to collect their possessions in preparation for another sojourn in the air-raid shelter.

At 6:20, over the hotel loudspeaker, came the sharp, authoritative voice of a young woman broadcasting from the city's Air Raid Control center.

"*Achtung, achtung*," came the words, clearly, slowly. "Several bomber formations have crossed the Dutch coast. They are now flying over Holland directly toward Bremen, at a distance of one hundred fifty kilometers."

Most of the hotel occupants had by that time come down with laden suitcases, hampers, and rucksacks. They paused while the announcement was broadcast, then settled into chairs to wait until the danger should become more imminent before proceeding into the stuffy cellar. I watched three truly inscrutable Japanese seamen who squatted solemnly around a coffee table in the lobby, saying nothing, watching and waiting.

At 6:30, the radio crackled back to life and the same voice rapped out, "*Achtung, achtung*. The enemy formations are now flying one hundred kilometers southwest of Bremen on a course due east." The atmosphere in the lobby, crowded with a hundred men and women, fully dressed with coats and hats, each with a small pile of luggage beside his seat, was charged with tension.

"*Achtung, achtung*," came the voice again at 6:35. "Enemy formations are now fifty kilometers southwest of Bremen, course east."

There was no pretense here. In England, during the blitz, it had not been "good form" to display emotion, fear, worry. But here, with a frankness approaching intimacy, no one attempted to cover the fact that he was waiting, watching, listening—would that terrible horror burst in a few moments over Bremen?

Five minutes later, a helmeted warden entered hurriedly from the street to announce that the flak was firing and everyone must go below to the shelter. As we filed down the steps, the radio snapped into action again.

"*Achtung, achtung*," we heard the woman's voice. "A few enemy planes have reached our city and the outer defenses are engaging them." To emphasize her words, came the dull, erratic rhythm of anti-aircraft guns, pounding distantly, hollowly into the night sky.

We sat for a while on benches in the low-ceilinged shelter, hearing nothing, for we were deep in the earth. Thick timbers supported the roof and the basement had been divided into a maze of interconnected rooms, separated by heavy steel doors which bolted on both sides.

From the shelter loudspeaker, lust before seven o'clock, came the control center again. "*Achtung, achtung.* The main enemy force continues to fly eastward. Leading elements are now two hundred fifty kilometers southeast of Bremen." Soon thereafter the sirens screeched a welcome but anticlimactic all-clear, and we emerged from the basement in time for a late supper.

Early the next morning, we drove southwest toward Osnabrück and Münster, along a good second-class road. The first town had suffered no visible bomb damage (my interest) and boasted fewer cultural residue (Borner's interest) than Münster, so we continued without stopping.

South of Osnabrück, we entered the religious, agricultural country of Westphalia. We stopped for gasoline at a blacksmith shop and, while an aged woman pumped the fluid into our tank in exchange for some ration tickets, we watched a fifteen-year-old apprentice shoeing a sturdy farm horse. An old man stood near by, advising and grumbling. He told us he and the boy now cared for nearly two hundred horses, for the whole district, as all the other smithies had gone to war "*für das Vaterland.*"

We passed frequent crucifixes and statuettes along the road, blurred by a sluggish mist which had settled over the low country. Each village had its quota of prisoners of war, working in gardens or driving wagons along the road. In each village too, there were scores of Russian civilians, of both sexes and of every age, each wearing an armband with the word "*Ost.*" These were the unfortunates who had been forcibly deported by the Germans from the occupied regions of west Russia. They helped fill the labor gaps in Germany, and deprived the resurgent Russian Army of help when they re-entered once-conquered territories.

The northeast suburbs of Münster had suffered little damage. As soon as we reached the city center, however, the vast wreckage was apparent on every side. The center itself was at least seventy-five per cent destroyed. In the middle of the town loomed a magnificent Catholic cathedral. It too was at least three-quarters destroyed.

Again, Borner contacted some city official, and after formal pseudo-introductions, we walked through the town with a guide end historian. For two hours, we toured the city, following its narrow, cobbled streets, framed by houses of the same type as in Bremen, and saw that the bombing had given Münster the same "chewed up" appearance as the city we had left that morning.

Official estimate of damage to Münster, said our guide, was fifty per cent damaged and a further fifteen per cent badly damaged. "But in the center of the city," he added, "the damage, as you can see, is over eighty per cent."

Münster had, in truth, been terribly hammered by the fifty-six attacks it had suffered to date. And this damage was largely the work of American Forts and Liberators, for the last RAF night attack had been nearly three years previous.

One of the most important Catholic centers in Germany, Münster in peace had been the religious hub of all Westphalia. And it had been a gay, busy town too, added our guide. Almost every Sunday saw the villagers and farmers from miles around driving into the city for the fairs.

Now the town center was all but obliterated. Nearly all the buildings walling the main market square were in ruins.

On one side of the large square had stood the home of the Bishop of Münster, von Galen. Previous to the air attacks, he had. been one of the most vigorous and vociferous enemies of National Socialism inside Germany, fighting from pulpit, pamphlet, and in outside speeches. He, along with a handful of resolute clergymen in Germany, had managed to stand up against the Nazis and, with the Church at his back, they could not silence him.

But American bombs had done what the Nazis had been unable to do. On October 10, 1943, over seven hundred high-explosives and nearly ten thousand incendiaries had tumbled in carpets from the sky to black out the center of Münster. Among the buildings destroyed had been von Galen's cathedral and his home.

(The deliberate target that day, the main point of impact for the cargoes of that bomber fleet, I learned much later from airmen who participated in the attack, was the cathedral and the main square.)

Bishop von Galen had joined a bucket brigade to help extinguish the fires that devoured his palace. But to no avail.

Today, he lived on his Private estate a few miles outside the city. "And," gloated our guide, "from that date he has not said one word against the Nazis."

Münster had been, in fact, one of the centers of anti-Nazi feeling in Germany. There had been no large, organized movement, hardly even an articulate, passive resistance—except from the pulpit of von Galen and a few other courageous churchmen—but the city had been a weak link in the new Germany, for its population was too devout to be recruited into the ranks of Hitler's new religion.

But the grumblings and the discontent were ended. Our bombs had done that. However much we might propagandize ourselves as twentieth-century crusaders, as defenders of religious and political freedom, our bombs had splintered the heart of Catholic Westphalia. Our bombs, in truth, had bridged the breach between the Church and Nazi Germany.

Our aerial warfare against Europe, I was later to find, had not only alienated elements of the German population who might have helped our cause, but had lost us many friends in the occupied countries.

Our bombs avalanching down on Münster had put the workmen, the churchmen, and the local Nazis in the same boat. Our bombs had threatened them all with an equally terrible death. It is no phenomenon that, because of our raids, Germans and Nazis became as one.

In one attack on Münster, the ancient city hall—the oldest example of Gothic architecture in Germany, where the Peace of Westphalia was signed in 1648—was destroyed. Most of the city's world-famous churches were ruined. And thousands of homes were wiped out. This did not result from a few misdirected bombs, nor from a temporary mania on the part of some air commander—it was the planned policy of an air force which was dedicated by its chief to prove that Germany's morale could be cracked through air attack.

What material gain could be hoped for in the destruction of Münster? There was a marshalling yard in one corner of the city; this was virtually untouched by bombs. There was a single, plane-component factory in another corner. This had never been hit.

A measure of damage had been inflicted upon the city's public services. After one raid, gas and electricity were nonoperative for five days. Time, labor, and material had to be diverted from the German war effort to repair some of the damage. But the cost of such raids to the *American* war effort was considerable. And, after long consideration and careful study of data on both sides of the question, at least one observer feels deeply that many of the raids-the "morale raids"-were a mockery of our vaunted efficiency.

Much of the population of Münster, nearly thirty per cent of the whole, had been evacuated to neighboring farms and villages or had joined families in safer regions of Germany. A few barrack towns had been constructed outside the city for the bombed-out families who had nowhere to go. But the evacuation problem for this city was not a great one, for it lay in the heart of a vast agricultural area that could absorb, as a dry sponge, thousands of families without serious inconvenience.

We left Münster in the late afternoon, driving southwest toward the industrial Ruhr. Borner, fatigued by his role as interpreter, for I still spoke only a mediocre German and very few of our guides spoke French, said little.

I found myself too puzzled to sleep or even to enjoy the rural loveliness of the rolling country through which we were now passing. His efforts to acquaint me with Germany's *Kultur* were falling flat. I was witnessing, instead, something else, an aspect of the war which was providing disturbing reactions. The only consolation, and that a dubious one, was that perhaps further along the line I would see evidences of success to balance the three clear failures so far.

CHAPTER 9

Ravaged Ruhr

The industry-packed Ruhr, arsenal of the Kaiser's imperialism in 1914 and again arsenal for Adolf Hitler's crusading National Socialism in 1940; a black-earthed valley, rich in coal and iron, and target for RAF and American bombs for three years: this was the vista that sprawled from southwest of Münster in a wide swath, far south to the broad bosom of the majestic Rhine.

Here was the home of Krupp, the munitions king, the home of a thousand coal mines and twenty thousand steel mills. Here was the home of twenty million Germans who, by their sweat and blood, made the Nazi gamble almost succeed.

And here too was the test and the proof of "Victory through Air Power." For here Allied bomber fleets had avalanched down a hundred thousand tons of bombs to blot out the throbbing industrial machinery to raze the workers' homes, to wreck the maze of railroads that carried the war weapons from the factories to the fronts. Here, air power had been put to the test: every one of thirty cities and fifty satellites had been flooded with the awesome destructiveness of incendiaries and high-explosives.

"Happy Valley," the airmen ironically called that oft-visited land and, though the Battle of Berlin may have been the more spectacular, the Battle of the Ruhr was by far the greater. Thousands of heavy British and American bombers were lost in the danger-fraught skies that roofed the Ruhr; fifty thousand airmen perished in that vast flak- and bomb-filled void. Fifty thousand more tumbled in parachutes to the solitude of prison camps. Five hundred million gallons of high-test gas were burned to carry the bombers to their targets and back. A thousand million man-hours were consecrated to building the planes and the bombs, planning the attacks, and carrying them out.

More than a hundred thousand Germans were killed, a greater number wounded in that valley of aerial death. Two million homes were blown up or gutted. For here the entire region was the target. Here, cities were adjacent; factories, mines, mills, it, and homes were sewn in a concentration unequaled anywhere else in the world.

The Ruhr was, in truth, the proving ground for the strategy of "Victory through Air Power." And, as late as February, 1944, Winston Churchill declared that the RAF's giant raids constituted "a fundamental principle of British war strategy." Here was evidence of success or failure in the Allied attempt to win the European war the easy way—the bombing way.

We entered the northeastern corner of the Ruhr Valley during the late afternoon, passing through Bochum and Gelsenkirchen, then drove into Essen where we spent the night. It was quickly evident: these were not separate cities, but the whole valley was one sprawling, industrial metropolis. Each town had grown and spread, fusing with its neighbors into one immense unit, one great arsenal of iron and steel—of weapons for German soldiers.

Both Gelsenkirchen and Bochum had been severely bombed. At least fifty per cent of each city was in ruins. But the amazing and disconcerting fact, immediately apparent, was that the heavy iron and steel works in each were still operating. Columns of black smoke surged from scores of looming chimneys on the outskirts of the towns.

And the reason was almost as immediately clear: the center of both cities had obviously been the main target and only stray bombs had fallen in the war-plant areas on the fringes.

The road into Essen was walled on both sides by the gutted skeletons of burned-out buildings. The destruction was complete, continuous, mile after mile. Utter lifelessness was the predominant impression; the streets were barren and the darkening sky was only half-occluded by the stark, jagged structures which had once been buildings.

We spent the night in the Essenerhof Hotel, one of the three remaining unbombed in the city. A few hundred yards from the disturbingly undamaged (or fully repaired) main rail station, our hotel had been built by the Krupp family. And its solid pomposity—ornate and heavy with useless steel fixtures—was typical of Krupp.

Early in the morning we acquired a *Gauleitung* chauffeur as guide and began an extensive walking tour of the city's center. "Twenty-two of our twenty-five major churches are gone," he announced as we picked our way through charred ruins. (Borner was having a difficult time finding residual specimens of German *Kultur* to show me.) On a barrier of the Münster Church, "the oldest Christian structure in Germany," we saw a poster: "Historical edifice. Nothing to be touched."

But the order applied to souvenir hunters, not to the RAF, for there was little left of the building. Inside was a tangled jumble of iron and leaded glass and mortar, where most of the dome and walls had been exploded inward.

The city's center had been obliterated by high-explosives. An area of six square kilometers in the heart of Essen was ninety to one hundred per cent destroyed. The city hall, museum, post office and almost every other building and store in the business area had, all been hammered into nothingness. And, because of the totality of the destruction, no effort had been made—other than to clear the main streets—to repair or restore the wreckage.

We came to an old man who was staring at the rows of destroyed buildings, as if fascinated by the sight. He was eighty-seven years old, he told us, and had been in three wars, a camp helper in 1870, and an infantryman in 1914, and he said, "The first two were wars. This is not war. I do not understand this."

Between wars, he had worked in the Krupp plants, being a native of Essen, and six months previously he had been evacuated with the women and children from the city. "Every Sunday since the *Angriffen*," he said, "I walk around the city and remember what it was like before."

For two hours we wound through the streets of Essen, from one corner of the city to another, crisscrossing and covering the entire area. The sights that walk produced were astounding. As badly damaged as was the center of the city, so its many factories were almost unanimously intact and working.

We passed a dozen large plants, branches of the Krupp organization, and, of these, one alone showed any evidence of damage. Pressed for an estimate of total damage to Essen's industry, our guide replied, "Perhaps ten per cent were immediately affected at one time or another. But the damage was always cleaned up within a fortnight, even after the heaviest attacks." I had no reason to believe that man was lying.

The locations of the plants, their present state, and the general impression gained from a tour of the city all bore out his statement. The railroad yards we saw were all completely undamaged and operating on what seemed a full schedule.

Later, we toured the surface installations of the *Zollverein* coal mine, claimed by its operators to be the largest in the world. Essen's suburbs had the same drab, coal-dusted appearance as mining towns in northeast Pennsylvania and the Midlands of England, the same atmosphere of goalless eternity, but the children were scrubbed dean and housewives polished their front steps.

Of more than a dozen mine fields we passed, the total apparent damage could not have been more than one per cent. Miners' homes, lining the cobbled streets, had suffered more heavily. As much as thirty pet cent were destroyed or badly damaged. But clustering around every mine shaft were several score wooden barracks where, explained the guide, German and prisoner miners lived. These, as the mines they surrounded, had suffered almost no damage.

Seventy-five hundred workers made up the labor in this single field, and nearly half of them were Italian, Russian, and French prisoners. The miners, claimed a *Zollverein* executive who showed us around his installations, were "the best-fed civilians in Europe," receiving three times as much meat, fat, and bread, and twice as much other food rations as civilians in other occupations.

Many of the French prisoners were *transformés*, having elected to leave prison camps and to live a relatively free life much the same as their German co-workers. The offer of leaving prison camps had been made to nearly all French prisoners in Germany, and of the million and a half only a few thousands had accepted; the remainder still considered their country at war with the Reich.

The mine official appeared unanxious to talk of the prisoner labor which made possible "the world's greatest coal output." When asked how they worked, he replied laconically, "The French are all right. But the others are not too enthusiastic."

Extraordinary bomb-proofing precautions had been carried out on all surface works by installing heavy steel girders and a one-meter layer of concrete on all roofs. All machinery was encased in brick walls and mortar. Nothing was combustible; even the office equipment and window frames were of steel.

We left the mine and drove south from Essen, passing several other mines and many large factories, none of which showed any evidence of damage. We passed through Oberhausen and Mülheim, both large cities, but both seemed to form only one immense metropolitan and industrial expanse that was the Ruhr. And here again the inescapable impression was the same: more than half the homes and buildings were in inescapable ruins, but the vast majority of the factories throbbed with life and labor.

Sometimes unguarded groups of French prisoners strolled along the road, their ancient uniforms apparently tidied and cleaned to retain some semblance of a Sunday dignity even after four years of forced labor for the enemy. And there were Russian women in evidence, on a Sabbath stroll like the French and Germans. Short, stocky women, the Russians, heavily booted and shawled with lengths of dirty white rag.

Solingen, our next halt, was the German counterpart of England's Coventry. It was known, in fact, as the city of a thousand factories. Almost every house, or the garage or shed behind the house, was a small industrial unit.

Here, in peacetime, had been the source of much of Europe's cutlery, scissors, razor blades, and other small metal commodities. But, so much like Coventry in most respects, Solingen differed in one important particular: here there was no evidence of bomb damage. This was a disconcerting discovery because I knew strong American formations had several times attempted to bomb the city's industrial targets.

Borner asked directions to one of the larger war plants in the city, and we were directed to a factory which we found to be the Rudolf Rautenbach Metallurgical Works, the largest light-metal plant in Germany, then engaged in constructing engine parts for fighter planes.

The French journalist and his officer-escort were shown through the many workshops, and halls which made up the factory. Hundreds of Russians, nearly half of them plump-faced women in heavy boots and white shawls, were working in the assembly shed, transferring light-metal parts from white-hot molds to long assembly belts.

In another shop were French and Belgian workmen, finishing and polishing shiny cylinder heads and carburetors. The only Germans in evidence were occasional foremen who walked among the lathes and benches, inspecting the work.

A large storage hall was half-filled with bricks of the gleaming metal to be melted and molded to create new *Luftwaffe* interceptors.

Dr. Nothling, general director of the plant, pointed to the metal and remarked jokingly, "The Yankee bombers are an important source of metal for us now. They use the best light metal in the world for their B-17's and B-24's, and we salvage quite a bit from the wrecks all over the Reich." In the guise of a Frenchman, I refrained from wincing at the thought of American bombers, shot down over Germany, providing scrap to build more Nazi fighters—to shoot down more bombers.

Over a vegetarian lunch, Nothling explained something of a classification system he had developed and which was now being widely used in German industry, designed to ensure a maximum per capita output and to eliminate sabotage by foreign workers.

"We photograph every new employee who is sent to us from the *Arbeitsfront*," he explained. "A man's physiognomy tells us a great many things about him, no matter what his country of origin.

"I have developed a system of classifying laborers, each into the special category of work for which he shows the greatest natural aptitude. We know better than anyone else the potential danger of employing millions of the enemy in factories all over the country. Only a small percentage of these foreigners is capable of becoming saboteurs or of leading other workers against us, however. But there is also the considerable risk of putting valuable tools in clumsy hands.

"So we study each one as he comes to us; we train him in the work for which he is best fitted. And if we find his nature is that of a saboteur, an agitator—or even a potential provocateur—he finds no opportunity to do us any harm.

"By continued study, we have developed our classification system into a science with the result that there has not been one act of sabotage here for the past two years. There is no one, I venture to say, among out foreign workers upon whom we cannot depend almost as completely as on our own workmen. And now this same system is in operation all over Germany."

In conclusion, I hesitatingly put forward the question: "Have you found, doctor, through your research in physiognomy that the Germanic type is generally superior to, say the Latin or the Slavic type?"

After a moments reflection, he answered: "No, I have not. There are many aspects to that question. But in general, no. The Germanic or Aryan physiognomy shows no evidence of an overall superiority above the others."

At last I had found a German who disagreed with Adolf Hitler!

We drove on to Düsseldorf which was ruined. The city's center was rubble. But the sprawling *Borzig* artillery works—where the 88 millimeter gun was produced to kill Americans—was still entirely intact. The bomb concentrations were in the business center; *Borzig*, and the apartment houses where lived its more than twenty thousand workers, was untouched.

The next day we drove to Cologne and visited the famous cathedral. Ninety per cent of the inner city was smashed, but miraculously the cathedral had suffered only minor damage.

Outside its main gate, I witnessed an argument between Borner, representing the Army, and a priest, representing the Church. The priest pointed to a sign which refused admission. Borner claimed the right to enter because of his uniform and the purpose of this visit: to show a French journalist Germany's most famous cathedral.

"You should have brought your friend before the war, before you and the rest of the world began this stupid struggle," admonished the priest. "The main altar and the organ have been ruined by bombs now and a part of the roof has been lost. But come in if you must. Be careful, there are dangerous spots."

I shall never forget the lofty serenity, the sublime aloofness of that structure. A haunting silence filled its great, domed interior. It loomed above the torn city, as the spirit it represented, a towering monument to faith amidst all that desolation.

That afternoon Borner telephoned Berlin and was informed that his furlough had been cut short, that we should have to return immediately. We drove east through Weimar, where two poets of another Germany were buried together in a sacred mausoleum, and through Jena where the great Zeiss optical works had suffered only one light bombing during the entire war, and north to Berlin.

I was just as glad the tour was ending. My memory was taxed with the details of what I had seen. I wanted to think about it and to plan an escape from this desperate country.

The most perplexing thoughts were those of the bombing. I had come to Berlin to witness one attack against one city, and now I had seen the results of hundreds of attacks against a dozen cities. It was not to be until nearly two years later that I could sort out my impressions and study the Allied version of the air war in Europe.

Today I feel even more strongly than I did then, in the middle of December, 1943. I have talked with thousands of British and American fliers, whose energy and whose blood were expended in a grand-scale test of a ballyhooed theory. I have checked the statements of Allied political and air-force leaders to analyze their chameleon-like reports to the people whose money and whose labor provided the machines. I have talked with Germans, Frenchmen, Czechs, Russians—people who had first-hand experience of our aerial offensive against Europe. I have covered a great part of Germany by car and by plane.

My sincere conviction is that a serious strategical mistake was made in trying to bomb Germany out of the war by destroying her cities. Chief guilt in this aim lies with the RAF whose main purpose was the razing of German cities. Only a very small number of RAF night attacks were carried out against factories or military installations.

Many American attacks, on the other hand, were directed against legitimate targets. It was only during a few months of 1944 that our Eighth USAAF was brought to follow the RAF strategy of deracination.

In the summer of 1943, Air Commodore George Jones, Chief of Staff of the RAF, declared: "I have no doubt that the bombing of Europe, if maintained at the present scale, might lead to the collapse of the Axis powers without any large-scale operations on land. … Other operations may be unnecessary except occupation." At the same time, reports were cabled from London that "British Air Marshal Harris, chief of RAF Bomber Command and Major General Ira Eaker of the 8th USAAF … believe that Germany can be bombed out of the war." This point of view was well known to correspondents in Britain at the time.

This is not an attempt to second-guess war strategy. It is all too easy to sit back now and, in the light of events and achievements, to denounce policy. But it is a serious warning that empty slogans must not supplant facts; that skillful propaganda must not be used to obscure murderous waste.

Harris and Eaker are sincere men. There can be no doubt about that. But Hitler was sincere too—and that does not lessen his guilt nor lighten the punishment of his nation. I condemn the bomber chiefs for lobbying extensions for their policy by presenting inaccurate reports of its effectiveness.

With clever public-relations officers, heavy losses were made to appear "a low cost for a great air victory." Reports of bomber losses were juggled so that the public heard of only half the blood spilled to test the theory. Hollywood's cameras, magazines, and newspapers were enlisted to glorify the Air Forces. Cartoonists imagined "Victory through Air Power" fantasies.

Fifty-six of Germany's major cities were destroyed. This forced a redirection of labor in Germany to clean up the wreckage, to build new barrack towns (but Germany had twelve million slave laborers for this work). The bulk of German city dwellers lost their homes (but this made them better soldiers for Nazism, for without possessions, without pride, they were the more easily led).

The destruction of fifty-six German cities, many of us are convinced, did not essentially alter Nazi production capacity. Note what Senator Brewster, returned from an extensive tour of Europe after the war was ended, declared:

"Had the European war lasted four months longer, Germany would have dominated the air." (Remember the number of bomber missions and the bomb tonnage employed to blot out the *Luftwaffe*? And Allied intelligence services knew full well that German aircraft production *reached its peak* during the late fall of 1944, within six months' of the war's end, and more than two years after its claimed destruction was begun.)

Four weeks after the war had ended, Leo T. Crowley, America's Foreign Economic Administrator declared: "... today, Germany—except for the United States—is the outstanding armament machine shop in the world. ... Practically all the great iron and steel furnaces of Germany are ready for operation or can soon be in operation with minor repairs. ... It would appear that little permanent damage has been done to most of the (textile) plants. ..."

Does not this official statement prove the futility of trying to deracinate a nation by scourging its cities? Essential Nazi industries were still fully operative at the end of the war, and those destroyed—by accident or by precision daylight missions—surely did not repay the cost of vast bomber fleets.

The Air Force publicists injured the Allied cause in another important aspect. Glamorized missions over Germany; fairytale-like combats above Europe; cheap, easy air victories against an "impotent" *Luftwaffe*—these widely circulated stories surely did not suggest the measure of titanic ground battles to come, surely did not assist a sober, realistic view of the struggle. "Why build tanks? We shall bomb them into Unconditional Surrender. The Air Force says it can do it alone."

Yet it was the tactical use of bombers and fighters which contributed so heavily to our victory in Europe, the scourging of enemy supply lines, dumps, and front-line areas, not the dumping of fire-bombs on residential areas throughout the Reich.

Yet first priority in metal, labor, shipping, and fuel was allocated the *strategic* Air Forces. The cream of youth in America and the British Empire were fed into the maw of Air Force training schools, Britain's ground forces suffered serious shortages of modern weapons and equipment so that a disproportionately large Bomber Command could continue razing Germany's cities at suicidal cost. The nation's best men were poured into an ever-emptying pool of flying cadets.

And those men and boys fought a terrific battle in the strange new arena of the world's roof. They flew and fought until death or the solitude of German prison camps plucked them from the skies.

The moral question has too many aspects to be argued here. It is clearly a historical crime that war was declared by both opponents against women and children. Bombing is a moral *wrong* no matter how *right* may be its ultimate purpose. But I argue not from the moral standpoint, rather from the practical point of view.

Air Marshal Harris argued his air bombardment tied down a million and a half German workers, rendered life difficult for millions more. He did not disclose how many millions of workers in the British Empire dedicated their time and strength to making possible the bombing.

It was not admitted until the war was ended how many of Britain's finest youth were sacrificed in the bombing: over sixty thousand killed and missing alone (from more than nine thousand lost bombers), and these figures did not include many thousands more from British dominions and colonies.

"Thousands of lives will be saved on the invasion beachheads," sloganed the Air Force publicists.

Those lives were saved not by deluging aerial death on German cities, by impoverishing and embittering a whole nation. They were saved by precision daylight attacks and by tactical bombardment. With its fire horror, the RAF proved Goebbels' sermon to his people "You are fighting for your lives"—and the German people did fight for their lives, as had no other nation in European history.

Our own Eighth Air Force expended over a billion gallons of high-test gasoline to check the theory. Many of its raids were fine examples of precision attack—against oil plants, plane factories, and rail centers. As many more, however, were wasteful dumping of bombs—and dead fliers—over German soil in pursuance of a stultified policy of morale bombing.

Ambitious Air Force interrogators, questioning Marshal Goering and other Nazi leaders after the war, sought to prove that air bombing had played a predominant role in Germany's defeat. Goering and the others, who should know, insisted that it was the ground forces and the *tactical*, coordinated, use of the Air Forces which obtained victory for the Allies, not the independent operations of a Bomber Command bent on pure destruction.

"Give us the planes and we will force Germany's surrender" called the office-desk generals and the air enthusiasts in 1942–1943. They were given twice as many planes as they called for. And they forced not surrender but a resistance and a fanaticism unparalleled in history.

We did not appreciate that Germany and Russia—both nations led by hard war realists—had expressly and specifically condemned strategic bombing as ineffective. Both nations employed their air forces *with* their ground forces, not independently.

Our air generals and Britain's air marshals were national heroes. Yet they sent scores of thousands of our best youth to death in flaming bombers, they twisted the truth to get more men and more planes. They promised to "soften up" Germany, but they produced instead a corybantic, brutalized population which murdered our fliers, which fought even to the women and children, which fought until the entire country was occupied and its government dead or captured.

I accuse the British Air Ministry of ignoring the true results of their bombardment and of authorizing more useless slaughter. I accuse the Eighth American Air Force commanders of sanctioning, for a vital several-month period, the British policy to be employed with our own bomber fleets: "Dump the bombs in the middle of the city ... that will discourage them from fighting and working."

I accuse the Fifteenth American Air Force of sending its bombers on "reminder raids," to avalanche their cargoes on the center of Sofia and other Balkan cities." "'Reminder raids,'" they called them, "to remind those people they're on the wrong side of the war."

I accuse the Air Force propagandists of concealing the fact that the Ploesti oil fields were practically untouched—despite two years of heavy bombardment—until fighters finished them off a few days before Russian ground forces arrived. Why did the Air Force refuse to admit that the Schweinfurt roller-bearing plants were virtually untouched by the highly publicized first attack which cost nearly a thousand American fliers?

Why did the RAF bomb the center of Essen instead of the sprawling Krupp works? Why was Leipzig, book center of Europe, wiped out instead of the Skoda works in Pilsen? Why did American soldiers stare unbelievingly at the Ruhr factories which—even after tactical bombardment and artillery barrages—were still operative at the end of the war?

This commentary does not consider the use of the strategic air weapon against Japan, nor the dramatic use of an atomic bomb which, with other factors, forced that nation's surrender. Japan, with its concentrated industries and population, offered a different problem. Moreover, the atomic bomb introduced a new element into bombardment which will reverse all previous consideration of the strategy. Neither factor was operative in the air war above Germany—nor was the "co-ordination" of which our generals have spoken—and an analysis of our air policy in Europe must be examined separately.

Why did the Air Force not realize that German factory workers did not live in cities, but in barracks around their plants? Why were the main rail stations in Berlin, Dresden, and Frankfort still handling a massive freight even at the end of the war? Why was it that the Luftwaffe was weakened only by trading American bombers for German fighters in terrible air battles and finally by precision campaigns against fuel plants?

And why did American Fighter Commanders order their groups to strafe cows, clotheslines, houses, pedestrians all over Germany so that open-season was finally declared by the Nazis on parachuting U.S. airmen?

If this butchery of Europeans, and the waste of Allied men, machines, and fuel could have brought the claimed result, if a surrender could have been forced, there could be no argument. If the invasion could have been made easier by the killing of women and children, by the deroofing of an entire nation—then the Air Force argument would be irrefragable. Perhaps, in wartime with such vital issues at stake, the end does justify the means.

But what was the result? A fanaticism in Germany, a bitterness throughout the Reich which made possible the *Volksturm* and the sniping by women and children, a tougher job for our ground forces because they had to fight not an army but an entire nation.

And, in the impoverishment of Germany by our Air Forces, one important achievement must be recorded: a long-range victory for Russia. If all Germany is to become Sovietized, it will be largely thanks to the bombing which proletarianized and dehumanized an entire nation.

CHAPTER 10

Escape

We arrived back in Berlin on the evening of December 16. I knew that the tour was at an end and that if I was to escape it would have to be soon, for my next destination was surely a prison camp.

Borner took his leave at the hotel, saying he hoped I had enjoyed our few days together and that he was sorry it had to be cut short. "I hope we shall meet again after the war," he added. "Good luck."

In his place a young East Prussian lieutenant, who spoke no English, was placed in charge of me. With him was an inarticulate corporal who sat up all night in a chair before the door. Escape was temporarily out of the question. I did not sleep, however, but dosed my eyes and lay still, trying to imagine some ruse whereby I could be alone for a few minutes.

The next morning at breakfast, downstairs in the hotel dining room, I evolved a scheme. It seemed harebrained, but I was becoming desperate.

As we rose to return to our room, where I believe the lieutenant was to await instructions, I asked if the corporal might buy me some matches. I had noticed several people standing in line at the tobacco counter of the hotel lobby. The lieutenant, an over-dignified, very soldierly individual, nodded formally and spoke to his man.

We waited a moment at the foot of the stairs, but as the corporal was fourth or fifth in line and the purchase would obviously take some time, the lieutenant called out that we would go on upstairs to the room. Half of the plan had succeeded, but now the time element was all important.

Once in the room, I walked over to the bed and lay down to carry through as much as possible an impression of casualness and nonchalance.

I called to the lieutenant to ask if he would send a message to Dr. Steiner's room, a few doors down the hall. (At breakfast I had scribbled on a sheet of hotel stationery: "Watch for me in the victory parade after the war—in Berlin.") The officer nodded, accepted the folded note and stuffed it in his pocket.

"It is rather important. Could you send it now?" I asked, taking off my jacket and starting to untie a shoelace. (Mustn't overdo this nonchalance, I thought.)

"All right," he agreed, buttoning his tunic collar and stepping out of the room. (You miraculous fool, I thought. It's worked!)

I flipped off the bed, slipped on my jacket, reached in the closet where the lieutenant's holstered revolver was hanging from a hook, snatched out the gun, and crossed over to the window. My heart was pounding and I could hardly breathe with excitement. I raced through a maelstrom of thoughts, considering that the corporal would be back in a moment, that the lieutenant might become suspicious and return immediately, that someone else might be watching the room.

I jerked open the window, climbed through, stepped out onto the fire escape, jamming the revolver into a jacket pocket. Then I changed my mind, climbed back into the room, tore the telephone wire from the wall and slammed the door's bolt shut. As I did this I realized I was wasting valuable seconds.

Back out the window and onto the fire escape, banging a knee on the ledge as I went, I started down the iron steps. Two floors to go, I thought; take it easy; cool off; act normally—how can you act normally going down a fire escape in the middle of winter when the building is not on fire?—don't hurry, stop panting, the worst is over. Despite all the silent conversation, I could not reassure myself. My palms were sticky with moisture; I felt faint with fear and excitement.

A swinging ladder dropped from the second-floor fire escape to the ground. I stepped out on it quickly and it lowered to the ground with a loud clang. I glanced back but no one was following me. Only about thirty seconds had gone by since the officer had stepped out of the room, but it seemed hours. Hurry, hurry, hurry, my heart screamed to my brain. Slowly, normally; think clearly, I tried to answer.

On the ground, I found myself in a large courtyard with two exits. Near one of them I saw an open window. I looked inside and saw an overcoat on a hanger just out of reach. I had thought of climbing in the window and hiding until the excitement, which I was sure had already started, should die down. But the overcoat brought different thoughts. I leaned far in over the ledge and reached the coat. It must have belonged to a much heavier man than myself, and it was several sizes too short—but these matters were of no importance.

In the pocket was a cap which was almost the right size. Once clad in coat and hat, I felt better. But I still imagined all kinds of happenings: the lieutenant banging on the door, calling the hotel servants, telephoning the Gestapo from the lobby. Still weak with nervousness, I stepped out of the nearest archway and walked quickly away from the hotel.

It was difficult to realize I was free, at least temporarily free. I felt certain everyone in the street was looking at me. Whoever heard of anyone perspiring at Christmas time? But it was consoling to remember Borner's words before our trip: "I won't have to lend you trousers. Yours are dark green and that is a neutral color here in Europe." For the coat came down only to my knees, although it was large enough around the waist for two of me.

It was incredible that the scheme had succeeded; it seemed Hollywood come true. That stupid lieutenant is going to be in trouble, I sang joyously and noiselessly to myself as I walked. Too bad, too bad, too bad. I'm free. I'm going home. But half-apprehensively, I still expected someone to come from behind and clap a heavy hand on my shoulder.

I must have walked for an hour, without knowing where I was going except that the direction was *away* from the hotel. I expected at any moment to hear the screech of police-car sirens as the Gestapo closed in on me. I was not a good reporter that morning. I noticed nothing, nothing except a multitude of faces, automobiles, soldiers, and wrecked buildings.

Once I bought a newspaper. There was a one-mark note in the overcoat pocket, so I stepped up to a newsstand and asked for *Der Angriff*, wondering if that was a mistake, if my accent would give me away—forgetting that in cosmopolitan Berlin worse accents than mine were heard those days. I received ninety pfennigs in change, and as I held out my hand, a German officer stepped up to buy a magazine, and I very nearly experienced a case of St. Vitus's dance.

After a while I came to a park in Berlin. I walked through it until I came to a row of benches, chose one, and sat down. I tried to look at the newspaper, but the words were blurred and I could not read many of them anyway. Ridiculous newspaper, ridiculous country. That lieutenant is going to get in trouble and I am going to get shot if I don't think of something fast, I thought disconsolately.

I walked some more, briskly and meaningfully. Finally, I came to *Unter den Linden* and stopped in front of a still-undestroyed opera house. "Today: *La Bohème*," read the poster. But ninety pfennigs was not enough for a seat, and I moved on. It was hard work to keep my thoughts from wandering. Why in hell do you want to buy an opera seat, I asked myself. Or a newspaper? The paper lends dignity; people will think I belong here. Talking to myself helped keep nervous strain from getting the upper hand.

I walked toward the *Brandenburg Tor* and there an idea was born. The American Embassy! That's where the Swiss Legation is located. There is just the possibility that I'll find someone who is friendly in there, and he will hide me.

I turned into the building, walked up a few steps, and entered the main door. A reception desk stood in the main lobby and two or three people were waiting in line to state their business. I went on past the desk, turned right, and started up a long flight of stairs which, I thought, led to the various consular offices. My aim was to get to one of the Swiss officials, to tell him my story, and to beg his help. I still had the gun in my pocket if he should try to phone the police.

Halfway up the stairs, I heard a voice calling from below. It was the receptionist who was beckoning me back down and saying something unintelligible in German.

"*Vous parlez français?*" I asked.

"*Mais naturellement, je parle français. Je suis Suisse*," he answered. "But you cannot go up there. First you must make an appointment. Whom do you wish to see?"

"The bureau that occupies itself with American affairs."

"Well, it is downstairs here. This way."

I was having a hard time controlling my voice trying to speak an accentless French and remain very formal at the same time. I walked back downstairs, hoping the revolver did not bulge too obviously and that the receptionist did not notice the strange-sized overcoat I was wearing.

We walked into a large front office, and the man called something in German to a woman who was just leaving another visitor. She came over to us, a tall, haughty woman, and the receptionist turned back to his desk.

"*Vous parlez français?*" I tried again.

"Yes, but not very well," she answered in guttural French. "How can I help you?"

"Are you Swiss, madame?"

"No, I am German. But I am sure I will be able to help you if you tell me what it is." (You old bitch, you couldn't help me if you were Hitler's wife. I'm stuck now. What'll I invent to get out of this situation?)

"Well, it's like this," I began, struggling for something to say. "You understand, my wife is American. I am French, myself. I work here in Berlin. But my wife, she is American." (Yes, you've made her American. Now what?)

"Yes, I understand," said the woman, looking at me queerly.

"Well, since my wife is American. I'm French. But she's American and she's over there now, you understand." (Wonder how the accent is making out?) "She's been over there since the commencement of the war. And, well, I would like to write her a letter. That's why I would like to be in contact with one of the consular officers here. To write to my wife, because she is in America, you understand."

"Yes, quite. But this is not where you apply for that. You must go to the German Red Cross. They will tell you how to write to her."

"Isn't there anyone here I could see about it?" I urged. (Damnit, I hate Germans and I'd like to talk to a nice refreshing neutral Swiss.)

"No. This is the Swiss Legation. We do not occupy ourselves with those affairs here. I will find you the address. One moment, please." She went into one of the smaller offices. (If you're going to phone the police you're going to get hurt, lady, I thought. I glanced around the room, noting a quarter-opened window through which I planned to evacuate in case of trouble.)

She returned in a moment with an office boy who brought a telephone directory. He checked the German Red Cross address, wrote it on a slip of paper, and handed it to me. I accepted it, trying to keep my hand from trembling, thanked them, and walked out the main door to the street. That was the first frustration.

I noticed a clock in one undestroyed shop which recorded 11:30. At least I had been free two hours. I had an overcoat, a cap, a revolver, and ninety pfennigs—and I was still free.

After that I walked westward, or what I thought was west-ward, keeping off the main streets in case patrol cars should be searching for me (did they have patrol cars in Germany?). Once I came to another small park and I sat down awhile and pretended to read the crumbled newspaper.

An old woman came past with a small cart of propaganda leaflets which she tried to sell me. I pretended I was deaf. "*Verwundet im Osten*," I told her and pointed dumbly to my ears. One of the leaflets she showed me had a cartoon of the "twin criminals, Churchill and Roosevelt," but I couldn't see the humor of it, so she went away. And I got up and continued walking.

I wished awfully badly I had a cigarette, and I was becoming more than a little hungry, now that the nervousness was wearing off. I tried to reconstruct the whole picture and plan the next move, but the very fact that it had all happened as it did prevented much coherent thought.

After a while I saw another clock and it read 3:45. I turned south and covered several more blocks. Everywhere was the same scene of debris. Sometimes in the cellar of a ruined house there was a fire burning in the coal pile, lit probably by incendiaries from an air attack.

Once I approached a French prisoner, walking alone and carrying a small suitcase. I decided to take a chance as there was no one else near us.

"Are you French?" I asked him.

"Yes, sir," he answered, stopping short and bringing both feet together. His obsequiousness was a jarring note; so that's how the Germans have their prisoners trained!

"Well, I need some advice. I'm French also." (I noticed he relaxed as I said that.) "I am en route home." (His eyes widened at that.) "And I want you to tell me the best way to get to France."

He studied me closely, and I dropped my hand onto the revolver (which I had switched to the coat pocket while walking). "Don't become excited," I warned him. "I am only asking for advice."

"I don't know what you mean. If you are going to France you can take the train. Have you permission from the Germans?"

"No, I have just arrived and don't have time to go through the formalities."

"I think I know what you mean," he replied, his eyes narrowing and his nostrils quivering. "You desire to go to France alone, without telling anyone? You can still take the train, but not the passenger train. But I know nothing of these things. You must find out for yourself."

He was plainly suspicious that I might be a German. I realized I would get no further information from him and that it was dangerous to be seen talking to a prisoner on the street, so I said, "Thank you, my friend. Good-bye."

I walked along more streets, sometimes coming to a dead end where hills of debris had completely blocked a road. It was tiring to appear always on business, to try to seem sure of every turning, when I knew neither where I was nor where I was headed. But I began to appreciate that no one was interested in passers-by; everyone in Berlin had sufficient problems to keep his mind fully occupied in those days. Yet a feeling of conspicuousness, an extreme self-consciousness, would not leave me.

Finally, very late in the afternoon, I came to a large railroad station, the *Goerlitzer Bahnhof.* I did not dare enter it for I was sure special police guarded all such places. I tried to calculate where I was in Berlin and where the trains from this station might lead. It began to get dark very quickly, at least one blessing. A light snowfall came down and soon the streets were covered with a soft white mantle.

Walking was rapidly becoming a real exertion; I was tiring fast. The section where I was now seemed less damaged. Whole streets were still intact and many shops were still open behind black-out curtains. Once I stopped in a doorway and stood there, leaning against the door-jamb to take a rest. Only a few moments after I arrived, a young woman stopped, stared kindly at me and said, "*Guten Abend, mein Liebling.*"

In her eyes, despite the darkness, I could read the question which requires no language which is basic and international. I did not then appreciate the scene as I do now in retrospect.

"*Ich habe nur neunzig Pfennig,*" I told her. "*Ich bin traurig.*" And, at the moment, I *was* sorry too. She smiled a weak little smile and moved off. At least it would have meant shelter for the night.

Later on, I walked back to the station and circled around it. I found a street which led into the marshalling yards away from the passenger station. The black-out, even more complete than in London, was nearly my undoing and it saved me. Twice I nearly bumped into workmen in the yards. And both times I managed to escape notice because of the pitch blackness.

The station end of the tracks was well lit, but there were only a few lights in the yards. I walked to a lumber pile in a dark corner and sat down to rest and to contemplate. From there, I could watch the trains being put together further along the track. I calculated that the lines led southward, so I followed several of them for about a quarter of a mile to see which way they went after leaving the station.

Finally, I found a pair of tracks which swung to the right—presumably to the west—a few hundred yards outside the yards. I came back to the lumber pile and waited until I saw a train being made up on that track. Two more hours must have gone by during that period, and I kept stamping my feet to keep them from numbing with the cold.

At last I saw what seemed to be a freight train coming out of the yards on the right track. I watched closely to see if anyone was near, then got to my feet and ran out to the line. The train was gathering speed and I had to sprint to keep abreast of it. I caught an iron step on the next to last boxcar and swung aboard.

There was a small compartment at one end of the wagon. I climbed down onto the coupling, got on a wooden step which led to the box, wrenched open the door, and crawled inside. I slumped down and waited, not sure if I had been seen, not caring very much, but waiting for what was to come next.

The exhilaration of being free, of having evaded the guard and gotten away, had by now worn off, and I was quite willing to allow events to take their own course. I must also admit of an inability to grasp the sudden change—from a reasonably comfortable hotel room to a box on a train—and to understand what was going on in my crazy world.

I turned up the coat collar, pulled the cap well down over my ears, and sat hunched up in the little compartment. I must have fallen asleep after a while, for the trip seemed much shorter than the five or six hours it lasted.

Sometime during the night, it was toward midnight I believe, the train came to a stop in a large marshalling yard. After the repose of the past several hours, I was now wide awake. I looked out to see two men walking toward me alongside the train, swinging lanterns, and checking the undercarriage and couplings.

I slipped out the opposite side of the box, dropped stiff-legged to the ground, and walked away from the train. One of the men came up between the boxcars, held his lantern high, and called something out to me. But I did not wait to answer; I raced down another track and caught hold of the last wagon on another train which, luckily, seemed to be moving in the same direction as I had been traveling—southwestward.

The train gathered speed and as we passed out of the station area, I glimpsed a sign under a floodlight: "Dresden." I did not know whether to feel elated or discouraged. Dresden I knew was quite a distance south of Berlin, but it was hardly in the direction of France. Still … luck had been good so far.

This train seemed to be made up of refrigerator cars, judging by the icebox-like hatches on the roof, and it also seemed to be empty. There were no compartments as on the previous train, but I found an iron ladder on the end of one wagon and hung onto it grimly. It was bitterly cold and the wind ate through the overcoat to chill my chest. The train seemed to be traveling extraordinarily fast and there seemed a serious danger that I would fall off. I buckled my belt around one rung of the ladder and entwined both arms around another.

I traveled this way for several hours. There were no thoughts during the ride except of the necessity of holding on tightly to stay alive. There was no danger of falling asleep; the slashing wind assured that. Driving snow blew under my collar and froze, it seemed, against my neck.

Toward dawn, as the first hints of gray streaked the sky, I watched the occasional stations through which we swept. I hoped to catch sight of a signpost to obtain an idea of where we were. Finally, I managed to read the sign on one station and it was perturbing. There were accents on the consonants and the town's name seemed twice as long as any I had ever before seen. I had no idea where we could be.

Eventually, the train began to slow down. We were drawing into a big marshalling yard. I watched closely to be ready to slip off at the first opportunity or at the first sign of trouble. We passed a large sign on which were words surely not German or French. I was beginning again to wonder if this was not all a nightmare. We could not have come as far as Poland or Russia.

As the train lost speed and began working its way into the depths of the yards, I slipped off the ladder and started to walk back out in the direction we had come. I took a few steps and fell down. I was stiff with cold and fatigue, and with the experience of having been so long in the same position.

I got up and started stumbling along the ties. A man called out from beside a vacant boxcar. He held a long water hose in his hand and had evidently been washing out the wagon. I believe I had reached a state of desperation, after that all-night ride without food or water, where I would have done anything. The workman put down his hose and walked toward me.

No one else was in sight. I drew out the revolver from my Pocket and held it at my side. "What do you want?" I called to him in English. He came closer. "I'll blow your head off, Kraut bastard," I yelled hoarsely. He said something in a language which was like nothing I had ever before heard.

"*Vous parlez français?*" I tried again.

"Yes, I speak French. Who are you? What is the matter?" he asked in good French.

"I am an American pilot," I answered grimly. "I have need of food and I will kill you if you raise an alarm." The man looked incredulous.

"American pilot? From where do you come?"

"From Berlin. I was shot down. I voyaged on that train to here. Will you aid me?"

He studied me an exasperatingly long minute, then gestured down the tracks toward a shack at the edge of a field. "Hide your gun and go there. There is a fire. You may warm yourself and drink the coffee there. I will come later. I will not betray you."

I quelled a deep suspicion within me and a deep self-pitying anger at this whole continent, deciding suddenly that I could not go on alone anyway, and even recapture was better than this cold, famished existence. I turned down the track and started toward the wooden shack. Then I remembered something.

"Where am I?" I called back to him.

"You are in Prague. Prague, Czechoslovakia."

CHAPTER II

Slata Praha

I lived in or near Prague for five weeks and must confess that I learned almost nothing of the Czech language. A few aspects of the people I could grasp, their attitude toward the war, toward the Germans and the Allies, their way of living and their expectations for the future—these I believe I glimpsed. But their language was a totally different matter and I now recall no more than a dozen words and a handful of phrases.

Slata Praha, Golden Prague, they called their beautiful capital, the city of a thousand spires. I shall return there one day to thank a few of its inhabitants, and in particular the family M, for their wonderful hospitality.

But that first morning, in a shack near the railway yards, I was far from feeling at home. I sat on a wooden box for nearly an hour, watching through a small window, before the workman returned. He knocked at the door before opening it and coming in, evidently made cautious by the sight of my gun at our first meeting. He was not a big man, but strength showed clearly from his broad shoulders and large, firm hands. I hoped I would not have to fight with him.

"Are you all right? Did you drink some coffee?" he asked.

"Yes. Did you call the police?"

"I told you I would not betray you," he answered in seeming anger. "Let us have some more coffee."

We talked together for a few minutes and I knew he was trying to understand how I could be an American flier. He explained that the Protectorate's border (enclosing Bohemia and Moravia) was guarded and that all passenger trains were stopped. "You were fortunate," he said.

"Many of the goods trains are also examined before they cross the frontier."

While he talked, I washed in a bucket of cold water, scrubbing prodigious quantities of railroad filth from my face and hands. I dried myself on a strip of lining torn out of the stolen overcoat.

He offered little hope of my continuing toward France. "If you stay here you will probably be safe. But if you try to leave you will probably be caught.

"I have a friend who lived for seven years in New York" he continued. "If you wish, I will take you to him and perhaps he can help you."

The family M, who lived on the western outskirts of Prague, were good friends of America. The father, Pappa Vlasiv—a small, humorous, bald old man—had saved three thousand dollars while in New York. before the last war and had returned to Prague for the sole purpose of bringing his wife and sons to the States. But the war had interfered and he had remained in Czechoslovakia, then a part of the Austrian Empire, and continued his cabinetmaking. His memories of New York, and of Chicago where he had once traveled, were those of a fabulous, story-book land where everything could happen and usually did.

The mother, a dark, energetic little woman of sixty-two years, was benevolently tolerant of her man's political and social dreams, but her real adoration focused on two sons, both of them working in Moravia. Pappa Vlasiv was still a skilled carpenter who spent most of his day in the city. One of his chief disgusts with the Nazis, as far as I could determine, was that they had changed the main station's name from "Wilson" to "Hiberner," and he told me almost daily how stupid a trick that had been.

The family M inhabited a white frame house on a street which resembled a street I knew in Lawrence, Kansas, and one in Hampstead, England. In fact, Prague was not nearly so exotic as I had first believed. The advertising in the butcher shop down the street was in unreadable Slavic; the books on the family's shelves were labeled with strange Czech titles; the furniture was mostly hand-carved and little of the food came from cans—but these distinctions were minor, and the family M seemed essentially quite similar to its counterpart in Britain or America.

For the first several days I spent my time eating, sleeping, and reading—not the ideal guest, but a most innocuous one—for when Vlasiv was at work there was no one with whom I could speak English. With Mrs. M I spoke a hybrid German-French, but while we achieved an understanding, conversation was impossible. One woman neighbor next door (the only neighbor who knew of my presence) brought two deep-dish pies one day and an interesting plate of Central European stew the next. She spoke fair French and it was from her and from Vlasiv that I obtained a fragmentary knowledge of their country and its unique wartime position.

The neighbor brought also a copy of *La Republique de Platon* in French, which I read twice. The only book in English owned by the family M was a novel, *Magnus Merriman*, by Eric Linklater, which I read more than twice. Other than that, there was little to do except spend hours examining a map of Europe and plotting further travels.

Many of those hours were spent in a rocking chair by a lace-curtained window in the living room where I could look down into the street below. German soldiers were seldom to be seen, but each time one passed in the street it was a blunt reminder that this was no vacation.

In the evenings, after a good meal, Vlasiv talked about America, about the war and the Germans, about the Russians and Dr. Beneš, Czechoslovakia's refugee Premier.

"You know, we are not badly off with the Germans here," he said mockingly one night. "Wages are higher than they have ever been before. The birth rate is climbing; there is a market for everything we make. If you mind your own business you may not be bothered by the Nazis.

"But we hate these animals for little reasons, sentimental reasons—and sentiment is more important with us than coins jingling in our pockets. We hate them because they gave some of our streets new German names. Because they added the German names *above* the Czech names on the other street signs. Because their dirty swastika is flying over our castle where our emperors once ruled the Holy Roman Empire. Because now that it is nearly Christmas, the Germans who live in Prague have been issued extra food rations, and there is nothing extra for us.

"We hate them because they print our newspapers and our books. Because they took away all our short-wave radios (or they think they got them all), and because they hooked up our sets to German transmitters so we can hear only what they want us to hear.

"We hate them because when their soldiers are here on leave they buy everything they can in our shops—and they have doubled the value of the damned mark just for that purpose. Because they are perverting our youth with their Czech Nazi Movement. They have taken nearly half a million of our workmen into Germany and they have killed hundreds of people who dared to speak their mind. We hate them because they want our girls to have children by German soldiers without marriage.

"They are like salesmen. They are always smiling—until they are worried about the war and then they are mean. They are always so polite and so damned understanding. They talk about *Kultur* as if it were something you could cook and serve as a meal. Crowds of them come to our castle and walk through it as if they owned it. They give me what you call in America the pip."

Always, when one of these sessions began, Vlasiv's wife would appear from the kitchen after a while to calm him down. "She says I will not digest my dinner if I talk about the Nazis," he explained. "And she is right."

Vlasiv and the woman neighbor had little sympathy for the British. "They promised help and they turned their backs on us," she said. "We shall not forget that. Many people here think England betrayed us and they are sorry Beneš and Masaryk stay in London."

For America, however, there was a profound friendship. From literature I was able to see it was clear that the Nazis were working hard to discredit the United States in Czech estimation. The jacket of one book then being sold in Prague had printed on it: ninety-seven per cent of the American Press is Jewish, eighty per cent of the American Radio is Jewish, and more than ninety-five per cent of Hollywood is Jewish."

Another book described the last American depression and graphically portrayed sharecroppers, tenant farmers, and slum dwellers as typical of life in the U.S.A. All kinds of propaganda pamphlets and leaflets were circulated free or for little cost. Each day, the Prague radio had something especially derogatory to say about Americans.

But the inoculations did not take. Too many Czechs remembered money orders and parcels from American relatives before the war and too many remembered the Hollywood films which pictured a quite different United States.

Moreover, even the methodical Germans were unable to halt Allied information and propaganda from reaching Europe's center. Almost nightly, after the two-hour dinner was finished, Vlasiv would lean across the table to say, "The BBC announced today that ..."

There was little homemade propaganda in evidence, however. Once I saw a single-page leaflet which showed an enormous bomb about to land on a swastika flag. Above the bomb were words which meant, "Don't Work for Skoda. It Will Be Bombed." (Skoda, however, was not bombed until sixteen months later, only eight days before American ground forces captured Pilsen.)

I asked Vlasiv if I could be put in touch with the Czech Underground and his answer was a negative shrug. "There is little left," he said. "Here it is very underground, very quiet. The Nazi animals [Germans to Vlasiv were always animals] have been so revengeful and so brutal every time something goes wrong that it takes the heart out of people. You remember Lidice where the whole village was wiped out? That was for the murder of Reinhard Heydrich, one man and a fiend at that. Once or twice there has been trouble at Skoda here in Prague [the great war plant had branches in Prague, Pilsen, Bratislava, and Brno] but the Germans caught the men and executed them."

Five years had been a long time. Czechoslovakia had had the longest term of *Wehrmacht* occupation of any non-German nation in Europe. The early fever of resistance and active dissidence was long since past. Most of those who could not or would not live under Nazi rule had long since disappeared to Britain or into Gestapo jails or concentration camps.

The extent of widely approved opposition was usually in the form of social boycotts against the more notorious collaborators, small-scale economic boycotts against shops which catered to Germans. Shortly before I arrived, there had been a city-wide boycott of the newspaper stands. Good Czechs had followed a Beneš appeal from London to refuse to buy German-authored newspapers. "But at night when it was dark," said Vlasiv sadly, "people went out and bought the papers anyway. People still like to read the news."

One evening I went for a drive in a fiacre, driven by a friend of the family. We rode across a bridge and below the historic castle of Prague. Black-out time had not yet come and a few shops were brightly lit. Pedestrians moved quickly along the streets, hurrying home from work. An occasional German soldier could be seen, usually alone, staring into display windows or walking aimlessly along the sidewalk. Only the sight of enemy soldiers, and of infrequent Nazi flags draped over the front of office buildings, gave this city any atmosphere of war. The drive for me, however, was a nervous one. I felt not at all secure, and finally asked that we return.

Halfway home, a German soldier stepped off the curb and waved a flashlight. My heart galloped and I put my hand on the revolver which I now always carried.

"Are you free? Can you take me to … ?" he called out.

"Sorry, I am busy," the driver answered in German, and we continued along the street.

The family took every precaution that no one should find out about their guest. I remained in the house all the time, except for the one drive, and only the single woman neighbor knew of my presence. Once, Vlasiv suggested that I go out into the country and live there until the war was ended. "You would be perfectly safe," he assured me. "There is plenty of food [Czechs officially received the same rations as Germans, but farmers naturally fared much better] and you would not be nervous as you are here."

I argued that I would have to leave soon, that I was grateful for their hospitality, but I had to be on my way. It was dangerous for them to keep me and I had to get back home soon to be present when a second child was born.

"That is too bad," he answered discouragingly. "It is almost impossible to leave the Protectorate. I have been trying to get you an identity card, but even that would not be enough. You are well off here. You can remain with us or go into the country. You would be safe. The war will not last forever."

But such a suggestion was entirely incompatible with a burning desire to get away from Germany. I decided to remain a few more days and then to try one of the several schemes I had worked out on paper.

The next day Vlasiv's cousin arrived from Vienna. Edouard was an important man; he traveled much and he knew a great deal about Europe and about the war. It was clear that the family M held the cousin in great respect. They also knew he was a good Czech, although his home was now in German Austria, and so we were allowed to meet. After the initial surprise was over, he turned out to be an interesting man who spoke almost flawless French.

His work was with a film-brokerage house in Vienna, and representatives with whom he worked traveled all over Europe to sell German and Czech films. "In a few days I will see a man who is going to Spain and another who is going to Switzerland. I'll bet you would like to be going with them," he said at dinner.

That statement birthed an idea. Vlasiv insisted it was impossible to leave the Protectorate. But now there seemed a possibility of getting word home. I launched a verbal campaign against the cousin. "My wife will have another child in a few months. She must believe that I am dead. It would be so wonderful if I could get news to her so she would know I am all right and in good hands."

The cousin was not enthusiastic. Yes, he knew the men who were going to Spain and Switzerland very well; they were business associates and they were also good friends. Yes, they could take a message with them. As a matter of fact (he lowered his voice) they brought silk stockings and coffee illegally into Germany on every return journey. But taking something out was a different matter.

The argument lasted half an hour. Finally, Cousin Edouard agreed that he would try. "It could be very embarrassing if we were caught," he cautioned. ("You don't know the half of it," I almost answered.)

Immediately after dinner, I went into the bedroom with an old French typewriter which the family possessed and wrote a letter to my wife:

"It is hard to believe that this will cross all the distance and danger which now separate us, but I am going to write this letter as if I were sure you will receive it. … I am free, unwounded and safe. I am on my way home."

When I had finished, I wrote a story addressed to Hector Licudi, International News Service, Madrid, requesting him to cable the information to New York and to say nothing of how or where it was received. A duplicate copy was addressed to the Press Attaché, American Embassy, Berne, Switzerland.

"Inside Nazi Europe (INS) ... This is the story of a one-way bombing mission to Berlin, a parachute jump from an aerial bonfire in a flak-filled sky down toward the burning city below, and of the action which followed. ..."

I sealed them in two addressed envelopes with the copies of the letter to Elisabeth and handed them to Edouard. He looked puzzled at the envelopes, probably having expected a tiny sheet of paper. "You have my word of honor that there is nothing in those envelopes which will in any way indicate where I am or who I am with," I hurriedly assured him.

He looked at them again, shook his head slightly and suggested "that must be a long message to your wife." But he finally agreed to give them to his friends for mailing in Madrid and in Berne. (Nearly two years later, I learned that the message to Madrid had gotten through—the duplicate to Berne is still unaccounted for—and was relayed to New York where the INS delivered the message to my wife and circulated the story to the press.)

At Christmas we dinnered on carp, rich soup, and a bottle of champagne. Vlasiv, slightly weathered by several glasses of after-supper brandy, toasted "to the next Christmas, when Czechoslovakia shall belong once again to the Czechs." But later, after more brandy and more toasts, he became somber.

"What is going to happen after the war?" he asked, speaking as much to himself as to us. "What is going to replace Nazism? More barbarism? Or anarchy? You Allies are going to have to tear down the whole structure of Europe before you can start to rebuild. For five years we have had nothing but Nazism. It has been good for us in some ways—it has taught us lessons—and it has been bad for us because it is a disease of brutality and a contagious disease.

"You are going to invade the Continent. You are going to win the war. I agree. Ninety per cent of us hope with all our hearts that you will win. Ninety-five per cent of us believe you will win. But there will be chaos and anarchy after the war. You cannot replace a whole system overnight. The only men in Europe trained to lead are those who have been collaborating with the animals and they will be done away with when it is ended. There are only a few others and they are wasting in concentration camps or trying to organize underground movements. Those in England and Russia are too far away, they cannot understand the changes that have taken place here.

"You will have to bring everything with you, not just guns and equipment, but even politicians—for we have lost the habit of administrating.

"And what is to be the 'New Order'? Is it to be made in Moscow or in Washington? It will not be made in London for we have had enough of that. Some of my friends fought in the Czech Legion against the Bolshevists after the last war. There are many people here who fear the Russians, who do not want that system for our country. But there are many more who want us to march with Russia, many who say the West has failed us and we must turn now to the East."

It was Christmas night, so Vlasiv's wife allowed him to talk on even after he became excited, even though she understood nothing of what he said, except occasionally when he turned to translate a phrase or two to her. "We hope so very much that your victory will come soon, that this animalism will be swept away," he said, suddenly appearing very old.

"Yet we are a little worried at what will follow. But perhaps anything will be better than this waiting."

Two weeks later I tried to get away. I had evolved an elaborate plan to reach the Slovakian Underground which was believed to be much more active than that in Bohemia, and hoped to pass through Hungary toward Turkey and neutrality.

Vlasiv's younger son, Jan, had come home for a visit. He was a fine-looking man of thirty-five with restless black eyes; he spoke good French (as did very many Czechs, I was to learn). He too was greatly surprised that his family should have such a guest, but he accepted it stoically. I asked if he would like to go to Turkey with me.

"That would be interesting," he answered. "I have always wanted to travel."

At first, however, he was not anxious to leave his work and to worry his family by such a project. Later, he agreed to accompany me, and we set out the next day with the city of Bratislava our first goal. Mother M had tailored my stolen coat so it fitted more adequately and the father had bought me, with a precious ration ticket, a new felt hat.

We rode about fifty miles eastward in the back of a truck. The driver, a friend of Jan's, knew we were traveling illegally and so made no stops which might have invited examination.

At the end of his run, we got out, had a meal in a small restaurant—Jan had brought extra food coupons along—and continued on foot. My companion had explained that it was quite safe voyaging in the Protectorate as only the frontier zones and factory areas were supervised by the Germans to any great extent. None the less, I could not suppress a feeling that we were heading into trouble.

Late in the afternoon, we came to a road tavern, outside which was parked a motorcycle. There were no other houses along the road and no one was outside the tavern. We both looked at the machine, then at each other, and Jan laughed softly. "It is time we stopped walking," he said.

He walked up to the motorcycle with a dignity and a casualness which suggested that he owned it, dropped it from the stand, and rolled it back away from the tavern. About fifty feet away, he got on the seat, kicked the starter, motioned me quickly to climb on behind him—and we were off. For two hours we roared along the road at breakneck speed and I wondered if I had not gotten into something too deeply—whirling around central Europe on a stolen motorcycle with a Czech who had turned out to be a perturbing daredevil.

That Jan was too much of a daredevil was soon to be proved. As we dashed through one village we cane to a half-blocked road where a policeman tried to wave us down. Jan added speed and sped past the officer who was nearly bowled over. I glanced back after a moment and saw the policeman tugging at his revolver holster. I leaned forward and shouted in Jan's ear, "*Vous êtes complètement fou.* You're crazy as hell. Now we're in trouble."

Jan was unimpressed. We continued undisturbed for another several miles until the inevitable happened: we ran out of gas. Still, the young Czech was unruffled. "Now we walk again," he said as he wheeled the motorcycle into the roadway ditch.

Toward evening we stopped at a farmhouse a few hundred yards off the highway and Jan talked the old woman into selling us a meal of soup, bread, and two eggs each. "I believe she is all right," he said. "I told her we were on holiday and that you are a French actor—which explains why you cannot speak Czech."

During the night, Jan talked with the farmer and learned that there was an "alert" in the whole region as it was suspected that Russian parachute-saboteurs had been dropped during the previous night. We took turns sleeping and standing guard to ensure that if the house were searched, at least we would have warning.

Early the next morning we prepared to leave. While we were eating breakfast, a car drove up in front of the house and three soldiers—either Czech or German; I did not see them closely—emerged. Before they reached the front door, we had left by the back and were running across the frozen barnyard toward the fields and a nearby woods. But the farmer or his wife had become suspicious and evidently warned the soldiers, for two of them chased out into the yard and called out after us. As stopping was the most remote of our inclinations, one of them kneeled and fired twice with his revolver.

I debated mentally whether to keep going or to stop and return the fire. The former won out and I tried to keep abreast of Jan, who was covering the hard ground like a college sprinter. We reached the woods and pushed on through it to a road which we followed, panting, for several hundred yards.

Miraculously, another car came down the road and Jan waved it to a stop. A man and a woman sat in the front seat and they agreed to give us a lift. We rode with them for about half an hour, recovering our breath while Jan spun a fine fairy tale to account for ourselves. In the back seat, I fondled the revolver, half wishing that something would happen so I could shoot back—being chased around Europe was becoming a very dull, very angering pastime.

Later that morning when we were alone, Jan urged that we return to Prague. "This is not the moment to leave for Slovakia," he maintained. "There are too many rumors about Soviet parachutists and the whole of eastern Bohemia is excited and nervous.

"We would do better to wait awhile. Or we might be able to obtain false passports so we can travel, at least to Bratislava, on a train." I argued that we were already nearly a hundred miles east of Prague, that we did not have far to go. But his view finally predominated and, after an icy night in another woods, we returned without incident to Slata Praha.

It was only after we were back that I made a discovery: the rucksack which I had been carrying slung over one shoulder had a neat hole which pierced both canvas sides, two handkerchiefs, and a pair of rolled trousers. The road-block policeman or the barnyard soldiers had almost been good marksmen.

CHAPTER 12

Gestapo Interlude

Once returned to Prague, Jan's enthusiasm cooled quickly and he urged that it was not a good idea to leave the Protectorate. Gracefully excusing himself from the other projected schemes I outlined, he declared that it was best to wait until the war would be ended, and after a few days he returned to Moravia.

This chameleon-like characteristic was not now so strange as I would have first found it. Life was not especially difficult in Czechia for those who did not interfere with the occupation authorities, Since the savage reprisals for the murder of "Butcher" Heydrich, Dr. Frank had been the Reichs Protector and his had been a policy of steadily increasing appeasement.

By the end of 1943, with a very possible defeat in prospect, the Nazis had become uneasily aware that they were virtually without friends in Europe. Their propaganda to the occupied countries was falling flat, while that from the United Nations was recruiting thousands of dissenters to the Allied cause. A turnabout in occupation policy was ordered by Berlin. And the first experiment in the new *grosser Perspective* was in Czechoslovakia.

"When they first arrived here they wanted to eat us alive," I remember Vlasiv saying one evening. "Now the animals are trying to cultivate us." It was true. A definite policy of appeasement was in effect throughout the Protectorate.

Coupled with the demand for everything that could be produced, with the increasing value placed on a man's workday and an apparently intelligent agricultural policy, appeasement was mollifying the Czechs, making them more satisfied with the lot of a subjected people.

Salaries throughout Bohemia were periodically boosted by order of the benevolent Reichs Protector. In January, 1944, while I was still there, the salaries of all Czech officials were raised thirty per cent. Men of the last-war Czech Legion, who had always been kept out of the peacetime governments, although they were popular with the people, were now being granted important posts.

More cattle was being raised in Bohemia than ever before. Although much of it was earmarked for German slaughterhouses, the Nazis paid good prices and there was usually enough left to ensure three reasonable meals a day for the average civilian. Dairy products and grains were also scientifically farmed and Czech citizens fared almost as well—though theirs had been one of the richest countries in Europe—as they had before the war.

Unemployment, of course, was unknown. With the transfer of many German factories into the Protectorate to avoid bombardment and with the natural boom of all war industry there was an unquenchable thirst for skilled labor.

And there had been no bombs. Once the RAF attempted to bomb the Skoda Works at Pilsen but missed the target by eighteen miles. After that, there were no heavy attacks until the tactical efforts which immediately preceded arrival of Russian and American ground forces at the end of the war. Prague still had all its windows, which was most unusual for a European city. There was a black-out, but after more than four years that was accepted as normality.

Finally, and surely not least, the Germans slowed down their efforts to Nazify Bohemia. The Czech government, at least nominally, was in the hands of the properly elected Czech Premier, Dr. Hacha, and his cabinet. Frank and his Protectorate staff made themselves as inconspicuous as possible—although this was difficult considering that they occupied the best half of the Prague castle.

What friction there was came in small ways. "We hate them for little reasons, sentimental reasons," Vlasiv had said. And he had put his finger on something very fundamental in the futility of Hitler's effort to unify all

Europe under Berlin. However much the Nazis might argue the legality of their occupation—Dr. Hacha, whose counterpart in France was Pétain, had invited Hitler's protection—Czechs simply did not like the troops of another country barracked in their cities and using their railroads. They did not like the one hundred and fifty thousand Germans who had settled in Bohemia since 1939 and who received preferential treatment in every way.

And however much the Germans might argue that America's greatness was illusory and superficial, Czechs felt differently, and propaganda could not alter their profound friendship for the nation where their own democracy had been born. Moreover, they had hated the Germans for a thousand years. Flamboyant posters and insidious "appeasement" could not reverse that in a few months.

Yet when it came down to hard facts and deeds, the problem was complex. "Come with me to England and join the Free Czech Army" had not been a tempting offer for Jan, nor would it have been for ninety per cent of his countrymen. Change suggested uncertainty; travel invited danger. "It is best to wait until the war is over" was the answer.

Active resistance in Czechoslovakia was now confined to small, almost unreachable cliques of patriots or of communists. Worthy of mention too were the groups of downright adventurers who could conveniently mask themselves as London-inspired patriots when in reality they were only the gangsters who in peacetime would have been hunted by their own police.

In the end, Czechoslovakia did redeem herself. Prague was liberated by its own citizens. Courage and resourcefulness unsurpassed anywhere was demonstrated throughout the country as the war was ending. But in 1944 the plans were inchoate and the courage was of a different nature, while Allied armies constricted slowly around Hitler's Europe.

"What could we do?" Edouard the cousin replied when I asked why there was not more resistance. "The Russians are a thousand kilometers away. Your people are not even on the Continent. We would be crushed immediately."

Despite the flood of stimulus broadcast daily from London and Moscow, most Czechs knew they must wait, knew opposition now meant death or a concentration camp—an official policy of "appeasement" did not alter the Gestapo's capacity for reprisal—and most Czechs waited.

After ten days with the family M, who proved their genuine hospitality by being neither surprised nor unhappy that I should have returned after a wordy, emotional farewell, I was ready to leave again. Anything, it seemed, would be better than waiting in Prague for the war to end.

Before leaving, I wrote two more letters to my wife and two stories to the INS in Madrid. Vlasiv promised that he would give them to his cousin on his next visit and would beg him, on my behalf, to forward them.

This time, I planned to travel via Brno and Vienna to Italy where I hoped to contact the patriots and to reach Corsica, by then securely in Allied hands. Vlasiv offered several suggestions, but each was so vague—and I recalled a memorable success in traveling from Berlin to Prague the previous month—that I decided to journey again by my own means.

I left soon after dark on January 25. It was nearly two miles to the marshalling yards, but I felt so exhilarated by the prospect of going on, of experiencing something new, and above all of reaching home, that the expected nervousness did not mature. My pockets were filled with breadrolls, a pound of meat wrapped in oil paper and a bottle of water. The revolver I now carried in a homemade shoulder holster and I felt completely outfitted for the thousand-mile trek to the Allied lines.

Once near the station, however, the tension increased and I slipped the revolver out and carried it in my right sleeve, with its barrel nestling in my palm. There were no melodramatic visions of shooting my way through a cordon of German guards, but I felt that if stopped by one man, I would be less molested if I had the gun within easy reach.

I circled the station and walked several blocks paralleling the freight yards, then climbed a low fence, skirted some barracks or storehouses and approached the railroad tracks. More than a month had elapsed since I had last been here, but the tang of burned coal, the clangor of activity further back in the yards and the frosted, gleaming rails were familiar and pulse-quickening.

Then it all happened so quickly I almost lost control. Someone stepped up beside me from behind a shed and demanded: "What are you doing here?" in German. I whirled to face him, dropping the revolver into my hand and raising it to point at his stomach. For a moment I lost my breath. Then I recovered and answered in English, "None of your goddamn business."

He looked down, saw the revolver, and registered more surprise than any actor could have done. My heart sank. I had a prisoner—he was only a civilian and not a very big one at that, but he spoke German and he was my prisoner. But I didn't want a prisoner, and I could not imagine what to do with him. Luckily, there seemed to be no one else near. I motioned him to turn around and to start walking.

As he turned, I pushed off his hat and hit him on the back of the head with my water bottle. It smashed with a loud noise and the water splashed over him as he slumped down. Christ, I've killed the guy, I thought desperately.

I tugged him over beside the shed, looked around quickly and walked away down the track.

Twenty seconds later, I heard a loud yell and saw two men with lanterns standing near the shed. This is where I need a train, badly, I thought. But no trains were leaving. The only activity seemed confined to a roundhouse area several hundred yards away on the left.

I crossed the maze of tracks to the other side of the yard and stood between two boxcars watching to see if there would be any more commotion. After a little while of breathless quiet, I heard footsteps crunching on the ash further up the train and on the other side. I climbed the iron ladder to the boxcar's roof and lay there a moment, expecting the footsteps to pass.

Suddenly there was no more noise; the footsteps had stopped. It was cat and mouse and I was again the mouse—a role of which I was beginning to tire. I'm going to shoot some of these bastards if they don't leave me alone, kept repeating itself through my consciousness. I crawled noiselessly along the boxcar roof to the other end, started down the ladder just as someone blew a whistle and came trundling up the gravel with a rifle across one crooked arm.

I aimed the revolver at him and squeezed the trigger. The damned thing wouldn't fire. I squeezed again and again as he came closer, but the trigger would not operate. When he saw the gun, he ducked back beside the carriage. I remembered the hours I had spent cleaning the gun in Prague, and cursed the Belgians for making such a poor weapon. I threw it far out into the tracks, climbed back up the ladder and ran down the train roof, jumping from one boxcar to the next. There seemed dozens of people chasing me.

I jumped off the roof toward the ground, intending to get far away from this unfriendly place. That goddamn gun, I thought. Those goddamn Belgians. The jump was badly aimed. I landed between two ties, twisting my ankle badly and fell forward across the track. For a painful moment I could not move. Then, as I started to get up, I realized that it was all over. One man was ten feet away, coming toward me at a dead run with a club in his hand. Another was close behind him, blowing a whistle as he ran.

I stood up straight and raised both hands high over my head. "*Kamerad,* you punks," I called out to them.

Within a few moments, there were four or five men around me, one of them patting my clothing for weapons. Then I was led to a barracks not far distant and we entered a brightly lit room. I was cold and exceedingly nervous so my observations were limited. There were several German soldiers seated around a table and a number of civilians, Czech railroad workers I guessed.

Noticing my overcoat and remembering something about the regulation of being in uniform, I gestured to it and asked, in barely understandable German, "May I take the coat off?" One man, evidently a sergeant, who sat drumming his fingers on the table and staring at me, nodded and I unbuttoned the coat.

Every man in the room started visibly and looked wide-eyed at the gleaming buttons on my tunic as I dropped off the coat. The sergeant stood up quickly and stared curiously. "*Ich bin Amerikanischer,*" I explained. "*Ich bin ein Kriegskorrespondent.*"

Again I was carefully searched and the food packages removed from my pockets. The soldier who examined me felt the cloth of my tunic and murmured "good."

The sergeant asked my name and rank. He then queried my serial number and my service, trying to find out what I was doing in Prague. I told him my name and rank, adding again that I was a correspondent, shot down over Germany. "When?" he asked. "I've forgotten," I answered. He asked, "Where?" and I answered, "Not far from here."

After a while a small truck arrived near the barracks and a German officer entered the room. He looked once at me, then spoke for a moment with the sergeant going over the details which I had offered of myself. Neither the sergeant nor the officer spoke any English and that precluded any serious conversation, for my German was still very basic and unfluent.

The next day I sat on a box in a cell in the Gestapo jail in Prague. Through the bared window, I could see the beautiful castle but was not impressed. I was deeply angry, at myself and at the Germans, that I should be once again in this predicament.

Also in the cell were two Czechs. One was a small, heavily mustached old man who played a game with two sticks of wood and a block which delighted him hour after hour. He spoke neither German, English nor French so our conversation was limited to gestures. The other was a larger man, powerfully built but very emaciated. A scraggly beard dirtied his face and his arms were covered with sores. I was not satisfied that they were real Czechs, and not Germans placed there to get information from me, so I sat on the box by myself in a corner of the room, leaning against the wall and trying to sleep.

Toward noon a guard called for me and I was taken to a room in another part of the building. There awaiting me were two civilians seated at a desk, both attempting to appear stern and authoritative. One of them motioned me to sit down and dismissed the guard.

"You are Mr. Bennett," he declared as if pleased with his knowledge. "We want you to tell us how you got here and what you have been doing."

"I was shot down over Berlin last month," I answered. "I walked here and have been living in the woods. I decided to take another walk and I bumped into your people."

(I will not attempt to quote the conversation, as I was then tired and worried, and now remember only fragments of it. The two civilians would not agree that I had lived more than a month in the woods. I insisted I had. They became alternately angry and ingratiating. After an hour of heavy questioning and innuendo, I was returned to the cell.)

Two days later, during which period I did little else than sleep and stare out of the window, I was taken to Berlin by train with a German sergeant and a corporal as guards. There was no opportunity to escape.

In Berlin, we rode a streetcar to a large building not far from the *Anhalter* station. The next day I was taken for interrogation to a schoolroom-like chamber and was heavily questioned by two other civilians who clearly registered their dissatisfaction with my answers.

"We have ways of making people talk," one of them warned when I refused to elaborate my story.

After two days things began to happen. A tall, austere man came to my cell one afternoon and announced: "We know all about you." He revealed that "the BBC has broadcast a story which they said came from you … from inside Nazi Europe. Did the International News Service invent this story in New York?"

"No. I sent it. I gave it to a French prisoner who was going to Switzerland and asked him to cable it to New York."

"Ah ha! You know that is a very serious matter. That comes under the class of espionage."

"I assure you I wrote nothing which would not have passed your censorship had I been a Swedish or Swiss correspondent. I am a reporter, not a spy."

My words made little impression on him. He left to return the next day and announce that I would be brought to trial. Until then, he said, I would remain in the cell and wait.

Twenty-four hours later, however, I was taken by a guard to another cell, a large, high-ceilinged room where nine other inmates were quartered. I thought at first that these men might have been placed there to discover the truth from me by posing as friends. But I soon discovered this to be wrong and that all of them were prisoners awaiting trial.

Three were waiting for sentence as black-market thieves. They expected nothing better than death and none of them seemed deeply concerned about it. Two others were Frenchmen, escaped and recaptured prisoners who had damaged German property during their escapade. Another was a Greek who suffered terribly from stomach ulcers and who should have been in a hospital. He insisted that he had done nothing except serve bad soup to a German officer in a restaurant where he worked. (Several of the others, however, confided their suspicion that he was a poison expert who had a peculiar perversion for *Wehrmacht* officers.)

Twice, the Greek was taken out of the cell and badly beaten. Each time he was returned, he struggled to his paillasse without a word and flung himself upon it, crying piteously. Curiously, no one exhibited any sympathy or interest in their fellow-sufferer.

Of all the prisoners, only the two Frenchmen were cheerful. They chatted voluminously about the "green things," which was their description of the Germans, and joked together about the other inmates who sat, dour and morbid, on their mattresses around the cell.

I spent five days in the room. We had two meals a day: a slice of bread and a cup of coffee for breakfast and barley-vegetable soup for dinner with herb tea. Our pastimes were confined to sleeping and waiting, with sporadic outbursts of conversation.

Twice more I was taken to another part of the building for interrogation. Each time the questions were the same: "Who sheltered you? Who took your message to Switzerland?" The questioners tried to confuse me by repeating and mixing up my answers. They suggested several times "We can *make* you talk," but each time nothing came of it. I held to my story and, after an hour or two, they called for a guard and angrily sent me away.

From the other convicts I learned a number of interesting sidelights on life in Germany during this next to last phase of her lost war. I repeat here only those which I believe were true.

To offset an increasing manpower anemia, the *Wehrmacht* had begun, as early as December, 1943, reconscripting discharged veterans who had lost an arm or leg earlier in the war. These men, after a concentrated training period, were directed into mechanized or armored units where their disability was of less importance than it would have been in the infantry.

More evidence of a soldier shortage: special SS units were being recruited from Allied prison camps inside Germany! A regiment of light armor had already been formed and was now training, composed almost entirely of British prisoners-of-war taken at Dunkirk. These men were guaranteed that they would fight only on the Eastern Front, never against their own country but the anti-Bolshevist propaganda had been so effective, along with alluring financial offers, that nearly three thousand prisoners had turned renegade. Other units were being recruited among Indian, French and Belgian prisoners with varying success. (After the war I learned that several such regiments had fought on the East Front and many of the soldier-prisoners had deserted to the Russians at the first opportunity.)

The non-stop aerial offensive against Europe was of assistance to at least one type of German. Many people who wanted to leave the Reich, usually for political reasons, stuffed some of their clothing and an identification card under bomb debris after an air attack. They then disappeared into Switzerland, via the "green frontier" (an area near Basle where the mountains were low enough to permit year-round crossing). As far as the Nazis were concerned, they had been killed in an air raid and their names were stricken from Gestapo records.

The air raids were also effective in destroying the police records of many German civilian evildoers, in wiping out debts by destroying loan houses and in confusing the banking system by destroying stocks of currency.

A favorite RAF trick was to pour down millions of ration cards over Germany, providing the enemy's housewives with extra food and clothing tickets. This forced the Nazis to alter their ration cards monthly, but Allied Intelligence kept up to date and each time Berlin issued a new set, London was ready with the perfect counterfeits.

Food rations for German citizens, however, were generally better than those in England—as long as the Nazis had all Europe on which to draw. The basic ration for a week was as follows: five pounds of bread, cake and flour; one and a quarter pounds of meat; one pound of sugar;

twelve ounces of butter, margarine and cooking oil; two eggs, a quarter pound of cheese and two ounces of bacon.

This ration was allocated to about fifty per cent of the population. Another thirty per cent received almost twice the foregoing quantities, being classed as "workmen." And twenty per cent of the people, in the "heavy workman" category, received nearly three times the basic ration. Steel workers, coal miners and opera singers, for example, were considered heavy workers. Foreign diplomats resident in Germany received four times the basic ration.

These rations were augmented by periodic bonuses, Christmas parcels, blitz-parcels and gifts from relatives who were farmers. Despite a hungry Europe all around them, Hitler's Germany did not fare badly at the dinner table.

It would not be an exaggeration to say that, next to the United States, Germany was the best fed and best clothed of the warring nations.

But even a totalitarian Nazi government could not keep closeted the twin skeletons of modern war, inflation and the black market. The latter flourished all over Europe to a far greater degree than in England or America. Prices in Berlin for black-market commodities included the following (cost is translated into dollars at prewar exchange):

> one pound of chocolate, fifteen to twenty dollars;
> one pound of coffee, sixty dollars;
> one pound of tea, fifty dollars;
> one pound of beef, twenty to twenty-five dollars;
> one suit of men's clothing, one hundred and fifty dollars;
> one bottle of imported cognac, thirty dollars;
> one English or American cigarette, thirty to fifty cents.

These prices rose steadily throughout 1944 and 1945 as Germany lost the war and today in central Europe money has ceased, in many respects, to have any value whatsoever.

The courtroom at first glance seemed not unlike an American Army courts-martial chamber. It was a small, drab room with a gray-painted ceiling and walls. A large picture of Hitler decorated one wall and below it there stretched a red banner with a black-stamped swastika. An armed guard stood at each of the two entrances and I noticed that both wore the skull and crossbones insignia on their uniform lapels.

Three civilians seated at a bench at one end of the room evidently served as both judges and jury. The prosecutor was a thin-faced young man with hard, intense eyes which glared every few moments at me as if angry that I was wasting his time. I had been accorded a defending attorney but this was a ridiculous gesture of Nazi justice.

Herr Stehlin, my counsel, was a bored, undernourished little creature whose sole use was as an interpreter, since the trial was conducted in German. And the trial itself was a classic farce.

My defense was a two-hundred-word statement, taken down by Stehlin and translated two days previously. In it I declared that I had lived the entire time in a woods near Prague, had stolen food from grocery stores at night and had met a French prisoner who was making his way to Switzerland. I had given him a scrap of paper on which was written a note to my wife and the story of my arrival in Berlin. I was not a spy but a reporter.

Even Stehlin, who in every other way seemed a fool, had not believed the tale about living in the woods. "If you tell the names and addresses of the people who cared for you, everything will be all right," he admonished. "What was the name of the Frenchman who carried your message? If you tell me these things you will be acquitted. Otherwise there is not much I can do for you. ..."

"I have told you what happened. That's all there is to it."

At ten o'clock in the morning I was taken to the courtroom. By ten-fifteen, the trial was completed. Stehlin had stood up and read my statement in an obviously bored voice. The prosecutor had rattled off a staccato speech, only a few words of which I understood—and one of these was the word *spion*—and the judges had sat on their bench with their decision already lying on the table before them.

When the talking was ended, the center judge looked up with noncommittal eyes and nodded to the attorneys. He ordered me to rise and to stand at attention. He then read a brief statement, pausing after each sentence so that Stehlin might translate to me.

"You have been tried and convicted on a charge of espionage," interpreted Stehlin. Espionage! I thought. These people are crazy!

"The sentence will be death," he added wearily.

I blushed like a reprimanded schoolboy and felt weak from the shock. "Ask for an appeal, a retrial," I blurted out to him.

"An appeal? What is that? There is no appeal from an SS court," he answered tonelessly.

CHAPTER 13

Illegal Tourism

Three nights later the RAF bombed Berlin again. I was quartered in a small cell, solitary confinement, in another part of the same building where I had been court-martialed and sentenced. As the sirens sounded, I realized this was going to be a very dull experience.

No indication had been given as to when the death sentence would be carried out and this made the waiting all the more difficult. After the first few hours of pacing the cell and of feeling hopelessly lost, I tried desperately to devise some escape from this trap. I called the guard and asked for paper and pencil which he brought after a three-hour delay.

I phrased an appeal to Adolf Hitler, pleading that my death was worth nothing to his government and that my life was valuable to my family. I addressed copies to Foreign Minister Ribbentrop and to Air Marshal Goering, but judging from the sneering disinterest of the guard to whom I entrusted the letters, I doubt seriously that they left the building.

There seemed no possibility of getting out of the cell. The tiny window was heavily barred on the outside and the bars were interlaced with barbed wire. The door was of thick iron and the locks and hinges were on the outside. The cell contained only a straw paillasse, a three-legged stool and a wooden container for toilet purposes. Walls, floor and ceiling were of cement, prohibiting any tunnel attempt. Escape was surely out of the question.

But when the sirens began their prophetic screech late that night, I felt a sudden elation: perhaps the Nazis would be cheated and perhaps even those ridiculous judges would be killed in the raid.

A few minutes later Berlin's anti-aircraft opened its booming defiance. I heard feet walking quickly along the passage outside my cell and thought for a moment that I would be taken to an air-raid shelter. The guards seemed interested in protecting only themselves, however, and after a while there was no other noise than the pounding flak guns.

Soon there came the sound of bombs and quickly the noise increased to a thundering cascade. Through the cell window I could see flashes and the bursting reflections of fires and explosions. Sometimes a ghostly searchlight swept past in the sky, seeking bombers in the night. The heaviest concentration of bombs sounded not far distant and I walked back and forth in the cell judging the nearness of each especially loud crump.

Suddenly, without warning, there was a terrific tug of wind; my chest felt as if a sledge hammer had struck it. Immediately there was a shuddering, enveloping roar. I was thrown to the floor against the wall as fragments of cement showered down from the ceiling. As I fell, I saw a long crack open in the far wall and I wondered if this was the moment when the judges would be cheated of their sentence.

Sometime later I awakened. The bombardment was continuing in full and terrible fury. As I got to my feet and brushed dirt from my clothing, I realized my head had been cut; blood smeared my face and trickled down my cheek. A piece of the ceiling had probably hit me on the head as I fell.

Supporting myself against the wall, I edged further back into the cell. My ears were deafened by the noise of concussions so that I no longer heard the scream of explosions and the clatter of incendiaries as they rained down. I followed the wall to the door, barely able to see in the dark, dust-laden air, and it swung open. The lock had been sprung by the concussion.

I staggered out of the cell and felt my way along the passage, stumbling over debris which cluttered the floor. Despite the noises and the disorder and the exhaustion, I felt my heart beating wildly at the prospect of getting away.

At the end of the hallway, I pushed forward to an iron staircase and started down. It was pitch black. As I took the second step, someone came stamping up the stairs from below, shining a flashlight ahead of him. I tried to shrink back to the side, but he came directly to me, seized my arm and hurried me downstairs.

We followed several flights of circular stairs to a basement which was lit by lanterns. There, several German officers and a score or more soldiers sat on benches in an air-raid shelter. One of the officers stood up as we entered and looked closely at me, then turned to the soldier who had brought me down and exclaimed something which I did not understand.

For the next half-hour, until the bombing and the flak had ceased, I sat with them on a long bench, wiping blood from my forehead on my uniform sleeve and cursing this series of bad luck.

One week later by which time my beard had grown to patriarchal length and I had become intimate with a variety of fleas and body lice, I sat brooding in a cell on a lower floor of the same building. The phase where anything mattered very seriously had by now passed and a complete lethargy had settled in.

I had been eating two slices of black bread and a cup of herb tea for breakfast, two slices of bread and a small bowl of watery soup for dinner. This supplied just enough energy to awaken for the next meal, not enough to sustain any mental labor.

It was late afternoon and I was awaiting the evening meal, no longer wondering if today would be my last as I had during the first week of confinement. A Guard stamped up the passageway, unlocked the door and a smartly dressed SS major entered the cell. This is it, I thought.

"Good afternoon, Mr. Bennett," he said as I got to my feet. "I have some good news for you. You were sentenced to death. Someone has intervened on your behalf and you will not be executed." I felt faint and stretched out my hand to the wall for support.

"The sentence has been altered to one of imprisonment, solitary confinement for the duration of the war."

At that moment, death seemed infinitely preferable to this soulless solitude. "Thank you," I answered.

"You will be transferred to another place. Now, for the moment, is there anything you would like to have?"

I thought of a number of things quickly, but knew that none of them would be permitted. "How about something to read," I asked. "Time drags pretty heavily in here."

The next day a guard brought me two books: *My Struggle* by Adolf Hitler, and *This Above All*, an English novel by Eric Knight. The latter was most welcome but Hitler's heavy-handed prophecies hardly helped dispel the gloom of four close walls.

My next residence was a cell, only slightly larger than the last, in the solitary block of a small prison camp outside Berlin. Food rations were again sufficient only to maintain life itself and interest was relegated to a wearying self-contemplation and, at times, to downright self-pity.

A French prisoner had the task of sweeping out my cell once each morning. For the first three days he was escorted by a German; the fourth day he came alone and as he swept the floor he talked softly.

"*Vous êtes américain?*" he asked, as if only seeking confirmation of what he already knew. He said he was a trusty; he had been a prisoner since May, 1940, and the Germans used him to help keep the officers' quarters clean in the prison camp.

"I can help you get out, perhaps," he said. "We must wait until I have papers arranged for you."

I begged him to help me now, immediately. "I may be moved again and then it would be too late." Without another word, he stepped into the hall, looked down both ends, then beckoned me out of the cell. I followed him and we moved down the corridor and out a door. My eyes ached with the glare of light.

"Quickly" he said. "Come down here." We trotted along a path, beside a stone wall and he led the way into another barracks and into a small room at the near end. Several prisoners were dressing themselves and they looked at me curiously as we entered.

"One man must stay home today. We have a friend who must leave," said my liberator. "Here," he added, turning to me, "put these leg-wrappings on and I will find you an overcoat and cap." In a few moments I was dressed almost identically with the other prisoners. I would accompany a corvée of workers, explained one of them, and would slip away at the first opportunity. The gate guards checked prisoners only by number so that there would be no trouble there.

We left by the camp's main gate within five minutes, after having been joined by several dozen prisoners in the main compound, and trooped out toward the road in a long column. Only one German guard accompanied us and he led the group.

After a ten-minute march, we reached a subway station. By that time I had dropped back to the end of the column and, as we started into the building, I turned away from it and entered a men's toilet. Several minutes later I emerged, went to the train platform and studied a subway map.

There was a choice of directions: north to Oranienburg; west to Potsdam or Wannsee; south to Lichterfelde. I decided to try to reach the Baltic Sea, for reasons which are still not quite clear, and took a train to Oranienburg. "Remember, prisoners going to work in Berlin do not pay fares," the Frenchman had cautioned me. "Just get on a train and act as if you were going to your employment."

A one-in-a-thousand chance endangered those who rode trains illegally in Berlin, they had added. Sometimes German guards went through the coaches checking identity cards but these inspections were very infrequent.

This time there was no mischance and, after a three-quarter-hour ride in coaches crowded with Berliners reading their morning newspapers, I reached Oranienburg. Only once was there a near incident: two German officers entered the train at one station and stood only a few feet from me.

After two or three more stations, I became uncomfortably aware that one of them was watching me closely. Once he turned away from his companion and, excusing himself through a cluster of people separating us, started toward me. At that moment we entered another station and as nonchalantly as possible, I stepped off the train and walked down the platform.

I waited in the men's room for a few minutes and caught another train going in the same direction.

At Oranienburg, I walked for about an hour toward the north and reached the far northern edge of Berlin's suburbs. The French had warned me that daytime travel was dangerous, that sooner or later someone would become curious and I would be caught. I found a large building which had been partly destroyed by fire and spent the rest of the day sleeping between some bales of paper.

That night, as I started to embark on a sixty-mile walk to the Baltic Sea, I was caught again. Just as I left the building, two men walked toward me and one of them called out in German, "What are you doing there?" Instead of answering, I ran back into the building and climbed a long metal staircase toward an upper floor where I thought I could evade them.

Revolver firing at twilight with the target a fast-moving person is a difficult enterprise. But luck, or skill, was this time with the other side. Halfway up the stairs I felt a knife-edge pain sear my left leg and at the same moment heard two loud reports from below. I twisted around, lost my balance and fell rolling down the stairs to the ground floor.

The two men jerked me to my feet, examined me, tried to question me and we went off to the local police station where my ankle was bandaged and I spent the night in a cell.

Next stop was Stalag III-D-500, a small French prison camp in the south of Berlin where I spent nearly a month. For the first two weeks, I was in solitary confinement, but evidently the camp commander did not know my past history for he relented and allowed me to mix freely with the French prisoners. My ankle healed almost completely within three weeks.

The camp contained eighteen hundred Frenchmen, war prisoners since May–June, 1940, a few hundred Belgian prisoners and two Russian generals. It was located close to *Tempelhof* airfield, within a mile of the great Siemens plant, even closer to the *Telefunken* electrical factory and only a few hundred yards from a large marshalling yard—not an ideal location from the point of view of air bombardment.

The two Russian generals, both captured near Vyasma in the fall of 1941, enjoyed the luxury of a single room between then and the services of a French prisoner who was their valet, cook, waiter, batman and barber. He also spoke a few words of Russian and so acted as interpreter, for neither of the generals spoke any language other than their own.

One was a swarthy, well-built man of thirty-five, a lieutenant general who had been seriously wounded and was only now, nearly three years later, able to walk easily. The other, a colorful little man with a snow-white beard, had lost his right leg. He was a major general and, claimed his batman, had before the war been a mayor of part of Moscow. Despite three years of captivity, he still wore a red-braided tunic and a high red cap. He saluted gaily every time we met.

They both cheated at chess. As the game required no verbal exchange, we were able to pass many hours in long-drawn-out encounters. One would invite me to a game and, after the initial moves, the other would draw up a box, sit hunched over the board and chatter interminably with his companion. That would have been all right, except that he pointed to various of the chessmen and indicated where they ought to be moved.

This resulted in heated Slavic arguments, in moves that took half an hour to execute and—at the end of two weeks—in a score that stood forty to three against me.

The spirit of the French prisoners, after nearly four years of captivity and of arduous work for their enemy, was truly inspiring. To hear their stories and to know what they had endured without losing hope or faith was to have my own self-pity wash away in a flood of deep-felt appreciation of these fine men.

They had been captured on every sector of the crumbling French front in 1940 and had been marched a thousand miles to prison camps in Poland, later being brought together to this camp on the outskirts of Berlin. Their privations had been so continuous as to have become accepted, finally, as normality. Punishment for misdemeanor was severe and penalties of up to three years of solitary confinement had been endured for misconduct. No one, I learned, had been executed by the Germans in that camp, but fifty-three Frenchmen had so far been killed or badly wounded by the Allied bombing attacks on Berlin.

Air bombardment sorely occupied the minds of these prisoners. The first questions I was asked, when allowed to talk with them, were, "Do they know in London that this camp is here?" "Are the fliers told to keep dear of the prison camps?" My reassurances, in view of their casualties to date, were not very effective. "You won't have to worry about daylight attacks," I assured them. "Those will be by the Fortresses and they will bomb military targets and factories."

During the daytime the prisoners worked in groups of fifty to a hundred in a wide variety of manual occupations. Most of them served in corvées which they called "Churchill Commandos" because their job was to clear the debris from the streets after the bombardments. Others worked on every type of construction, helping to build new factories, barrack cities for the bombed-out Germans, and hand work in factories of every kind.

Some worked in tailor shops, some with cobblers, with bakers, butchers, in retail stores and barber shops. They were part of the vast labor pool of twelve million slaves and were employed as their masters saw fit. Representative French soldiers, they came from every walk of life and could fill every type of job.

There were stolid, big-boned Bretons and miniature, excitable southerners from the Midi. There were bachelors and fathers, and the most tragic were the latter, for they had not seen their children for nearly four years.

One evening just before lock-up time, I stood in the doorway watching rain splashing into puddles outside the barracks. The perimeter lights of the camp and the rain glistened on the barbed wire and I thought of New York and another life over there.

A Frenchman whom I had met the day before came out and watched the night with me, standing there by the barrack door saying nothing. I wondered why he was so quiet, for normally he exuded that French ebullience, joking about the Germans ("Green Beans" they were called because of their uniforms) and about the war. Tonight, however, he seemed unusually quiet. Finally he spoke.

"I have a heavy heart tonight, *mon ami*," he said. "My daughter has died." I could think of nothing to say and felt suddenly deeply embarrassed.

"Yes, my little girl would have been seven years old next month. She was only three when I last saw her, before going away in the army. Now I shall never see her again because she is dead." He said the words slowly, pensively, pausing a moment after each phrase as if unwilling to go on and yet unwilling to bear the burden of this news by himself.

"Was it from bombs?" I asked, trying to think of something to say.

"No, not bombs. My wife's letter came today. She said it was just sickness. The baby had been sick for almost a year. Not bombs, just not enough food, not enough medicine no doctors. She would have been seven years old next month."

I realized suddenly the full tragedy of this man's life. Four years of exile had been terrible, but there had always been the hope and the horizon of returning one day to his wife and his daughter. Now that was gone. His daughter had died and his grief was overwhelming.

One night a concert was given by the prisoners. Their instruments and music had come from France through the Red Cross and the concert hall was a large wooden barrack filled with benches and boxes for the audience. The musician-prisoners had practiced and rehearsed for a month to ensure that the program would represent their very best.

The conductor, Raymond Ley, was a wiry, nervous southerner who before the war had won several French national awards for his music. He listed the program and it included the *Barber of Seville* Overture and several other full-bodied offerings. It seemed almost too pretentious for an orchestra composed of men whose hands were gnarled and worn by hard labor. But it was the most successful concert I have ever attended.

Several French Army doctors, employed by the Germans in Berlin hospitals, attended, and along with the Russian generals, we enjoyed front-row seats. The hall was packed with an audience of more than two thousand but there was only a small group of Germans standing near the exit, evidently to ensure that it was really a concert as scheduled and not a scheme of some sort.

The horns sometimes threatened to stampede the strings, the woodwinds were occasionally drowned by the trombones, and the drummer's enthusiasm sometimes surpassed his abilities, but the ensemble was inspiring. Ley was a fervent conductor, music seemed to flow from his animated body through his fingers to the players, and both the musicians and the audience forgot for a while that they were prisoners.

At the conclusion, Ley announced a surprise, "We shall now play our own *Marche Lorraine*," he said. The orchestra played with a feeling and a vigor such as I had never before heard. The audience stood, and when the march was ended, clapped and cheered hoarsely for more than ten minutes. Ley could not quiet them. Finally, the orchestra repeated the march and it was followed again by the same tumultuous, deafening applause.

Afterwards, I asked the conductor, "Didn't you know that the *Marche Lorraine* is associated with General de Gaulle and the Germans might not like that?"

"That's exactly why we played it," he answered happily.

CHAPTER 14

Chain-Letter Sabotage

Almost every Frenchman in Stalag III-D-500 had attempted many and varied escapes during the previous four years. They seemed to regard it as a game and, along with their black-market activities, it ranked among their few diversions in an otherwise very drab existence.

French imagination was given full play in devising the periodic escape attempts and it was combatted by a less imaginative but much more methodical German perseverance. Nazi prisoners-of-war authorities, I learned later, cataloged all unsuccessful escapes, listing carefully and completely all the ramifications of which surely only a French mentality was capable.

German punishment for apprehended escapes ranged from three weeks to three years of solitary confinement or hard labor. A vast horror camp existed at Rawa Ruska in the southeast of Poland, recounted the French, where unreformable prisoners were confined for "correction." The camp was notorious for its pitiful food rations and overcrowded accommodations, but its real terror was its proximity to a political concentration camp where the inmates died at the rate of several hundreds weekly and were buried—by the war prisoners from Rawa Ruska—in great lime pits near a forest.

The sights, odors and noises of the region, said those Frenchmen who had sojourned in the camp, were the major corrective influence. Yet despite such an experience, and the more severe physical punishment of months at hard labor, escape attempts remained a frequent monotony-breaking pastime.

Colorful stories were told of the efforts to regain freedom. One man in the camp claimed he had escaped nineteen times in three years. Twice he bad reached France only to be picked up at his home when the Gestapo paid his family a precautionary visit. He had spent, he boasted, a total of two and a half years in solitary confinement or at hard labor for the nineteen attempts. "I don't try any more," he said. "I will stay here instead and become rich on the black market."

Once, three prisoners had slipped out of the camp and posed as a family on the long walk to France and hoped-for freedom. They had previously obtained civilian clothing on the black market and were completely outfitted for the role. One was the father, the second the mother, and the third—a much smaller man—posed as the child. They walked and rode trains from Berlin to Kassel in Western Germany, but they were caught when the "child" momentarily forgot his role and lit a cigar.

On another occasion, the father and mother attempted an escape without their cigar-smoking offspring. This time they were dressed as nuns and succeeded in walking all the way to a Rhine River bridge at Cologne before being caught again.

One prisoner recalled stealing a milk cow after escaping to Brandenburg and leading the animal from there to Karlsruhe where he was recaptured and sentenced to nine months for evasion and theft. During the daytime he had walked along side roads, leading his cow with the air of a prisoner-worker who belonged in whatever locality he found himself. It was not until he made the mistake of trying to go through a city with the beast that he was questioned and arrested.

The most popular escape methods, however, did not involve disguises or theatrical props. The majority of attempts were by way of the railroads, riding the bogies, under fast passenger trains or by hiding in boxcars. Sealed freight wagons offered no problem; the escapee would break the seal, enter the boxcar, climb out to reseal the door and then re-enter the window and ride to his destination.

I heard tales that *Luftwaffe* pilots would fly a prisoner from *Tempelhof* airfield in Berlin to a point over Switzerland or Sweden where he could parachute to safe neutrality. The charge was reputedly ten thousand mark, but I cannot vouch for the story as I personally had no interest whatsoever in trusting another parachute.

Forged identity cards and travel permits were difficult to come by and these were only infrequently employed. Sometimes a prisoner might purchase the furlough papers of a French civilian worker and go home for a two-week period, to return afterwards to his camp and submit to a three-week or three-month hard labor punishment.

That escape was almost purely a diversion for most French prisoners was quite clear. I heard the question "Why escape?" many times. "The situation is worse in France than here," argued the men. "At least in prison we have goods." There was little temptation to escape to France, unless it was the desire to see family and friends again, for France before the Allied invasion was virtually a blind alley.

The French Underground, until it became ridden with Nazi agents, did gallant work in funneling Allied fliers into Spain. Because of the growing traffic, however, a priority system had to be set up which left little room for refugee French prisoners. Moreover, while the U.S. government offered thirty thousand francs to any Frenchman who brought out an Allied flier, the German government offered thirty-five thousand francs to anyone who turned in a prisoner.

There were the alternatives of joining the *Maquis* or some other group of dissidents, of returning to civilian life and trying to evade the German protective police, and of escaping via Spain to England and the Free French forces. The last mentioned, however, held little glamor for most prisoners who, after four years of passivity, were hardly anxious to risk their necks again by carrying a gun for De Gaulle and a dubiously free France.

The *Maquis* offered a precarious, hungry, hunted life which was also too great a change from the protection of prison-camp barbed wire. Of course, over a period of three years, many hundreds of French prisoners did escape to join the revolutionary groups in France and to contribute valiantly when the hour of national resistance arrived. But these amounted to only a small percentage of the million and a half Frenchmen imprisoned in Germany. Most of them had lived too long without good food, had become too accustomed to taking orders from the Germans—no matter how much they hated them—and their policy, not unlike that of the Czechs, was to wait.

To escape to civilian life in France was also a doubtfully inviting experience, for the Gestapo's ubiquitous hand sought out, with an almost canny precision, those who were out of place. Families and former employers were closely watched and evading prisoners were usually picked up soon after their arrival in France.

It was chiefly the desire for change and for amusement that prompted escape, for the life was surely not an easy one. In Stalag III-D-500, the prisoners lived in wooden barracks, six to twelve men in a small room with tiered bunks, and their few embellishments in furniture were handmade after working hours.

Their food rations were sufficient only to enable them to go to work from six in the morning until six at night, and consisted mainly of soups, barley stews, ersatz sausages, cheeses and jams and a half-pound of bread daily. At Christmas time and on other holidays they were allowed a small beer and wine ration, but except at these infrequent intervals there were few delicacies for Hitler's slave prisoners.

Monthly "Pétain parcels" increased the rations somewhat. These were five-pound packages distributed to all French prisoners in Germany from their government in Vichy, consisting of Swiss cheese, Argentine beef, French jam, army biscuits and one hundred *Gauloises* cigarettes. Additionally, the families of prisoners managed to scratch together a few oddments of food each month to make up a personal parcel for their exiled men. But many prisoners wrote home to insist that whatever food could be obtained was for use at home, for they knew that France's plight was worse than theirs.

Moreover, because of the thriving Berlin black market, prisoners were able to carry on quite an underground trade. Quantities of extra food were obtained and small fortunes were actually accumulated by the more enterprising, and nearly every one of them had a finger somewhere in the illicit food trade. Best method, they explained, was to steal food and clothing from the Germans and to sell it back to them at exorbitant prices. Much of the money gained was converted into francs and smuggled home by returning civilian workers.

A pair of good *Wehrmacht* boots, for example, brought upwards of fifty dollars; a good civilian shirt was worth thirty dollars; a suit of clothing could easily fetch two hundred dollars. All of these things could be stolen, with careful planning, from the Germans at the places where the prisoners worked.

For Christmas, 1943, French prisoners in Germany had received two American Red Cross parcels and one Canadian parcel each—it was a windfall and, as late as March of the following year, the foods and cigarettes were still being stretched out. It was indeed embarrassing to be told by scores of Frenchmen each day: "Thank you, American, for what your country has given us. We are very grateful."

Something else happened at Stalag III-D-500 which made one American realize that we have good friends in Europe. The French knew that I received no parcels and no cigarettes and that I had spent the past weeks in solitary confinement. A collection was taken up without my knowledge and one evening, against German orders, I was brought dozens of packages of American cigarettes and a large quantity of long-hoarded foods by a spokesman of the prisoners.

"We received these for last Christmas from America," he explained. "It is too bad we were so greedy, but there were a few things left and we want you to share them with us."

Another interesting diversion of French prisoners in Berlin was the encouragement of adultery by German wives whose husbands were busy retreating in Russia. It has been claimed that the amorous magnetism of a Latin is mythical and illusory, but to hear the stories prisoners told was to be convinced that at least some German women were still subscribers to the legend. Sunday afternoons the camp was emptied and the prisoners were allowed a free four hours in a specified area of the capital. This was their weekly holiday and they used it to the fullest. Many men claimed to have a mistress or two among Berlin's female population and it was with deep satisfaction that they regarded the cuckolding of German soldiers away on a front.

"I've got two fat fraus," said Raoul LeJean, a tall young prisoner from Lyons, "and they are wearing me out although I only see them once a week and sometimes on the way home from work. Both of them have husbands in Russia and I am wearing their underwear and drinking their wine ration. The fraus save their cheeses and their liqueurs for me and—although I only give them an hour each on Sunday—they are madly in love with me. After the war one of them wants to desert her husband and come live with me in Lyons."

Another claimed quite proudly that he operated a small brothel in Berlin. "I have three women who think I am wonderful," he explained. "I receive more than fifty mark a week from each of them, and I send the money home to my wife to feed our son."

Most of the prisoners operated less extravagantly, however. Usual quota was one lover with absent husband who supplied her prisoner paramour with little delicacies and her attentions each Sunday afternoon. The very severe penalties, reaching to the death sentence for both offenders, were evidently not effective as dissuaders, for—unless the storytellers were exceptionally careless with the truth—few of them ignored this prison-life diversion.

Surprisingly enough, the Sunday afternoon freedom was not used as a medium for escape. It was too easy to leave the camp any day of the week, and the Germans banned Sunday promenades for a month every time the privilege was abused. Usual method of escaping was to slip away from work during a weekday, after long months of planning and of gathering together the pieces of equipment. There seemed an understood agreement among the prisoners not to misbehave on Sundays so that their fellows would not have to forego the four-hour freedom.

The camp was equipped with a library of battered, paper-covered books which were supplied by the Red Cross and by libraries in Germany. For a population of twenty-three hundred prisoners, there were four thousand books so that in this matter at least they were not too badly equipped. Concomitant with a contemplative existence, the works of Racine, Corneille, translations of Shakespeare and Milton were as heavily read as were the lighter, more modern volumes.

A weekly newspaper, the *Trait d'Union*, supplied French prisoners with up-to-date, heavily pro-German news and views. The paper was printed in Berlin by renegade Frenchmen and contained contributions from the prison camps to encourage circulation. It is easy to see how such a journal was renamed *Le Trahison* by prisoner readers.

In a multitude of other ways the Germans sought to convert their charges to the ideology of National Socialism. Pamphlets explaining the "New Order" filled the camp and were used appropriately as toilet paper. Posters lined the walls of the barracks with panegyrics of the New Europe and cleverly turned philippics on the Soviets. America too received her share of vitiation and prisoners were exhorted to beware of the lying rumors from the Allied transmitters. The German radio was piped into the barracks by loudspeakers and the camp guards preached their propaganda at every opportunity.

One prime example of self-stultification was contained in *L'Echo de Nancy*, a Nazi-supervised French newspaper which enjoyed a wide circulation in Germany. I saw the copy for March 9, 1944, which contained a well-displayed account of the previous day's American air attack against Berlin.

"The enemy formations were not able to penetrate to the center of the Reich's capital," read the article. "Losses were excessive and it is doubtful if even the generous Americans can afford to give away so many bombers so they may report that they bombed Berlin.

"Authorized circles in Berlin declare," it continued, "that after yesterday's hecatomb of losses it may be assumed that the Americans will not attempt to bomb Berlin again for many weeks."

Probably in the interests of editorial accuracy, the article was followed by: "PS. Berlin was again heavily attacked in daylight today by strong formations of American bombers."

Excepting for that single humorous aspect, there was nothing comical for us in the series of American air raids on Berlin early in March of that year. In the first attack, four of the camp's prisoners were killed in a hospital where they worked as orderlies. A notice was posted in each barrack asking for contributions for the families of "our unfortunate comrades who were killed yesterday in the bombardment."

The second raid was noisy. It lasted nearly two hours and the roar of airplane engines and the staccato thunder of bombs and flak was an unpleasant discord. There were no casualties, however, and no bombs fell nearer than five hundred yards from the camp.

The next raid was terrible. For two and a half hours there was a giant battle above Berlin, and the bomb carpets rumbled down with the crescendo thunder of express trains. With several Frenchmen, the two Russian generals and a half-dozen German camp personnel, I took shelter in an underground bunker a short distance from our water reservoir.

The two generals and about half of the Frenchmen sat impassively on their benches in the dimly lit vault. The others of us displayed our emotions more frankly. Surprisingly, the Germans were the least brave and, with one exception, they showed sheer terror in their eyes as they sat waiting with their jaws clenched and their hands clutched tightly together.

The raid far surpassed the RAF attacks I had experienced, though this may well have been because the bombs were nearer and not because the tonnage was greater. Instead of finishing within half an hour, it seemed to go on forever and, with the pounding of bombs and guns, there was a continuous whining roar of engines above.

Once a bomber dived into the ground not far away and exploded with a yawning, gushing boom. A few minutes later, a carpet of bombs screamed down, immediately above us it seemed, and hammered violently into the earth very close. After that it was a wall of sound and the shelter shook with near-misses.

Two Frenchmen who had been wounded in a previous raid and who had been carried into the shelter from the camp hospital upstairs, were stretched out on benches, trembling beneath their blankets. Both of their white faces stared out at me and I read a mute question in their frightened eyes: "You said there was no danger from the daylight attacks. What is happening now?"

Sometimes one of the Germans would look over at me and narrow his eyes or mutter. But the Russians were on our side: every few moments the colorful little general, still clothed in his red tunic and high red hat, looked over at me, winked and raised his fingers in the V-sign.

After the raid was over, we left the shelter and surveyed the wreckage. Smoke billowed up from several sections of Berlin and the sky was still half-occluded by patches of black smoke. Leaflets dropped by the bombers drifted and tumbled downward, and once when a prisoner ran to pick one up as it blew across the compound, a German guard fired over his head in warning.

A carpet of eight bombs had fallen across the camp, the nearest having dropped into the water reservoir not fifty feet from our shelter. Dead prisoners, seven in number, were being brought out of a half-demolished stone building which had been the storehouse. Nine men had been wounded, but these were already attended to.

Jagged blocks of ice and cement from the reservoir littered the compound. Most of the barrack windows were out and a part of one roof had been torn free by concussion. A row of circus-type tents, where until a few days ago several hundred Italian prisoners had been camped, was completely demolished.

As I started back to my barracks, I saw a parachute dropping just outside the main wire. An American flier, dressed in a blue heated suit, fell to the ground, quickly unbuckled his parachute and started running across a field. In a moment, however, he was surrounded by guards from our camp and was brought into the *Hauptquartier* block. I asked permission to speak with him but the camp commander, overwrought by the raid, completely lost his temper, screaming at me to get to my room out of sight or I would go back into solitary confinement.

Apart from reading and talking with the prisoners whose work kept them in the camp, I found little to occupy me. Some of the prisoners gave me their letter forms—which were rationed, three per man per month—so I was able to write home to say that although once again behind barbed wire, I was safe and well.

Most of the men had learned German in their four years of captivity and so spoke it with a reasonable fluency. A few said they had steadfastly refused to study it, that soon it would be a dead language, and if the Germans wished to address them it would have to be in a civilized tongue.

There was no universal consensus of attitude toward the enemy. Most of the prisoners hated the Germans generally and only disliked them personally and individually. A few were quite outspoken in their bitter hatred of everything German. Some of the more thoughtful ones had examined the Nazi literature which flooded the camp and had sought to understand why this unhappy situation had come to pass in Europe.

Only a handful openly approved of the Nazis and the new ideology. These men kept their opinions within themselves and it was only by slips of the tongue that any hint of their attitude could be heard. Most of those who agreed with National Socialism had, naturally, accepted the German offer to become civilians and to work at standard wage levels in factories.

The attitudes of the prisoners toward France were equally divergent. Most of them approved of Pétain. They accepted that he was "a poor old man whose voice is not strong enough," but they were grateful to him for having the courage to remain in France and to try to maintain some semblance of national order and dignity. "Without Pétain," said one prisoner, "we should long ago have been conscripted by the Germans to fight on the East Front."

As had been the Czechs, many were worried about the future of Europe, and I sat in several evenings on heated arguments of what would and should be the postwar course of France.

Those arguments disclosed at least that there was no mental apathy in this camp, that however long had been their sentence these men had not forgotten how to think and to analyze. But they showed too a certain tragic aspect of the prisoners.

They themselves realized all too well that they had been left out of the stream of life, that during four years of continuous labor for their enemy they had missed the changes which had come to their homeland. Letters from home, rumors and distorted newspaper articles could hardly bridge that gap and there was the unhappy realization that readjustment would be a difficult task.

Their whole life was now centered on their daily work, on their increasingly vague dreams of home and of the future. Their dealings with the Germans overrode all these and it was a negative delight for them to call the guards "Sche-leu" behind their backs. (This was the name of Africa's most primitive tribe and replaced the last-war name, *Boche*, which was by now too well known to the Germans.)

I tried to discourage the prisoners from working so hard. "Why don't you take longer to walk to work in the morning? Why don't you make more mistakes and work more slowly?" Those who were honest argued that their work was routine, that it was—despite themselves—all they had with which to occupy themselves. Moreover, most of the work was by daily quota and it was difficult to cheat.

I found one prisoner, however, who took my words seriously and we set to work on a chain-letter idea to help slow down the contribution of prisoners to the German war effort. The result was a single-sheet letter addressed to the "soldiers and citizens of France" and it argued, in the name of the Republic, that all loyal Frenchmen must slow down their work so as to assist in the defeat of the Axis enemy.

"We have worked long enough for the enemy," it read in French. "Now the hour has arrived to work for ourselves, for our families and for our motherland. In a few weeks, the United Nations will invade Europe and will march to Berlin to destroy Nazi Germany. We must not be left out of this historic triumph; our honor and our national pride are at stake. We, prisoners and slaves of the Nazi war machine, must assist our allies and assist ourselves…"

The letter exhorted all readers to lose one hour of work each day, to delay on the way to work, to make mistakes at the tool bench, to lose equipment and to pretend illness. "If each of us does his part, our enemy will be deprived of millions of hours' work weekly."

In conclusion, we asked each reader to make three copies of the letter and to pass them on to other war prisoners and to slave workers. The letters were signed, "Committee to Redeem the Honor of France." We were careful to disguise our handwriting and to use new paper brought into the camp from another part of Berlin.

Four hundred copies were written secretly during the following week and went on their way through trustworthy prisoners to all parts of the capital. First reports of their reception were favorable the idea was catching on, but I did not hear the full story of their result because eight days later I attempted another escape.

Toward the end of March I managed to leave the camp by the same means as I had the other French prison compound, by being included in a group of prisoners leaving for work early one morning. This time I carried with me a small knapsack filled with bread, sausage, two cans of beef and a bottle of red wine. I carried also a compass and a quantity of German and French currency borrowed from the prisoners with a promise of postwar repayment.

Leaving the column at the Lichterfelde Süd railway station was not difficult, nor was catching a train after a few minutes' wait in the men's lavatory. At a station in the center of Berlin, I changed to a westbound train and traveled toward Potsdam. So far everything was going well; I had elaborate plans worked out to go from Potsdam to Frankfort on the Main and from there into France and Spain—and home.

A few stations before I was to get out, I heard a voice say behind me "Your papers, please." A German sergeant stepped up beside me and held out his hand. He had evidently approached from the rear of the coach while I was watching in the wrong direction.

A dozen ideas presented themselves. I chose one, reached into my pocket and brought out a red folder on which was stamped "British War Office License for War Correspondents." The sergeant accepted it, opened it to the picture, glanced at it a moment, then at me and seemed as if ready to return the pass and move off.

Suddenly a frown furrowed his brow, and he knew something was wrong. He looked closely at the printing in the folder, looked again at me—with honest-to-goodness bewilderment spread across his face—and announced: "*Das ist englisch.*" He thumbed through it and studied the British seal on the covet, then drew out his revolver and told me to put my hands in my pockets and stand away from the door.

Two days later, after another interrogation and another two nights in a prison cell in the center of Berlin, I was taken to Stalag Luft I by a German sergeant and two privates. The soldiers sang strains of opera music on the way north from Berlin in the third-class compartment, and I looked across the sergeant out of the window at the green hills rolling past.

CHAPTER 15

The House That Flak Built

Stalag Luft I was located between the Pomeranian cities of Stettin and Rostock on the Baltic coast of northeast Germany. Its population, which increased until by the war's end it numbered more than nine thousand, was composed of shot-down fliers from every one of the United Nations.

These were the men who tested with their skill and their blood the theory of "Victory Through Air Power" and their bonus was temporary exile to a barb-enclosed enclave on the bleak shore of a northern sea. The community eventually became one of the largest prison camps for officers in all Europe and our most enduring recollection is of the simplicity of our society.

The Germans deserve most of the credit that our life was simple: they supplied us only with basic, life-sustaining necessities. The Red Cross, the YMCA and associated organizations—along with a true ingeniousness on the part of the prisoners—were responsible that the existence was more than merely bearable.

In 1942, Stalag Luft I was a small camp for sergeant fliers; by the end of 1943, it had expanded to contain over a thousand officers. From that time until the end of the war, it was an ever-growing haven for parachuting and crash-landing airmen from every corner of the Continent. But only from a safe distance can it be called a haven, for while we vacationed there on the Baltic, our chief interest in life was to leave the damn place.

That only one man, an RAF flying officer, was able during the entire war to escape all the way to Allied territory reflects much credit on the efficiency of our German guards. It certainly does not mean the prisoners did not *try* to escape. Catalogued tunnel attempts numbered over three hundred; escape efforts by deception counted above two hundred and the times captives sought by stealth to leave the camp were innumerable.

German guard personnel included a battalion of nine hundred soldiers who patrolled the fences, manned the watch towers and wandered around the various sections of the camp. Additionally, there was a company of two hundred German escape experts whose sole job was to keep one jump ahead of every evasion attempt. Two dozen well-trained and vicious shepherd dogs, a scattering of seismograph instruments around the camp (to detect tunnel digging) and an assortment of searchlights, thousands of miles of barbed wire, guard towers and lookout posts encircled the camp and completed the defenses. Machine guns, mortars and tear-gas grenades were at the ready disposal of the Germans.

We called ourselves "kriegies" because the German word for war prisoners, *Kriegsgefangenen*, was too unwieldy for Anglo-Saxon tongues. We called the Germans "goons," until they learned that it did not mean German officer or noncom and forbade it as an insult. And we called the camp a variety of unpleasant, uneuphonious names.

Our home measured ten acres and was divided into four main compounds, each separate from the others and each individually guarded and administered. A compound contained upwards of two thousand prisoners who lived in long, low barracks. Depending upon rank, the men lived two, four, fourteen or twenty-four in a room. From the point of view of accommodation, our colonels—many of them young fighter aces before their last mission over Germany—were hardly conscious of being prisoners for they were quartered by twos in reasonably large rooms and were served by sergeant-orderlies. The thousands of second lieutenants and the several hundred sergeants who also sojourned at Stalag I however found their surroundings less comfortable.

The Germans supplied us with two army blankets and a sheet which was changed biweekly. Sergeant prisoners were not allowed sheets, but Lieutenant Leo Oldmixon, an RAF volunteer from Long Island, New York, handled the laundry service and—with the worldly wisdom of a former seaman—found means to supply them with the same ration as more fortunate officers.

Mattresses and pillows, placed on slat-board beds, were filled with a rough excelsior or straw. Room furnishings were rudimentary but adequate: a table, benches, a twenty-five-watt electric bulb, stove and one pound of coal per man per day.

In the matter of food, our captors were less generous. We received the basic German civilian ration and when Allied bombing attacks became more severe, a full quota was not always received. Red Cross parcels, paid for by the U.S. Army and packed by civilian volunteers in America, were—as has been reported so many times before—truly lifesavers. They were planned to arrive weekly, but this was not always the case, and once for a two-month period early in 1945, none was received at all. The food packages were distributed upon arrival by a crew of prisoners, one to each internee.

These included a gallon of powdered milk, a pound of luncheon meat, pound of margarine, half-pound of sugar, and an assortment of biscuits, chocolate, sardines, paté, cheese, jam, cigarettes, and soap. Similar parcels arrived sporadically from Britain and Canada. Not least of their contribution was the color the tin-can labels brought to our lives.

A bartering system was set up in all the compounds, whereby a cigarette was listed at one point and was the exchange medium. Powdered milk was valued at eighty points, a pound of margarine at fifty, half-pound of sugar at sixty and these prices fluctuated according to the market. Speculating by the more business-minded prisoners was discouraged by the community. Exchange was effected daily at central stores, and the system permitted a variance of diet and a ready disposal of surplus stocks.

Cooking was handled by two of the compounds in the individual rooms; in the other two, through large mess halls where hard-working staffs of airmen KPs and chefs struggled with poor equipment to feed the rest of us one, two or three meals daily, depending upon the quantity of food available. The work of these men, day after day for long months, testified both to their versatility as amateur cooks and to their good will in helping fellow prisoners to keep as well fed as possible.

Early one April morning, 1945, the mess hall of one of the compounds burned to the ground. It was a strange sight, that of hundreds of prisoners and German guards working together with buckets and antiquated fire hose to save what they could from the blazing barracks. And it was only after the fire had abated that the Germans realized it might have been an elaborate decoy to assist an escape—although it had not been—and they set to work to discover where lay the blame.

Monotony, sheer soul-searing boredom, was the chief problem in a prison camp. Average age of the fliers was only twenty-two years, and their background was that of energy-expending activity rather than a passive, contemplative existence where reading, sleeping and talking were perforce the chief pastimes. For men whose out-of-school history had been almost entirely dedicated to flying and to furlough hell-raising it was a difficult, tedious existence behind barbed wire.

Frequent reminder of our status came with the sight of *Luftwaffe* training planes which flew acrobatics and buzzed the camp, and the deep-felt longing in the prisoners' eyes was plain to see. To offset the monotony and to establish an intra-camp discipline, the senior Allied prisoners took it upon themselves to set up an organization, "Wing X," which sought to control and to correlate the various kriegie activities. As a disciplinary effort, Wing X was an unamusing farce for its purpose was directly antithetical to the orders airmen received before flying over Europe: "If you are shot down, make as much trouble as you can for the Germans."

Moreover, the psychology of war prisoners was hardly adaptable to a strict military discipline, with saluting, parading and periodic inspections intruding upon their own activities to disperse boredom.

Most of those activities were spontaneous and individually inspired; they had little to do with the well-meaning but officious interference of youthful flying colonels. In fact, Wing X became almost as cordially disliked as the Germans who guarded us, and its nicknames varied from "kangaroo court" to some which ought not to be recorded in print.

What occupied most of the prisoners most of the time were thoughts of home, of the future, talk about their last mission and their experiences before reaching the camp. Furlough orgies in London, Algiers and Naples—and in all of the in-between cities and towns—were choice reminiscences. There was a certain quality of whimsy and sometimes of downright *cafard* in prison-camp conversation. This accounted for much of the exaggeration, for many of the heated arguments over trivial details, and for much of the persistent sadness of the boys.

Conversation in the crowded rooms at night, with the lads dropping off one by one to sleep, frequently ran something like this:

"That flak was terrific the day I got it over Bremen ... there was striped flak, polka-dot flak, rainbow-colored flak ... " "Save your horror story for the civilians, fella. Let's talk about the women in England. Remember the gals who set up a trailer camp near the base? And the engineers used to line up every night ..."

"That's nothing! Let me tell you about San Anton. That was a town ..."

"You know, one guy got a V-pack from his folks yesterday in a parcel. What the hell do they think we're doing over here? ..."

"And another guy got a white feather in a letter. They think just because we got shot down we're cowards. That's Hollywood for you ..."

"Let me tell you about the flak over ..."

"Flak? That reminds me, we gotta play the Flak Dodgers for the league championship tomorrow ..."

"You married guys, what do you think your wives are doing? Sitting home knittin'?"

"Wonder if I've got a son or a daughter. Jeez, it would be good to get a letter ..."

"Now if I wuz Eisenhower, this goddamn camp would get rescued by air, that's what ..."

"Hell, we'll be here till Easter."

"What Easter?"

"Sure, but think of the guys in Japan. They've been longer, and they're gonna be longer ..."

"... I could see that sonovabitchin' fighter crawling in at us, winkin' his cannons ..."

"Aw shut up, fella. Let's hit the sack. I got a big day tomorrow. Got to go to French class and sew up my sweater ..."

"Wonder where the RAF is tonight ..."

"Wonder where my *gal* is tonight ..."

Time was the luxury and the bane of our lives. A few men, crazed by monotony, tried to commit suicide but only two were successful. A few others had to be hospitalized with a special neurosis born of boredom. But the vast majority of the prisoners found ways to occupy themselves and may look back today on time not too badly spent at Stalag Luft I.

Big deals and riotous gambling games filled much time. Non-smokers sold their cigarette ration for the duration to their addicted fellows for fifty or seventy-five dollars (to be paid after the war). Others stored their tobacco ration (of one hundred cigarettes per week in the Red Cross parcel) and sold them at prices from one dollar to five dollars a package when, toward the end of the war, the supply was cut off. Chocolate, jam, articles of clothing and watches were similarly bought and sold, prices depending upon the extreme variations of the market demand.

Several enterprising young men set up a "Sunshine Laundry Service" which offered to wash clothes for two dollars a week or fifty dollars for the duration. Despite the abundance of time at our disposal, many of the prisoners—being born airmen, they claimed—frowned on so mundane an occupation as laundering. The scheme was imitated by other groups and the workers collected sizable postwar nest eggs of IOUs.

Gambling games flourished as much or more than at any army camp at home. The few complications such as an absence of currency, hand-carved dice and a fairly constant, immobile population did not adversely affect the trade. Cigarettes were the substitute for money and several clever airmen set themselves up at casinos. The most successful was "Lucky's Casino," operated by Lieutenant Lo Presto of Walsenburg, Colorado, who retired after a few weeks' operations with five hundred packages of cigarettes as profit. This did not mean he was forced to smoke like a chimney to consume his winnings, for he used them as the exchange medium for food, watches and extra clothing.

Such outdoor gambling games were usually attended, in addition to the legitimate kriegie gamblers, by several tobacco-famished German guards who would have liked to play but hadn't the ante.

Private bets, chiefly concerned with the expected date of the war's ending, also caused a large-scale transfer of wealth earned in absentia. Colonel Jean Byerly, of Estes park, Colorado, one-time senior Allied officer at the camp, managed to lose several thousand dollars in IOUs because of his unquenchable optimism.

For more general entertainment, there was a band in each compound. Best was the "Round the Benders," eleven-piece swing orchestra under the direction of Lieutenant Mike Spodar of Cleveland, Ohio, who had trumpeted with several well-known bands at home before joining the Air Force. All instruments were from the Red Cross, but before these arrived the musician tried to create trumpets and saxophones from food cans and wrote the sheet music on toilet paper from memory.

Several glee clubs were also formed and real musical talent was discovered among the men who, to the Germans, were terror-fliers and barbarians.

A hard-working crew of stagemen, actors and playwrights also helped greatly to relieve monotony. Leading among these was Lieutenant John Coppinger, from Brooklyn, who had been associated with the theater before the war, and who directed and acted in several of the plays produced. He consolidated Shakespeare's *Julius Caesar* into a one-act, ninety-minute, modern language show and was preparing its production when the war ended. The Germans permitted the showing of several movies, sent from America through Switzerland, and along with skits, musicals, phonograph sessions and lectures, we were not shy of formal entertainment.

Of sports we had a sufficiency, using more than thirty thousand dollars worth of equipment sent through the YMCA. Baseball, basketball and football games flourished when the frequently inclement weather of northern Germany permitted, and leagues were set up to determine compound championships. Names given the teams by the prisoners keynoted the psychology of the camp: there were the "Draft Dodgers" and the "Flak Dodgers," the "Terror Fliegers" and the "Luft Pirates," the "Wingless Waifs," and the "Moraleless Morons."

Garden-plot farming was another widespread pastime. Seeds for the more common vegetables and flowers were received both from the United States and from Germany. Kriegie "victory gardens" covered a total of several acres and during the spring and summer our fare was embellished by bumper crops of fresh radishes, carrots, tomatoes and onions. Chief obstacle to our agricultural aspirations were the German police dogs who nightly trampled the gardens.

Most of the entertainment was individual and a good example of the lengths to which it went may be provided by Lieutenants Barris and Jellison who became the camp's self-styled doctors of entomological aviation. They selected sturdy, intelligent-looking flies, stunned them, harnessed them with thin thread and experimented on wing-load capacity and versatility of performance!

Barris deduced that "Flies have proportionate wing-load capacity to the P-40, otherwise they are aerodynamically like the B-24. All flies have retractable landing gear. To land on the ceiling, they half-roll and sometimes, just to be ornery, they loop."

Jellison explained that they had stolen a march on evolution by attaching a tail to the fly—a small paper triangle—but that they had found it wrecked their control and stability.

The doctors tried to teach flies formation tactics by harnessing them together in threes, but it was found that the middle man usually lost his head, literally. Transport flies, however, lifted amazingly heavy loads. Gliders, slightly larger than postage stamps, were made airborne by teams of rehearsed insects. But again the problem of co-ordination was a major one.

Sometime before the war ended the fliers schemed out a plan to train ten thousand flies which they calculated would carry one glider and one prisoner to safety outside the camp. The war's end interfered with the training program and both Barris and Jellison returned by other means, quite sanely, to their West Coast homes.

When mice became a problem, hundreds of fantastically elaborate traps were constructed throughout the camp. Mouse traps do not have to be elaborate to be effective as has been proved by standard types, but they had to be fanciful to fill time and to satisfy a kriegie longing to accomplish something. There were guillotine types, sledge-hammer types, hang-yourself-mouse types—all made without tools and employing only scraps of wood, bits of string and metal from food cans.

Lieutenant James A. McAvoy, a pilot from San Francisco, California, had another use for the camp's mouse population. He caught several, caged them, fed some vitamin tablets, powdered milk and other luxuries. Others he fed from his German rations to observe comparative growth. Opposition to the menagerie from McAvoy's roommates finally ended the experiments.

Shoestring lathes, operated with trouser belts and shoelaces, were created to turn out first-class chess and checker sets for the camp. One of the most clever endeavors was a supercharged kriegie stove with a thirty-four to one ration which, claimed its builders, cooked a meal on a two-ounce lump of coal. Yet the only materials used in its construction were empty tins, scraps of wood and a pair of suspenders.

Powdered-milk mixers, model planes, airfields, prison camps, flak guns, statuettes, model homes—these were all turned out by the hundreds by men who worked with virtually no tools and no guidance except their own ingeniousness. The drawing of blueprints for postwar homes, designing new planes and cars, these too occupied many prison hours.

But it must not be suspected that even this imposing list of activities succeeded in dispersing boredom. The barbed wire and the German guards were still with us and it was not easy for young fliers to reconcile themselves to such an existence.

Endless hours were filled with talk of home, of flying, of past—and imaginary—sex experiences. At night sometimes could be heard, from behind a blacked-out, shuttered barrack window, a plaintive call, "Come on, Ike," "Come on, Joe."

Our camp library expanded gradually to contain over ten thousand books. Most were received through charitable organizations at home or in Switzerland, but German libraries and personal book parcels sent to prisoners provided many more. At first, complained Lieutenant Marcus Dekle, the camp librarian from Cordele, Georgia, prisoner readers were employing the book pages for a wrong use, but later on, Red Cross supplies of toilet paper saved the remaining volumes.

Many of the young airmen, whose transition from high school and college to a German prison camp had been a rapid one, delved deeply into the philosophies, histories and weightier classics to compensate for an incomplete education.

After many months with virtually no literary facilities, shipments of college texts began to arrive in the camp and formal classes were organized in the mess halls and larger rooms. A serious effort was made at self-education and a wide selection of studies was made possible by enlisting teachers among the prisoners themselves. Courses ranged from languages, music appreciation and salesmanship to the highest mathematics.

Lieutenant John Burke, one of the community's most active workers and one of its most talented citizens, instructed classes in algebra, geometry, trigonometry, calculus and German as well as helping to edit a clandestine camp newspaper. In their lust for knowledge, and for something to pass the time, prisoners studied architecture, radio and television, insurance, banking and business, labor relations, history and economics, public speaking and most of the modern languages.

A mercurial morale, juggled by war news and by the arrival of mail and food supplies, rendered the studies somewhat haphazard. And periodic escape attempts—with inevitable failure resulting in two-week solitary confinement—hampered both teachers and students.

Medical facilities at Stalag Luft I were adequate to handle all but the most delicate surgical operation. Chiefs of the medical staff were brilliant British doctors, captured in 1940, whose skill and fortitude helped largely to explain the camp's high health standard. Although they had little to work with, and German co-operation left much to be desired, they helped maintain a health standard unsurpassed by most army camps in Britain or in America.

Shortly before the war ended, the senior medical officer, a Harley Street physician before 1939, told the writer that "Generally speaking, the men in this camp will leave here in as good health or better than when they arrived. Some weight has been lost ... but the fliers here are on the whole in better health than civilians of their age group. ..."

Surely our camp boasted, at least, the lowest venereal rate of any comparable-sized community in the world!

The one activity which filled more hours—in planning, in execution and in solitary aftermath—of most prisoners was the subject escape. A fantastically wide range of methods were employed but the results were singularity alike: failure. Undaunted kriegies tried again and again, suspecting spies among the prisoner population and hidden microphones in the barrack walls, but never completely frustrated nor unalterably discouraged.

Summertime, with its enervating heat, brought lulls in the cadence of attempted evasion. Other seasons, however, witnessed a fairly constant effort at illegal migration from every corner of the camp. A Wing X "Escape Committee" was established, but its sole effect was to formalize the game and so to decrease the kriegie's chances of success.

Tunneling was the most favored medium. Tunneling was also the most work and, because of the belatedly discovered seismographs, was the most hopeless.

Excavated dirt was disposed of by flushing in barrack toilets, by strewing it under floors, filling lockers and mattresses. Ventilation for the two-man digging crews was supplied by Rube Golberg type contraptions: chains of cans and hand-built air pumps. The work sometimes lasted a month and the tunnels sometimes continued as far as two hundred feet before emerging above ground.

The strictest security was observed; our own guards were posted everywhere to warn of "snooping goons" and even mention of the word tunnel was forbidden. But every time a group of prisoners, their pockets laden with long-hoarded chocolate bars and cans of beef, crawled underground to a point outside the camp there was the saddening anticlimax of finding German guards pointing rifles into their exit hole and ordering them to solitary confinement.

Escape by deception was also popular, and when apprehended was rated an extra week solitary punishment, as trickery constituted "an insult to German honor." Some prisoners tried to leave concealed in the garbage cart, others sewed potato sacks and bits of tin to themselves in abortive attempts to simulate refuse. Others created German uniforms from scraps of colored cloth, fashioned wooden revolvers and sought by bluffing the gate guards to walk out.

Once Bolton, my pilot who had arrived before me at Stalag Luft I, another British pilot and I tried to leave the camp at night with one of us feigning violent illness on a stretcher. The guard was not fooled.

Of the few who managed to get outside the camp, to be caught days or weeks later somewhere in Germany, most succeeded by simply climbing a less-guarded section of the fence at twilight. Those who reached the surrounding countryside usually fared badly before being returned to the camp for they were jailed in Gestapo prisons, heavily interrogated, sometimes roughly handled by the civilian population and always, believe it or not, quite happy to be back in the relative security of our kriegie community.

In October, 1944, escape "ceased to be a sport" in the words of an official German poster nailed in each of the camp barracks. In vivid black and red print, the announcement read:

"TO ALL PRISONERS OF WAR

"Escape from prison camps is no longer a sport. Germany has always kept to the Hague Convention and only punished recaptured POWs with minor disciplinary punishment.

"But England, besides fighting at the front in an honest manner, has instituted an illegal warfare in non-combat zones in the form of gangster commandos, terror bandits and sabotage troops.

"They say in a captured secret and confidential English military pamphlet, 'The Handbook of Modern Irregular Warfare': 'The days when we could practice the rules of sportsmanship are over. For the time being, every soldier must be a potential gangster. …'"

Because of this claimed abrogation of international conduct in warfare, the German retaliation, continued the poster, would be to forbid escape from prison camps under penalty of death.

"Urgent warning is given against making future escapes!

"The chances of preserving your life are almost nil!

"Escaping from prison camps has ceased to be a sport."

Reaction of the prisoners was to chalk V-signs, to scribble "Buy War Bonds" and "Come on, Ike" across the posters. Escape efforts, however unsuccessful, were not discontinued. And no lives were lost in the attempts.

CHAPTER 16

Not as Briefed

To visit Germany by parachute or by crash-landing bomber was hardly an unusual experience in the eyes of some nine thousand prisoners who had all arrived at Stalag I by one or the other means. But even among such a blasé audience of experienced young fighters there were some tales which stood out as spectacular and incredible.

Storytelling was a popular time passer. Most yarn spinners began with "We were at twenty thousand feet and the flak was so thick you could walk on it. ..." or "There were four hundred German fighters around us and they were all shooting at me. ..." Sometimes a new arrival would bring in a fresh twist, but generally the pattern would be the same and the novice kriegie would soon find himself without an audience unless he had something really spectacular to recount.

It worked both ways. Reception committees sometimes met the incoming groups of new prisoners and the ensuing scenes were not unlike those at a fraternity hazing session. When a new group was scheduled to arrive, hand-drawn signs would be put up around the camp: "Dance Tonight. Date up your Luftwaffette now." "Golfing and horseback riding Sunday." "Boat to Sweden leaves Barth (the nearby town) every four hours. Get your furlough papers from the German HQ." Less elaborate posters advertised "Soft Drinks and Ice Cream now on sale at the PX" and "Fly a Focke-Wulf for an hour: *10 marks* at the local airfield; get your tickets here."

Once, a newly arrived prisoner, not yet accustomed to the rigors of a POW camp, asked the mess-hall waiter for more sugar. "This coffee is sour," he complained. "Get me some more sugar. I'm a combat airman." There was no scene, but it was later pointed out to the complainer that his "waiter" had earned the Congressional Medal of Honor and had been exploded out of a B-17 over Berlin a year previous.

On the other hand, to temper the enthusiasm of arriving kriegies, sometimes a veteran prisoner would be wrapped in blankets and laid on a bunk next to the newcomer's bed.

"What's the matter with him?" would ask the new citizen.

"He's dead," replied a roommate in a matter-of-fact voice.

"Dead! Jeez, why don't you bury him?"

"Oh, the guys are dying off like flies. Haven't time to bury them all. This one won't bother you. He's been dead three weeks from starvation."

Life, however, was neither so difficult nor so rosy as it sometimes appeared. During the summer of 1944, when there were rations and sunshine aplenty and when the Germans permitted periodic swimming parties in the nearby Baltic, few complaints were to be heard. The Allies were galloping across France at blitz pace and the war seemed nearly won. Much satisfaction was to be derived from the discomfort and worry of our German guards.

During the following winter, however, Red Cross supplies were cut off by the intensive tactical bombardment of German railroads and we fed on one half-rotten potato and a few slices of bread for breakfast, and a plate of thin, tasteless stew for dinner. For brief periods there was no water and no electricity in the camp. Our German guards drew fresh hope from their counteroffensive in the Ardennes and kriegie morale was at its ebb.

It was a true compensation to remember then, despite present hardships, that life had been much more difficult *before* reaching Stalag Luft I on the Baltic and we were now relatively well off.

Many of the fliers had experienced strange adventures in Europe's skies on their last missions. I gathered together a number of the stories which should disclose some of the unpublicized misfortunes of airmen who had only a one-way ticket to Germany, and whose missions were not as briefed. I include these stories as they were told to me, without any attempt at enhancing them with added words. I believe they are all true.

Lieutenant Greenwood Gay (of Pensacola, Florida) left England on his twenty-fifth and last mission as pilot of a Liberator on February 25, 1944. The target was Nuremberg.

Shortly before bombing, flak injured the right wing and the Liberator fell out of formation to be attacked by four FW-190's. Cannon fire chopped up the loaded bomb bay and damaged the controls. Gay tried to swing off toward the French border, but six more fighters attacked and the bomber was very seriously damaged. Wing gas tanks were aflame and incendiary bombs in the hold were exploding into furious, phosphorous fires.

"I had to order everyone to bail out," reported Gay. "After I checked fore and aft to see if they had left, I prepared to get out. As I started climbing out of the seat, I felt a terrific impact on the nose of the plane and heard the top-turret guns firing. Sergeant Gery Brown (of Indiana) had stayed with his guns despite the order to get out."

A German fighter scorched in from dead ahead, all guns firing into the stricken Liberator. Gay felt a hammer blow on his chest. He fell back into the seat, unable to move. Blood spurted from his chest. Nearly unconscious, he decided to ride the ship down and to take his chances in an uncontrolled crash-landing.

Suddenly, Sergeant Brown appeared from the top turret, dragged the pilot from his seat by the harness, struggled with him back onto the flight deck and fastened his parachute. The rip cord had been torn away.

"I kept telling Brown to get out, but he ignored me," said Gay. "He turned me over, jerked my parachute free from the pack and carried me into the bomb bay which was burning. He dumped me out through a gaping hole in the side. I felt the chute drag along the fuselage for a moment, then I was jerked upright as it opened.

"As I glanced down, I fell through a small tree and landed on my back in about a foot of snow. I felt blood gushing from my chest."

Gay managed to reach a handkerchief in his trouser pocket, to wad it up and to stuff it into the gaping chest wound. Then he rolled around until he was in position so that a rock pressed into the back wound. "Both sides coagulated and I settled down to wait for the Germans to find me."

Three hours later, a group of *Landwehr* scouts arrived and the pilot was eventually taken to a hospital, after having been given first aid by a local midwife. A Catholic priest administered the last sacraments and the doctor advised him that there was no hope. But blood transfusions from the German soldiers the next day, and a phenomenal constitution, saved Gay's life.

A twenty-millimeter cannon shell had gone right through his chest, he learned, missing his heart by a quarter inch and nicking the lung and main artery. After several months in German hospitals, Gay recovered completely and eventually came to Stalag Luft I where he awaited the war's end.

Sergeant Gerald W. Brown, who had destroyed two fighters during that last mission, never reached the safety of a prison camp. He was killed in the crashing Liberator. He gave his life to Gay, for it was too late to help himself after saving his pilot.

Lieutenant Robert E. Paine (from Baltimore) bailed out of his bomber at eighteen thousand feet above Germany after a severe fighter attack had set the plane afire. He had unknowingly failed to fasten the leg straps of the parachute harness.

When he pulled the rip cord and the parachute opened, he almost fell out of the harness, but the tightly fastened arm straps prevented this. As he floated earthward, however, he felt himself gradually slipping out of the harness. Every movement to make his position more secure made it more precarious.

Finally, still several thousand feet above the ground, he slipped completely out of the harness. As he fell, he grabbed the straps with both hands and hung on—not unlike a trapeze acrobat—until he was safely on the ground.

Lieutenant G. J. Thom (from Budington, Wisconsin) was the pilot of a heavy bomber over Germany. Flak and fighters knocked out three engines and the plane lost altitude rapidly. At three thousand feet, north of Hanover, he ordered the crew to bail out and then jumped himself.

The rip cord of his parachute would not work, due to a bent cotter pin. He fell three thousand feet without a parachute, crashed through a tree to the ground, unconscious. When he awakened, the unopened chute was still in its pack attached to his harness. Thom suffered no more serious injury than sprains.

Captain Raymond P. Sanford (from Alhambra, California) was the pilot of a B-26 Marauder bomber. On December 13, 1943, his group bombed Schiphol airfield in Holland.

As Sanford entered the bomb run, flak struck the port engine and the fuselage. By manipulating the controls, he held the ship on course for a moment until the wing exploded away from the plane. Then, completely out of control, the bomber spun down toward the ground.

At four thousand feet it exploded. Sanford next remembered tumbling through the air, still seated in his armor-plated pilot's seat. He managed to reach around and to pull the rip cord, then to release the fifty pounds of armor plating, after which his descent slowed.

Examined a few hours later by a German doctor, Sanford learned that his right arm, shoulder blade and collarbone were broken. His back was dislocated and he had several serious wounds.

The other six crewman did not survive the explosion.

Lieutenant Hampton Pugh, heavy bomber pilot (from Hamburg, Arkansas), was shot down on February 22, 1944. German fighters had sieved the plane with rocket and cannon fire. The crew was forced to bail out, but as Pugh was preparing to follow them, he realized the plane had straightened itself out and was still flying.

He returned to the pilot's seat, nosed the bomber down to within a few feet of the ground and set a dead-reckoning course for France and England. He passed directly over the flak-infested Ruhr, skimming factory roofs and banking to avoid church steeples.

Sometime later, when he calculated he was over southern Belgium or France light flak chained upwards and further damaged the plane so that it fell off and started earthward. Pugh crawled to an escape hatch and jumped. Below, he saw water and something which resembled a canal system.

Five days later, he regained consciousness in a railroad station at Frankfort on the Main, where he was told that he had been picked up near Brussels, Belgium—more than five hundred miles distant. He did not recall, and still does not, being transported to Dulag Luft near Frankfort, nor being interrogated, nor being started out on the long boxcar ride to Stalag.

Lieutenant R. H. Cooper, a B-17 copilot (from Los Angeles, California), and his crewmates encountered an unusual experience early in April, 1944, On a mission from England to central Germany, one engine was lost near the target and a second was put out of action by oil trouble.

The remaining two engines were not strong enough to carry them home, so the crew was ordered to prepare to bail out. Just before the "jump" order was given, a small landing strip was sighted far below. The ship's captain made a snap decision, decided to land the bomber and to try to repair the damaged engines before being captured.

Gunners remained at their posts while the pilots managed a trick landing on the short runway. For the next hour, the pilots and engineer worked over the engines, while the other crewmen held off civilians and police with the bomber's machine guns.

Finally, they ran out of ammunition before the engines were repaired. Civilians overpowered the crew and the Fortress was captured intact. But the next day, just as the unfortunate airmen were embarking for a prison camp, a P-51 fighter flew over the airfield, strafing and destroying the grounded bomber.

Lieutenant W. L. Kalman (from la Crescenro, California) was returning from a bomber mission over Germany when his plane was directly hit by flak over the Ruhr. The bomber fell into a tailspin and Kalman struggled toward the escape hatch just as the fuel tanks exploded.

He regained consciousness floating down several thousand feet above the earth, absolutely nude except for his parachute harness. The explosion had blown off every stitch of clothing and opened his parachute. Total injuries on landing were a few cuts on his feet and a serious case of embarrassment.

Lieutenant Ted J. McDonald (from Rochester, New York) was the pilot of a heavy bomber in a mission over Germany. Before reaching its target, the bomber was crippled by attacks of from thirty to forty fighters. Two engines were knocked out and the starboard wing and radio compartment were set afire. McDonald salvoed the bombs and ordered the crew to bail out. Lieutenant Jacob Moskowitz, the bombardier (from Brooklyn, New York), was unable to leave as his parachute had been shredded by cannon fire. McDonald ordered Moskowitz to take his parachute and to bail out.

This left the pilot alone in a burning plane with no parachute. He pushed the wheel forward and dived toward the ground. Fighters followed him down, pouring machine-gun and cannon fire into the blazing bomber. The plane's air speed reached three hundred miles an hour and the fire was fanned out.

McDonald managed to straighten out the bomber and to slow it to two hundred miles an hour, but the fires broke out anew. Nearing the ground, he attempted to crash-land in a swampy field by first dragging the tail to lose speed. He managed to stop and, after a few moments' struggle, forced open the copilot's window and crawled out onto the wing which was afire.

Just as he reached the wing, the plane exploded. He was blown nearly fifty feet across the field and awakened sometime later to find a German police dog licking his face. When asked if he was injured, he answered, "I have a headache."

Lieutenant W. W. King (from Kingtree, South Carolina) piloted a B-17 from a North African base. He arranged a business deal with an Arab native who agreed to supply him with a dozen eggs daily in exchange for ownership of the bomber. It was understood, however, that King would continue to fly the Fortress and, for the time being, the Arab's title would be an honorary one.

The withered up little man took extreme pleasure in ownership, directing the ground crew to polish the plane carefully and admonishing them to keep it in the best condition. They humored him and begged his forgiveness whenever the Fortress returned damaged by shell or flak holes.

Finally, there came a "last mission" and Lieutenant King crashed his wrecked bomber in Germany instead of returning it to North Africa.

and to its Arab owner. King, who spent the duration at Stalag Luft I, wondered sometimes how chagrined the Arab was at losing his B-17 pride.

RAF Flying Officer C. E. Smith (from Portsmouth, England) was the pilot of a Lancaster and was shot down over Berlin during a night raid early in 1944. He bailed out, landed safely on the outskirts of the city in pitch blackness. He unhooked his parachute and started walking away.

After a few steps, he fell forty feet, breaking his right leg and seriously straining his back. He had unknowingly landed on the roof of a two-story building and walked off the edge.

Lieutenant R. A. S., a Fortress navigator (from Chicago, Illinois), was shot down near Budapest in July, 1944. He landed in a grain field and was surrounded by irate Hungarians. One of them shot him with a small-caliber pistol and he collapsed on the ground.

A fortnight later, he awakened in a Budapest general hospital and learned that the bullet had lodged in his heart. A Catholic priest administered the last rites several times, as the surgeons refused to undertake such an operation, and the navigator was given up as a hopeless case.

But he survived and, several months later, arrived at Stalag where he was active, healthy and cheerful. The camp doctors told him that if the bullet moved a fraction of an inch he would die. As a unique example of a man living on borrowed time, R. A. S. refused to be discouraged and explained, "I'll just go on living until I stop. There's nothing I can do about it."

Sergeant Robert B. Reed, a B-24 tail gunner (from Indianapolis, Indiana), suffered no more than a few bruises and a brief case of nerves from his four-mile death ride in the tail of a bomber.

Shot down by fighters at twenty-three thousand feet in March, 1944, Reed's bomber was exploded into several parts as it fell through the sky. He tumbled down, trapped in the burning tail section which had torn free.

He fell over four miles, unable to move and resigned to what must come. Just before striking the ground, he lost consciousness, to awaken sometime later on the earth near the battered, splintered tail section. His leg and back were slightly bruised.

Lieutenant Henry V. Markow, a B-17 pilot (from Brooklyn, New York), took off on his seventeenth mission over Germany on February 22, 1944. Not far from the target, the bomber was crippled by German fighters and the bomb load of incendiaries was set afire. Controls were almost useless and nearly all the plane's guns were shot out of action.

As Markow prepared to follow the other crewmen out of an escape hatch, he saw the bombardier, Lieutenant George Littleton (from Mississippi), crawling through the ship without a parachute. Markow returned to the pilot's compartment, after learning that the bombardier had no chute, and fought the plunging ship as it swirled earthward.

They crash-landed nearly a hundred miles an hour faster than normal landing speed and plowed along a field before stopping. Both men crawled safely out of the plane only a few seconds before it was covered with flames.

Lieutenant John C. Morgan, a Fortress Pilot (from New York City), had earned the Medal of Honor for gallantry and courage on a mission to Hanover in the summer of 1943. Two missions later, he was shot down over the center of Berlin, in a B-17 which was leading the entire Eighth Air Force in a maximum-effort attack.

Immediately after his plane entered the bomb run, flak set the wings afire, but the first pilot, Major Fred Rabo (from Chico, California) held on to the controls so that their bombs would go down accurately to direct the avalanche to follow.

A few seconds after "Bombs away!" the Fortress exploded, and Morgan was blown free with his parachute grasped in one hand.

As he tumbled downward, he buckled the chute to his chest harness, then pulled the rip cord and, swinging once he landed abruptly at the edge of a small lake in Berlin.

Bombardier Lieutenant Angelo F. Malerba (from Brooklyn, New York) was shot down over Austria in a B-24 on April 2, 1944. Nearly all of the crew members were wounded by the persistent attack of fighters which brought about the disaster. But ten German interceptors were destroyed by the gunner in the furious battle.

The Liberator fell off into a flat spin and the centrifugal force was so great that the airmen were pinned to their positions Malerba, a man of tremendous strength, fought his way through the falling, burning plane, pulled the copilot from underneath a mass of wreckage and threw him overboard. He then released the trapped engineer and threw him out of the plane. Both men parachuted safely to earth.

Malerba landed near the crashed bomber, from which ammunition was exploding dangerously. He heard cries for help from within the plane. Four times he smashed his way with bare hands through the blazing fuselage and each time dragged a crewman to safety. Then, before thinking of himself, he supervised the removal of the three badly wounded fliers to the hospital and attended the burial of five of the men at a nearby cemetery.

Although the vast majority of parachuting airmen were treated fairly by both the German civilian population and by the enemy's armed forces, there were occasional cases of serious mistreatment, torture and murder by their captors.

One example was contained in the story of eleven hundred American prisoners who arrived at Stalag XII-A, near Limburg, Taunus, on December 21, 1944. The Germans seized all their overcoats, blankets, sweaters and personal valuables, then ordered them into boxcars which were equipped with neither straw nor heat.

Despite the sub-zero temperature these men were freighted eastward for thirty-two days to another camp in Pomerania. Only infrequently was there an issue of water or food during the entire trip and, upon arrival, four hundred of the men were so badly frostbitten that they were unable to walk.

On arrival at Stalag I, Lieutenant Kenneth R. Murgatroyd reported what had happened to three of his fellow crewmen when their bomber was shot down near Weimar on July 20, 1944. The navigator was shot and killed by a civilian as he removed his parachute. The radio operator and tail gunner were beaten to death by members of the *Volkssturm*. The other crewmen were marched nude through a small town where they were kicked and stoned by the local population.

Many of the airmen who tried to reach safety through the French Underground, but who were intercepted by the Gestapo, were roughly handled before reaching a prison camp. Up to six months' solitary confinement was not unusual; severe beatings, devious medieval tortures and starvation were employed frequently by the sadistic protective police to force airmen to disclose information.

Most of these stories will never be told, however, because the airmen concerned were killed rather than allowed to come into a large prison camp where they could tell their story and, in so doing, add to the condemnation of Nazi barbarism.

On file at Stalag Luft I, nonetheless, were the names of four hundred Air Force personnel who had suffered serious mistreatment by the Germans. Although these represented only four and a half percent of the camp strength, hundreds of other cases never came to light for there was no one left to tell the story.

Exiled solitude was not the only price Allied airmen paid to test the theory urged by office-desk generals. There are thousands buried today in obscure graves across the earth of Europe.

CHAPTER 17

Pow Wow

Food, mail and war news were the foundations of kriegie morale. By the quantity of the first two and the quality of the third was our collective spirit sustained.

Prisoners were permitted three letters and four postcards per month as outgoing mail. These underwent the scrutiny of Wing X, to prevent information from reaching the Nazis, the inspection of the Germans to glean scraps of news and opinion for propaganda purposes, and finally a censorship in America and Britain. Partly because of the public nature of all letters home and partly because of the non-stimulating sameness of prison life, mail home was usually uninspired. Moreover, a letter from Stalag to New York ordinarily was three to five months in transit.

Incoming mail, however, sometimes contained choice excerpts. One RAF sergeant pilot received this letter from his wife in Liverpool: "Darling, I've been living with a private since you've been gone. Please do not cut off my allowance, though, as he doesn't earn as much money as you. …"

Captain R.A.L. once received a sweater from a woman through the Red Cross and wrote her his thanks. Months later, he received the following reply: "I am sorry that a prisoner received the sweater I knitted. I made it for a fighting man. …"

Lieutenant J.M. heard this unhappy news from his wife in New Orleans: "James, I will be glad when you get home so I can get a divorce. I have been living with an infantry captain for some time. He is really swell. …"

An RCAF flying officer was told by his wife in Ontario: "Dear John, I gave your golf clubs to a German colonel, a prisoner of war in a camp near here. I hope you don't mind." Unconverted John wrote his wife to get back his goddamn clubs and not to give anything to the goddamn Germans. He heard later that his country club had canceled his membership for not being a gentleman.

Another RCAF flier, shot down eighteen months previously, received this word from his wife: "Dear Harry, I hope you are broadminded. I just had a baby. …He is such a nice fellow … he is sending you some cigarettes."

Lieutenant R.S. received a letter from his adult sister in Des Moines who had this to tell him: "Dear Bob, I am really so worried over Tommy, the cat. I took him to a veterinarian yesterday and he said his diet is insufficient."

A complete letter from his father to Lieutenant H.L.A. contained: "Dear son. Hello. How are you? We are all well. With love from all, Dad."

One that was more appreciated came to Lieutenant K.R.B. from his father. "Dear son," it read. "I knew I should have kept you at home and joined the Air Corps myself. Even when you were a kid I expected you'd end up in prison. …"

Lieutenant C.P.N. received a letter from a girl he had met in Florida two years previously, and after one date had not written her since. "Dearest Charles," she wrote, "I am going to spend the summer with your folks. They are fine and all your relations are very kind. The girls around here are all worried about the man shortage and becoming old maids. But we can beat that when you get home. …"

From many letters, it appeared also that the Red Cross publicity department was taking liberties with its advertising. Mothers wrote of their happiness that "you can play golf again" or that "you can go to school and learn a trade" or that "I won't send any parcels as I understand that you can go into town and buy things." There were occasional suggestions that prisoner-of-war life was one grand paid vacation with all the comforts of a luxurious country club. These hardly encouraged a reasonable morale, although some of the boys believed themselves better off than they really were.

Other mail, sometimes the first letter received by a prisoner, contained mess bills, advertising circulars and uniform bills. Once the long arm of the Hague political machine reached all the way to our Baltic prison camp when Lieutenant C. E. Faller, from Jersey City, New Jersey, received a form letter from a local ward heeler urging him to vote "no" on some local referendum. War ballots arrived in profusion, but all of them too late to meet the 1944 national election. One young flier received an envelope full of pin-up girls' pictures from a friend in Hollywood. The prisoner in question enjoyed a sudden great popularity in camp.

Most pathetic were the boys who watched every mail call with eager, anxious eyes—waiting for news of their offspring, born while the father was a prisoner in Germany. Proof of Air Force fertility; in one barracks of a hundred and thirty fliers, no fewer than fourteen "sweated out" their children's arrival while in Stalag Luft I.

Complex codes, set up in advance, were used by prisoners to communicate with the British Air Ministry and the War Department. Instructions and advice were also sent to us in seemingly innocuous letters from Military Intelligence officers in Britain and America. Unfortunately, the Germans learned of the system and intercepted many of the letters.

Prisoners sometimes were quite blunt in their mail. One wrote to a big U.S. steel corporation, requesting "a catalogue of alloy steel escape tools so I can get out of this place." Another wrote to say that football, baseball and tunnel digging were the most popular sports, "and the last named is always won by the Germans."

Periodic personal parcels from home—although delivery took four to nine months—helped food rations and morale. Tobacco packages were also authorized and the U.S. government encouraged the sending of more cartons of cigarettes than necessary as it was known that the common cigarette had a high bribing value in Germany. Book and clothing parcels also arrived and, generally, there were very few instances of looting or pilfering while the consignments were en route from Switzerland in German freight trains.

No liquor was allowed into the camp, however—although we dreamed of parcels of dehydrated whisky—so the more imaginative airmen constructed their own distilleries with lengths of pipe and empty food cans. Kriegie "brews" were usually based on fermented prunes, raisins or potatoes and the resulting concoctions, however welcome to parched POW throats, hardly resembled the Olympian nectar. German search parties, frequently bursting into a barracks to seek out tunnels, the storage of escape tools and the unaromatic breweries, sometimes interrupted the liquor-making and seized the *verboten* distilleries.

Once Lieutenant Leo Oldmixon, one of the camp experts on fine liqueurs, saved a barrel of brew—when intruded upon by German guards—by throwing a pair of trousers and a scrubbing board into the stewing raisins. When the Germans had left, he calmly removed the trousers and board, and the raisins went on fermenting—to be heartily imbibed some weeks later when they had reached a more interesting stage.

Christmas time in a prison camp was not quite like Christmas time at home. Nostalgia reached its peak when cold northern winds blew snowdrifts around the barracks, when the coal ration was insufficient to keep frost from the rooms and when, in 1944, the German offensive in the Ardennes threatened to prolong the war indefinitely.

But even a barbed-wire exile could not prohibit a holiday spirit and the airmen set to work decorating the rooms with scraps of paper and metal, fashioning Christmas trees and preparing for a feast with special parcels from the Red Cross.

A camp Christmas tree, ersatz in its every aspect but the symbolic, was made with a broom handle as its trunk and a log as its base. Strips of wire, cut from powdered-milk cans, imbedded at one end in the trunk and arching outward, served as branches.

On these were mounted carefully cut lengths of toilet paper to simulate needled foliage in a natural conical form. Slivers of cellophane from cigarette packages were strung out like tinsel. The varicolored paper of soap wrappers, tin-can labels and note-book covers were meticulously cut to make decorations.

Red Cross water paints, applied with homemade brushes of human hair, colored other bits of paper—glued together with barley-flour paste—to make other ornaments, and razor-shredded paper produced "snow." That pattern was duplicated and varied all over the camp, and almost every room had its Christmas tree.

The Reverend Charles R. Charleton, a British Army Catholic chaplain captured at Dunkirk in 1940, conducted a Midnight Mass in one of the camp's mess halls. Nearly two thousand fliers gathered together in the barracks from the several compounds and the combined glee clubs were accompanied by a small, portable YMCA organ. It was the first Angels' Mass ever held in a German prison camp and was truly an impressive ceremony.

It was also about Christmas time that a new kriegie racket was innovated: extra light for the barracks rooms. A single twenty-five watt bulb was hardly sufficient to illuminate the large rooms, so prisoners bribed their guards for larger bulbs, secretly constructed appliances and nightly tapped the wall wires for as much as twenty times the allotted ration of electricity.

During the spring of 1945, when the military ledger began to run heavily red for Germany, Max Schmeling paid our community a propaganda visit. The bulky, genial, ex-world-champion boxer was mobbed by autograph-hunting kriegies wherever he went in the camp.

His excuse for the visit was that his wife had been evacuated from Berlin to a nearby town and he "wanted to visit my American friends while in the neighborhood." Wing X colonels sought to keep him to themselves, but the common kriegie would have none of it, and if Schmeling had prepared a propaganda line he was given no opportunity to introduce it, for the exuberant welcome he was accorded left him no time to make a speech.

He explained that he had been wounded in the right knee and suffered fractured back bones while a sergeant parachutist in Crete in 1940. Until a year and a half before his visit, he had been in and out of German hospitals recuperating, and now he was a civilian managing a small restaurant in central Germany, "if it hasn't been bombed yet." He still spoke choppy, friendly English, still grinned like an embarrassed schoolboy instead of a world-famous sportsman, but his hair was graying and, when no one else was present, he admitted that it was nearly all over for Germany.

After he left, Colonel Hubert Zemke, the camp's senior prisoner, commented: "Next we'll get dancing girls. ... Then they'll tell us the war's over and we ought all to be good friends."

A week later, Berlin's printing presses stamped out a curious invitation to treason. Thousands of circulars arrived at our camp, ludicrously begging our assistance on the crumbling East Front. If we would carry a rifle and "help defend Europe against the encroaching horrors of Red Bolshevism," the circular promised that we would be released to return as free men to our homes "at the conclusion of the present offensive."

The men at Stalag Luft I—not one of whom accepted the offer—did return home as free men at the conclusion of that offensive. It was the middle of April, 1945—and three weeks later, Germany was destroyed.

Pow Wow was the largest circulating daily underground newspaper in Germany. Its headquarters were at Stalag Luft I and, at its most successful period, it boasted editions in three languages and a circulation that reached seven prison camps. Its masthead somewhat libelously read: "The Only Truthful Newspaper in Germany."

The Germans did not like *Pow Wow* and made strenuous efforts to eliminate it, but from March, 1944, until May, 1945, not one edition was missed because of enemy interference. It served a continuous and vital kriegie need: the urgent necessity to be kept informed on what was happening outside our barbed-wire isolation.

Chief among its editors and compositors were Lieutenants Parker, Austin, Gallagher and Burke. They hailed from California, New York, New Jersey and Massachusetts. Their prewar work had varied from reporter to factory foreman to metallurgical engineer and their Air Force profession had been as combat airmen, destined to be shot down and to turn out a professional clandestine newspaper in the heart of Germany.

Pow Wow covered two sides of a large sheet of writing paper, was printed and duplicated by carbon paper on a battered Swedish typewriter and circulated each evening throughout the camp. When supplies of carbon paper were exhausted, new stocks were made by smoking sheets of paper over lamps and sizing them with smuggled kerosene. (The lamps, incidentally, were cans of boiled margarine with a strip of web-belt as wick.)

News was drawn from four main sources: from German newspapers and magazines brought into the camp, from loudspeakers which broadcast the

Nazi war communiqués and from newly arrived prisoners who brought fresh news from home. The fourth source was a tiny radio set, in part handmade and in part smuggled into the camp by bribed guards, which was hidden in the wall of one of the barracks rooms.

Lieutenants Burke and Tiffany (the latter from Syracuse, New York) labored daily over all German periodicals which found their way into the camp, translating thousands of words of fact and propaganda which were carefully analyzed, condensed and each evening presented, in *Pow Wow*'s four news-packed columns, along with excerpts from the broadcasts.

Best news source was the hidden radio set which was strong enough to pick up one BBC broadcast each evening from London. The receiver was hand-built by imprisoned radio operators except for the miniature tubes which were purchased from German guards for several hundred cigarettes each.

Only two almost invisible points on the wall disclosed where the radio was secreted. When these points were joined by a short length of wire, the set was automatically switched on to the correct wave-length and the chimes of London's Big Ben could be heard preceding the nightly newscast.

The report was taken down in shorthand, transcribed onto sheets of toilet paper which were rolled into a small wad and brought to the publishing corner of the camp inside a hollow wrist watch. There, the BBC news, the German radio broadcasts and translations from the newspapers were edited together to make up the day's columns.

Pow Wow's news was not stale news. Its first bulletin of the invasion of France was circulated twenty minutes before New York "extras" reached the streets. Within an hour of the liberation of Paris, our camp newspaper headlined the great news. On many occasions, because of the variety of its sources, *Pow Wow* was ahead of American newspapers with war news.

Young Lieutenant Raymond A. Parker, whose previous journalistic experience had been as copy boy on the *San Francisco Examiner* and whose wartime occupation had been as navigator-bombardier of a B-24, demonstrated a remarkable talent as editor-in-chief. Hard work, an honest attempt at objectivity—which sometimes annoyed Wing X as much as it would have the Germans—and good nerves were required for the job.

Moreover, with so much time on their hands, kriegie subscribers were perspicacious readers. They demanded a variety of style and of content, a speed and a condensed completeness which would have taxed the most experienced newsmen. And, thanks to Parker and his team, the kriegies were usually satisfied.

Good nerves were primary requisite. German interest in *Pow Wow* was unabating and attempts to disestablish the newspaper were frequent. Often after midnight, a platoon of guards would burst into the barracks and order its occupants outside while they went to work on walls, floors, mattresses and furniture to discover the suspected radio. Sometimes, snooping "goons" would intrude in the middle of publishing time and there would ensue several hectic minutes while the paper and all attendant fixtures were hastily hidden from prying eyes.

Only twice did copies of *Pow Wow* fall into enemy hands and while these further excited German interest, they did not mean an end to the underground press.

A daily Russian edition was published from the original by Lieutenant John Durakov, of San Francisco, and the thirty-five Soviet fliers who were also interned in the camp had means of communicating their news to other Russian compounds in the vicinity. For a time a French version also appeared regularly, but the American-language edition was the continuous backbone of the venture.

For several months, Parker's team also managed to produce a weekly Sunday Supplement, eight pages of news summaries, features, contributions and analysis. For this, a fighter ace, Captain Donald Ross from Los Angeles, supplied a weekly page of comics, entitled "Klim Kriegie" which parodied the more amusing aspects of camp life. Other columns featured analytical articles on German and Allied propaganda and on camp policy.

One feature, which may be interesting as a record of the kriegie outlook, was a weekly poll, whereby *Pow Wow* representatives canvassed the camp for opinions on timely subjects. In the middle of July, 1944, prisoners voted that September of that year was the most likely month for the war in Europe to end. Only two weeks later, optimism soared even higher, and August, 1944, was chosen as the likeliest month for victory. The Normandy breakthroughs had clearly upset a sober survey of the war from a prison camp as well as from home.

Asked "Will you volunteer for the Pacific War?" twenty-five per cent of the prisoners answered an emphatic "Yes"; fifty per cent were equally emphatic in the negative, and twenty-five per cent were uncertain.

Paulette Goddard and Lana Turner ran neck and breast in a poll, "Who is your choice for a non-platonic week's companion in Stalag?" In another poll, ninety-six per cent of the kriegies approved the suggestion that there be compulsory military training in postwar America. During the 1944 national election fever, which swept even a distant prison camp, Roosevelt drew ten to one votes against Dewey.

One light poem which appeared in the Sunday Supplement and which had a lot to do with helping maintain morale was written by editor Raymond Parker. I quote it here as perhaps of value in disclosing another aspect of kriegie mentality.

> When your day is too lengthy, your temper too thin,
> And you fret o'er this God-awful place we're in
> (Tho' it's twelve bucks a day for a Second Looie,
> Too much of this stuff and you're apt to go screwy)
> Think of the alien friendless Kraut
> Whose future is only a nagging doubt
> As to who'll be the first to invade the Reich
> And plan him a life he is sure not to like.
> When *you* leave you'll go back to a land where no stint is
> Where standards are high; where the old dollar mint is
> But the Kraut? The alien, friendless Kraut
> Has naught save a thought of a life so fraught
> With troubles he's nearing hysteria
> 'Cause who the hell wants to go live in Siberia?
> And you? Why you'll have a Ford V-8
> Or even a Buick that's up to date
> With radio, top and chromium plate
> While Jerry, the hapless war-losing jerk
> Will be glad to be cycling off to work;
> He'll be happy to have a home to phone to.
> (You know where most of his neighbors were blown to.)
> The position you're in isn't very exemplary
> But, thank Uncle Sam, kriegie life's only tempor'ry.

Quite soon when the whistles begin to toot,
'Cause the day has arrived when the Reich is *kaput*,
Address these words to the nearest Kraut:
"Are you set to move in? I'm moving out."

CHAPTER 18

May Day Liberation

Liberation is an exhausting experience; about once per lifetime is about as often as a normal set of nerves could endure. Months and years of stored energy, enthusiasm and expectation were blitzly drained and the adventure was one no man among the nine thousand at Stalag Luft I will ever forget.

Although we followed the war closely by tracing military changes from the daily German war communiqué and the nightly BBC broadcast, its developments became increasingly hectic as April, 1945, drew to a close. First sure word we had that the end was near came one afternoon over the German radio.

Normally, the communiqué was broadcast at one o'clock, preceded and followed by brief interludes of martial music. But on that day, April 27, the communiqué was long delayed. From one o'clock until after three the radio offered instead the solemn, weighty tones of the Overture to *Tannhäuser*. We knew something important was coming; this was one of Hitler's favorite operas and the Pilgrim's Chorus was his favorite march. Its ponderous, dramatic chords echoed forebodingly through the crowded barracks.

Finally, at 3:15, a solemn-voiced announcer interrupted the music to read the High Command communiqué. "*Das Oberkommando der Wehrmacht gibt bekannt,*" he began slowly. "... The colossal battle of Europe against the Bolshevist hordes is raging today in Berlin. Red Army battle groups have broken through our capital's outer defenses and are attacking the center of the city. Berlin's defenders are battling with unsurpassed courage … the fate of all Europe hangs in the balance."

Four days later, Berlin had fallen and—along with most of eastern German-Pomerania and Stalag Luft I—had been overrun by the "Bolshevist hordes."

On April 24, Reich Home Defense Minister and Gestapo Chief Heinrich Himmler arrived with a skeleton staff at the town of Zingst only seven miles from our camp. He had flown from Berlin in a French passenger plane and, from Zingst, was to make his first contact with the United Nations for peace terms. Because he offered to surrender Germany only to the western Allies, he was rebuffed and thereafter, as a common refugee, he fled westward toward Denmark until captured three weeks later by British soldiers.

While he was at Zingst, I requested an interview, through our German camp commander, but Himmler replied that he had no time or interest in interviews at that moment.

On April 27, it was ascertained that Stettin, seventy miles to the east and the last important bastion in Pomerania, had been captured by the Red Army. The Second White Russian Army then struck westward, smashing the scattered resistance before its tidalwave fury and driving to link up with the British near Wismar.

On April 29, permission was obtained from the German authorities to dig slit trenches inside the camp. This was done with tin cans, broken shovels and sticks within six hours, and by noon of that day ten thousand foxholes pocked the prison camp. Although new to ground warfare, Air Force kriegies dug their foxholes a veteran depth.

The next day, Hitler's embattled headquarters in Berlin found time to order that Stalag Luft I be evacuated immediately to the west. A colonel at Himmler's headquarters rescinded the order and commanded that the camp guard personnel evacuate themselves, leaving the prisoners where they were. By nightfall, the camp was virtually unguarded. A few interpreters, censorettes and grandfather-guards too old to make the hazardous trek remained.

Wing X, long prepared for such an emergency, went into action. The camp's perimeter guard towers were manned by crews of ex-Fortress and Liberator gunners. A skirmish and picket line was spread out over a wide area around the base, armed with clubs and knives to prevent any looting attempts by the local German citizenry, and our headquarters staff moved into the abandoned quarters of the German *Kommandantur.*

As May Day's dawn approached, patrols of former prisoners were accepting the surrender of the local towns of Barth, Prerow and Zingst. Weapons and vehicles were being rounded up to establish an armory and a motor pool. Forage parties scavenged food and drink.

Meanwhile, an engineering outfit seized the *Luftwaffe* airfield three miles south of the camp. Six planes were taken intact, fourteen others were found only partially damaged. Several thousand gallons of high-test fuel and a full array of airfield equipment were captured from the bewildered, unaggressive Germans. The engineers set to work clearing the runways of mines and preparing the field so that an air evacuation might be arranged.

Versatile radio men rigged a homemade transmitter in the camp and began signaling, attempting to contact the British and Russians and to tell them of our presence. The receivers picked up tank-to-tank signals of both nationalities but the transmitter was not strong enough to break in with calls for aid.

Simultaneously, a telephone crew had repaired the camp exchange system and was phoning eastward, hoping a Russian soldier would answer. Lieutenant John Durakov stood by to take over the phone and to formalize the affair in Russian. But the telephone exchange in Barth was being handled by a female comic who evidently appreciated neither her country's death nor our unique plight.

"Telephone the police station and the mayor's house in Stralsund," said our operator.

"No use," quipped she, "the police chief has sprouted wings and the mayor has taken poison."

A looting attempt by Germans and freed slave laborers interrupted all other activities. Thousands of our Red Cross parcels were stored in a nearby flak school which had been partially destroyed by scorched-earth demolitions the previous day, and Barth's citizenry had heard rumors that there was food for the taking. Two thousand parcels were lost before a guard line could be established, but no blood was spilled in dispersing the looters.

Most of the kriegies were still prisoners. Wing X imposed a discipline on the camp at least equaling that under the Germans. Periodic roll calls were held to determine if there were any "deserters" and our own guards were posted at the gates to keep the jubilant kriegies from making their way homeward individually.

German women from the nearby towns came up to the fences, begging for food and offering themselves in exchange for temporary shelter from the oncoming Russians whom—thanks to Goebbels' persistent propaganda and a flood tide of rumors—they deeply feared. A few got inside the camp, later to be removed by search parties. Several others, frantic at the disaster which had come over their country and their homes, committed suicide near the camp. Two women first shot their children, then themselves.

Five German censorettes, who had previously befriended the kriegies by supplying information and radio tubes, were sheltered by the camp chaplain in the hospital. They were five terror-stricken girls whose homes were in western Germany and who were deathly afraid of the Russians. Uniforms were supplied them; they bunched their hair under kriegie caps and tried hard to hide their femininity beneath tightly fitting tunics.

A short-wave radio set was repaired and London's BBC was openly broadcast throughout the camp for the first time. Kriegies who for long months and years had awaited this wonderful day were overcome with emotion, delirious at the prospect of soon going home and angry at Wing X for keeping them behind barbed wire.

Colonel Zemke, Wing X Commander, and his staff of nearly a hundred field-grade officers occupied the *Kommandantur*, stared glaze-eyed at maps and charts, held conferences and periodically made futile announcements over the public-address system.

During the afternoon, small patrols were dispatched to the southeast to effect a link-up with the advancing Russians. It was dangerous work;

Red Army advance guards were notoriously trigger happy, but there were volunteers aplenty. Major Braithwaite, a South African paratrooper captured in Italy in 1940, and a Londoner, Flight Sergeant Korson, were the successful team.

In a seized German car, they raced twenty-five miles south-eastward, armed only with the order: "Find Uncle Joe." They picked their way through thousands of refugees, passed houses draped with white and red flags, defying a rumored Soviet order which was about as brief and emphatic as their own: "Everyone stay put. Anyone seen moving will be shot at sight."

All afternoon they pushed along the main road toward Stettin. No one knew where the Russians were. The BBC had been vague—"streaming across Pomerania and Mecklenburg" was the most exact information London could offer—and refugee tales were of no value.

At eight o'clock that night came our own historic link-up. Braithwaite and Korson had deserted their disabled car and were moving on by foot. Suddenly, there was "Uncle Joe," or rather one of his ambassadors. A chunky little Dead-End guy loomed up from behind a hedgerow and flashed a variety of lethal weapons and a cacophony of Slavic challenges.

"Amerikanski, Engliski," shouted our scouts.

Without further ceremony, they were trotted to the nearest Soviet officer. It was Marco Polo all over again. East met West; there was hugging, back-slapping, cheek-kissing. Then they kidnaped the officer and brought him back to the camp.

He was First Lieutenant Nickolai Karmytoff, a twenty-two-year-old infantryman from the town of Tula near Moscow. He had fought his way from Stalingrad three years across Russia, Poland and eastern Germany to the relief of Stalag Luft I. Wild cheering went up from nine thousand kriegie throats as it was announced that the "Russian vanguard" had arrived.

Karmytoff entered the camp's main gate. He had been celebrating it seemed, en route westward from Stettin during the past six days. Asked our MP gate guard, quaking with cold and that special kind of anticipatory fear we were all enjoying: "Is the whole Russian army coming in that way?"

Colonel Zemke and Wing X staff received Lieutenant Karmytoff. The Red Army representative mashed several Allied hands in enthusiastic greeting, speeched at us in bewildering Russian. Long-hoarded, long-hidden bottles of hospital spirits were opened and the articulate young fighter toasted us: "To the destruction of Germany—she will newer rise again. And to our solid and enduring friendship." (Exact translation by Lieutenant Durakov.)

Schnapps seared kriegie throats; glasses smashed Hitler's picture which until then had decorated the Kommandant's office. The barracks jiggled with cheering and back-pounding. Karmytoff showed curious airmen how he operated his automatic rifle and worried us by the nonchalance with which he handled so deadly a weapon.

After a while Karmytoff went to the Russian barracks in another part of the camp. There he told our coprisoners about himself, about their victorious army and about the new life that was beginning. That was an unforgettable experience: a flood of Slavic, Lieutenant Durakov translating, and, believe it or not, "Cocktails for Two" backgrounding it all over the barracks radio.

Explained Karmytoff: "No opposition for six days and nights. ... We crossed the Oder River south of Stettin. Many of our tanks were lost but we encircled the city and it surrendered. Then we headed west, and fast. The Germans kept ahead of us and there was no real opposition. Those who opposed us were wiped out."

That was the first contact. Karmytoff, finally worn out, bedded down on the floor. "Rather the floor than a Fascist bed," he said. The BBC announced Hitler was dead and his nation dying. Long-exiled kriegies heard the "Hit Parade" direct from New York. The excitement was overwhelming, exhausting.

During the night, eight Frenchmen were stretchered into our hospital from a nearby concentration camp. They were starved, dying. But good food and attention from the hard-working medics (captured at Dunkirk, Cassino and in the Ardennes) started them back to life. They whispered a real horror story of starvation and mistreatment.

At five o'clock on the morning of May 2, a party of three—led by Lieutenant Westerfield from New Orleans, Louisiana—drove out of the camp to a crossroads south of Barth to prepare for a formal junction of the East–West allies on the Baltic coast. With them went this reporter, one camera, one pad and one pencil.

Halfway through sleepy Barth, we passed another civilian car going in the opposite direction. We stopped, swung around and raced back after the vehicle. It was as we had thought, a Soviet reconnaissance. Chief of the four-man party was another Russian first lieutenant, tough, all soldier; even Hollywood could not have reproduced him. A huge-handled revolver jutted from his tank jacket, a furred hat covered his head, under which was a stern, tanned face—that symbolizing the conquering nation he represented. We were allies, and the exuberant greetings were repeated.

A barking dog interrupted the parley. The Russian lieutenant nonchalantly shot it. A car drove toward us from Barth. With equal nonchalance he stepped into the road, held up his hand and requisitioned it. The two German occupants walked back into Barth, happy to be alive.

Thus, in a three-car convoy, we drove south to the nearest Soviet headquarters. A handsome, female Russian MP—leisurely handling a sizable machine gun—motioned us to a car park and we entered a farmhouse where the division's officers were quartered. A magnificently attired Soviet major met us and returned in the car to camp.

There, Colonel Zemke and his chief of staff, RAF Group Captain Weir, joined the party and we returned to the major's headquarters for a champagne-vodka-fried-eggs breakfast. After twenty minutes of toasting, few remained sober—and those few were the humble, obsequious Germans who acted as waiters.

It was an emotion-stunning panorama. There was accordion music by a Leningrad commissar whose confusing chords became the more exotic after each vodka toast. In the kitchen, a German woman was trying to open cans of Spam—our contribution to the party—while her dirty-faced children hid frightened, in an unused corner of the room. Nearby, a bronzed Russian infantryman was shaving and incoherently cursing the kitchen's broken mirror. Another polished his officer's boots with window curtains which he had torn down. In a bedroom, the officer was preparing to join the party, dressing himself in embroidered shirts and copiously spraying himself with a prurient perfume.

Outside, Cossack cavalrymen were stabling their mounts after a night patrol. Mongolian infantrymen were deploying across a planted field to eliminate a handful of fanatic SS-men hiding in a wood. One soldier was chasing chickens in a farmyard to obtain a breakfast. An occasional tank rumbled past—westward where there was still fighting. Horse- and oxen-drawn wagons rattled along, loaded down with crates, bundles and women. Caucasian, Siberian and Ukrainian soldiers—representing every color and every ethnic group—marched westward in long, loose columns by the side of the road.

A Russian orderly came outside where I had gone to breathe fresh air. He spoke French. "My officer told me to give you this bread toaster as a souvenir and a gift," he said, handing me a cheap German camera. "Thanks," I replied, and added undiplomatically, "but it's not a toaster."

"I know," answered the soldier. "But my officer says it is a toaster. So it is a toaster."

Back in the farmhouse dining room, the toasts were continuing ad infinitum and ad prostration: toasts to Roosevelt, Stalin, Churchill and Truman; then all of them over again. "The men in my command are all wearing black armbands for the death of your great leader," said one Russian colonel. "And I would like your men to exhibit the same mourning." (That day a furious search was conducted in Stalag to find remnants of black cloth so that we might wear a more apparent mourning.)

Then back to the camp and to the hard work of bulldozing some order into the chaotic maelstrom which everywhere surrounded us. Until forty-eight hours ago, we had been kriegies, waiting passively, patiently for the end of our exile.

Now, in an overwhelming metamorphosis, we had a grandstand seat at the death of a nation. Now we were masters, we and the Russians. A Soviet colonel had said to us: "Germany is ours and we share it with you. ..."

But all we wanted was orderliness and a quick evacuation. New York radio, swing music and the fresh, crisp-voiced newscaster from home had been the stimulants. Now we wanted to leave this continent gone mad. The Russians, however, had different ideas.

We were well dressed, we exhibited a good discipline, we had impressed them—now they wanted to fete us. The complication in this was that the Russians had just won the most terrible war in their history and they were bewildered and overwrought with their total victory.

One young soldier marched through the gates of our camp, gesticulating with two enormous Luger revolvers. "Tear down the fences. Go home. You're free!" he shouted to all present, shooting off his guns in the air. The prisoners did not understand the words, but the suggestion was clear. Within ten minutes much of the barbed-wire fencing was lying strewn on the ground. There then followed a mass exodus from the camp. "We'll court-martial every one of them for desertion," fumed Wing X martinets.

"You go to hell. We're going home," answered the kriegies.

Rape, looting, orgying—these were the order of the day. And some of the liberated prisoners were not immune from the fever. The Russians arid the freed slave laborers set the pace with their drinking and debauching. The next morning a score of German women were found dead, strangled or shot, within a three-mile radius of the camp. Plundered watches, cameras and jewelry appeared everywhere.

Germany had lost a war which the madness of her leaders and the enthusiastic consent of her people had begun. Now she was beginning to pay the terrible, unprecedented price.

Special groups of Russian soldiers were detached to collect and to drive herds of cows, pigs, sheep and horses eastward. Everything with wheels rolled back toward Russia, laden with linen, cutlery and every other transportable household utensil. One Russian colonel, who had partied with Wing X the night before, redirected a herd of a hundred and fifty milk cows into the camp. These were slaughtered by the best means available: machine gunning and clubbing. Kriegies that night enjoyed steak and schnapps for dinner.

The next day, a herd of sixty fattened pigs were driven into the camp, but our doctors advised against their consumption. That morning, thirty women who had been inmates at a nearby concentration camp were touted out of prisoners' rooms and the doctors had another headache.

Another group of fliers found the stores of Red Cross toilet paper. They threw hundreds of rolls high into the trees of a nearby pine forest and the wind swept them around the branches in a wild, Bunyan-scale Christmas scene.

Others seized horses and carriages, rigging them like old Roman chariots and drove, shooting revolvers off in the air, through the streets in mad chases. Still others saddled German farm horses and held steeplechases across the fields. Months of barbed wire had produced inhibitions; now there were no restrictions and the aphorism was changed to "all's fair in victory."

Many were too overcome with the emotion of liberation, however, to indulge in such riotous celebration. These men went on swimming and boating parties on the Baltic, walked around the camp or just sunbathed, purposely oblivious to the chaos outside.

The vast majority of Stalag I prisoners remained good soldiers, following Wing X orders and patiently awaiting evacuation. They continued a routine prison existence, enjoying only an extra issue of Red Cross food and occasional bottles of liquor brought in by the friendly Russians.

Their attitude was typified by Lieutenant Edward L. James, from Warsaw, Illinois, who—with a crew of sergeants—set up a mess for the busy camp leaders and for a week ignored the turmoil, preparing three fine meals a day for more than a hundred officers. Other airmen were in charge of the motor pool, which sought to keep our fifty vehicles in good condition and operative so there might be a constant liaison with the Russian headquarters. Still others operated the water supply, guarded the food stores and policed the camp. Stalag Luft I remained a quiet, sane enclave in the midst of the extreme and indescribable confusion everywhere outside.

Several of our doctors drove to the concentration camp just south of Barth and set to work to clean up its diseased squalor. I accompanied them and witnessed for the first time the horrible aftermath of one of history's most terrible crimes. The camp was not a large one; it had contained fourteen to fifteen hundred political prisoners, chiefly Germans, with a scattering of men and women from every country in Europe.

Its inmates had been imprisoned there for every possible crime: desertion from the army, listening to foreign broadcasts, black-market offenses, espionage, sabotage. Three hundred of the prisoners had committed the sole crime of being born Jews. Some had lived there, and in other camps before being transferred there, for as long as ten years.

The area was entirely surrounded by electrified wire and ringed by guard towers and searchlights. Until a few weeks previously, it had been run as a business operation: slave manpower for the Reich. It had been clean, orderly, and had supplied an important labor pool for that section of Pomerania. But as Germany's eastern defenses crumbled, the camp's SS guards had deserted it and fled westward, leaving the prisoners to starve and to die.

Nearly three hundred had subsequently perished, a small number in comparison with the stupendous death toll in the larger horror camps at Buchenwald, Belsen and Dachau, but the sights here were a small-scale facsimile of the most frightful corollary to Hitler's New Order.

Excretion, garbage, tattered clothing and refuse littered the camp. Dead bodies, many of them in grotesque positions, were scattered through the brick barracks. In many of the rooms, the fetid odor of death and disease was so strong that we could not enter. Men dead for five hours and others dead for five days hung from their tiered bunks, their arms outstretched stiffly, their faces twisted in agonized predeath pain, their spider-like bodies recording slow starvation. Above and below them were skeletons still alive, but dying as the minutes went by.

Here were scenes that no camera could picture. The cries of the living; the otiose, retching odor of filth and disease; the stupefying, unbelievable horror of the place—this was no subject for photography or words, but one for bitter personal experience. We heard of the beatings, the tortures and the crematoriums which were a part of the camp. We were told by still living prisoners of Nazi surgical experiments on prisoners of both sexes—stories that transcend the imagination's capacity to visualize.

We heard of children being born in the barracks, of "kangaroo courts" set up among the prisoners themselves, of sadistic SS women who surpassed the male guards in cruelty.

We walked into one room which contained nine dead bodies and one man who was still alive, propped up on the floor against a wall. He was crying, weakly, piteously. "You're all right now. You'll be free. The war is over," a doctor called out reassuringly to him.

"They came and hit me," he wailed plaintively. "The Russians and the others—they beat me because I am a German. And I have been here nine years." He died within an hour, still propped up against the wall.

Diseases varied from typhus, ulcer and dysentery to inanition and diarrhea. The camp was a terrible danger for the entire region because some of the prisoners had escaped after their guards departed and were loose in the neighborhood, looting and raping, spreading their diseases wholesale. Our doctors isolated the whole camp, commandeered burial parties from among local Germans and tried their very best to clean the filth.

A French doctor, Lieutenant Jean Fraisse from Paris, a fine-looking young Frenchman who could easily have been celebrating the great victory in Paris, was already there with a crew of fifty-five Frenchmen who were working hard to establish some order in the camp. Fraisse, wearing a pistol in his belt, driving a Red Army jeep and accompanied by a Russian interpreter, had been working twenty hours a day when we arrived.

"You've been prisoners for five years. Why don't you go home now that it's finished. Don't you want to see Paris again?" I asked one of his assistants.

"Yes, we're impatient to go home," answered one. "But first there is work to be done here." We who heard that answer, and who realized it represented all the Frenchmen there felt suddenly a profound respect for those wonderful men. It was revivifying amidst all this death and horror, to know that there was still a clear sense of moral duty left in Europe.

The Germans who dug mass graves for the dead were initially uncertain whether the trenches were for themselves or the prisoners. No lime could be found, so sacks of potassium from a nearby factory were dumped in on top of the bodies. "We heard about these things on the radio from London," said one German. "But we thought it was just some more of your Allied propaganda."

"You can see now that it's not," answered one grim-faced Frenchman. "Keep digging, and fast."

I went into another room with a tough-looking Russian lieutenant who had fought at Moscow and Stalingrad. We saw bodies lying athwart one another, stiff and malodorous. I choked at the terrible air and turned to say something to the Russian. I noticed he had left.

He was outside, leaning against the barracks, retching.

CHAPTER 19

Flight to Civilization

After one exhausting week with our Soviet allies, nine thousand kriegies became painfully conscious of an almost permanent hangover and of an increasingly fervent desire to go home. It was not just the vodka and champagne, although there was plenty of both; it was the whole setup which transcended understanding and control. Too many different things were happening at the same time.

Once a Russian private wandered into our motor pool and demanded the best-looking vehicle, one which had taken three days to repair. The airmen mechanics were seriously unhappy, but the private flourished two large pistols and the car was his. As he prepared to embark, a Russian major walked past. Through an interpreter, the motor-pool chief protested that we needed the car badly. The major understood immediately and ordered his soldier to leave the car and evacuate the camp.

"If my men give you any trouble, just shoot them," he advised calmly as he walked off in search of a party.

On another occasion, two Russian colonels drove into the camp, reported that their men needed trousers and asked to be shown our stocks. They examined the khaki trousers, shaking their heads dolefully. "Whatever are these?" asked one of the colonels, Pointing to the creases. When told that trouser creases were normal with Anglo-Americans, he shook his head again. "Sorry" he said. "Good cloth. But we must have red stripes down the side, not creases."

A crew of airmen took over Barth's printing presses and set to work to produce a single-edition newspaper which would serve as a souvenir for the kriegies. They left the camp with a handful of copy, extravagant ideas of make-up and layout and the good wishes of both Russian and American authorities. The name of the paper was to be "Barth Free Press." Two days later, it was produced after back-breaking work and heart-breaking complications.

Freed slave workers had smashed up the linotype machines and thrown the typewriters out of second-story windows. The paper had to be set up by hand and, although it was a workmanlike job, it was entitled "Barth Hard Times" when produced.

Two peripatetic airmen wandered off a few miles from the camp and encountered a Russian woman doctor who worked in a field hospital. One of the fliers sought to expand on the theme of interallied relations with their new-found friend. The other airman helped him home with a black eye and sprained back.

By the third day of our liberation—when the Russian private had ordered the barbed wire torn down—nearly three hundred kriegies had disappeared into the roads heading homeward. Some rode bicycles, others requisitioned horses and carriages, others introduced the American highway technique of hitchhiking to the Russian supply columns. One group got an engine working and steamed off toward Rostock on the railroad. Yet another group seized a forty-foot sailboat and set a course due north—toward Sweden.

Three men decided they did not want to go home yet, that they wanted to see more of Europe. They drove off in a car toward the east—into Poland and Russia. Two others narrowly escaped being shot when they tried unsuccessfully to steal a Russian tank to drive down to Berlin. Several others forgot all about the war, the victory, and the opportunity of going home. They went out into the countryside, found sympathetic farmers' wives and settled down to good food and a long rest.

Once, a German woman telephoned the camp and excitedly complained that an airman was trying to violate her. A colonel and a major went down to Barth from the camp to straighten out the matter. When they arrived at the woman's home, they found the telephone operator had misunderstood her: she *wanted* an American flier in the house so the Russians would not molest her! A number of fliers, it was learned later, unofficially filled that role, receiving in return a plentiful supply of food and drink and a soft bed.

Eventually, as some order was being restored, a system of passes was set up whereby ten per cent of our camp strength was allowed in Barth each day. Unfortunately, as one interpreter explained it, "Even Joe Stalin's signature on a pass wouldn't do any good these days."

Most frequently, the Americans were well treated by their Russian allies. A few incidents were reported where friction had come about and the ex-prisoners had returned to camp to be patched up.

A hint of Soviet occupation policy toward the Germans was contained in a speech-making rally held in Barth before our departure. There was that day a plan laid before the people of one zone in Pomerania, nearly a hundred miles behind the Soviet demarcation line, and it may well have been a small-scale outline of what was contemplated for all of Germany occupied by the Red Army.

A crowd of nearly ten thousand gathered in the main square, anxiously, nervously waiting to hear from the Soviet zone commander and the "Free Germany" leaders what was planned for their future. The bulk of the crowd was composed of refugees from East Prussia and eastern Pomerania, swept westward by the tidal wave of Soviet advance.

Several speeches were made in Russian and the translations were carried out by Lieutenant Henry S. Levine, a Fortress navigator from Syracuse, New York.

The first speech was made by the new Communist *Bürgermeister* of Barth, Lemke by name, who appealed to the people for co-operation with the new administration. "Return to your work," he urged. "The disgrace of Nazism has finally been removed and a free nation will arise if everyone does his duty." He concluded with the promise that all Germans herded into labor detachments would soon be returned to their families.

Next to speak was Colonel Zhovenik, a thrice-wounded veteran of the Moscow and Stalingrad battles who was the zone commander. "We did not expect the Nazi attack in 1941," he said. "But the whole population of Russia arose to defend its homeland, and finally halted the Germans at Stalingrad. ...

"Nazi propagandists have said that the Russians want to destroy the German people. That is not true. We have orders from our leader, Stalin, to preserve your culture. But we have sworn to hunt down and to annihilate the militarists who began this terrible war.

"The German people, as a people and as a nation, will live but Nazism will be eliminated. The war is ended now and there shall be no more destruction of human life. Germany may now in its own land enforce order as its people wish. You may have the political parties you wish. Germany will arise again as a free country, working closely with our great Soviet Russia."

He then enumerated the martial-law regulations: no weapons in the hands of any Germans, a curfew between eleven o'clock at night and five o'clock in the morning. No troops would be billeted in homes without their commanders' permission. Young women must be kept in during the night. "German girls have been calling to Russian soldiers from upstairs windows, inviting them to visit them, and later they have complained of the consequences. You must see to it yourselves that this does not continue."

After several more speeches, including one by a blind old man from East Prussia, Zhovenik again mounted the platform and added, "A new Germany and a new Europe are being reborn. We must work together to cure our mutual ills and repair our mutual hurts. We are going to be your leaders. We are going to replace the Nazis. We promise you fairness and an opportunity for the little men and women to get the place they deserve in society."

Lieutenant John Burke, Staff Sergeant William Medill, a former newspaperman from Marlboro, Massachusetts, Flight Lieutenant Ian Bolton and I decided that to await official evacuation was decidedly the slower of two exits from Germany. We obtained a small, two-cylinder car from the motor pool, loaded it down with our personal possessions, Red Cross parcels, and glued a paper on the windshield, announcing in Russian: "Press—Pass Freely."

We drove out of the camp, along a dirt road toward Barth. As we entered the town we decided it might be best to have a senior officer's signature on a sheet of paper which would facilitate our departure.

We drove to the Soviet headquarters and requested an interview with the commander. The Soviet captain who took the message into the requisitioned house accomplished more than we anticipated or desired.

"Interview with the general?" he returned to ask. "It's all fix. Come this way."

The next four hours were spent with a colorful, highly articulate character who became known to us as General Borrisov, second in command of the Second White Russian Army. Hero of the Soviet Union and many times wounded veteran of every major battle fought on the East Front between 1941 and 1945, Borrisov was a gracious host. His stock of vodka and champagne was inexhaustible and his prolix of highly personalized war stories resulted in a tongue-wearing job for translator Flight Lieutenant deLage of the RAF.

We sat around a table laden with plates of *hors d'oeuvres*, varying from delicately sliced Spam to bowls of gleaming caviar. Also present was Lieutenant Colonel Mark E. Hubbard, fighter-ace from St. Paul, Minnesota, who was the camp's liaison officer with the Russians, and several British officers stationed in the town as his assistants.

Stern, swarthy, bulky Borrisov was a former commander of a Soviet Guards Division, that nation's finest infantry unit. At forty-three he had spent twenty-one years in military service and he regarded fighting as the highest possible earthly profession. His teeth were platinum to replace the original set lost at Stalingrad by artillery shrapnel. His body was marred and scarred with nine distinct wounds and Borrisov raised his shirt and lowered his trousers to show each of them to us.

He was an eloquent speaker, making full use of his arms and available cutlery to describe his battle tactics, and the interview was punctuated with frequent toasts. After the first two hours, Borrisov's remarks became less and less coherent, and my pencil found difficulty in staying on the page, because each toast meant draining a tumbler full of vodka or champagne.

Most important of the battles in which he had participated had been those of Kiev, Stalingrad, Danzig and Stettin, each of them milestones in the bitter three-year struggle which had cost Russia nearly five million dead. "Now," he said, raising his glass in another toast, "we have together

beaten the Fascist wolves and together we shall rebuild a better world."
We drank to the better world, deLage translated the toast and I scribbled
the words in a Red Cross POW notebook.

"I was a divisional commander at Kiev in June, 1941," began Borrisov.
"'We were encircled twice and each time broke out to fight our way
back to the east. We fought terrible rear-guard actions all the way to
Stalingrad where I was deafened in my right ear, lost all my teeth and
was wounded in the left thigh.

"That was the turning point of the war. My divisions remained on
the west bank of the river and defended the factory area in desperate,
close-quarter fighting. Since that time, long ago, we have driven forward,
encircling and annihilating the Fascist hordes." We drank another toast.

"I and my army pushed forward across the Volga, Dniester, Berizina
and Vistula Rivers to Stettin and the Oder. There we fought one of
the hardest battles of the war. For the Nazis, it was a last stand and they
fought furiously.

"Our soldiers had to fight waist-deep in muddy marshes. A frontal
assault was impossible, so we brought up machine-operated saws and
cut down the woods. We constructed hundreds of boats and rafts, and
my units crossed the river south of Stettin in a mighty flood. Many of
our tanks were drowned by artillery fire until pontoon bridges could be
built, but we pushed around the city and forced it to surrender.

"In the following six days and nights we drove westward through
Pomerania without opposition except for a few SS-men who knew they
would be killed anyway. Some of them escaped to Rugen Island (off
the Baltic coast) and if they do not surrender, I will order the assault of
the island.

"You Americans will be able to help me. I will have all the boats
collected together, and you—as expert mechanics—will operate them
in the assault." We all nodded vigorously, wondering what in the world
was going to happen to us next. (Fortunately, the SS-men on Rugen
capitulated the next morning and the assault was unnecessary.)

"Yes, we have used great quantities of American equipment, particularly
transport. As we advanced, we had to widen the German railroads to fit
our trains and this slowed us up many times, so your trucks have been most

valuable. We prefer our own tanks, however, because yours are too high and they tip over too easily. Ours are the T-14 and the Klim Voroshilov; they are the best in the world. And our Katusha, 132-millimeter artillery is also, we believe, the best in the world.

"I have seen cities struck by your air forces and I know of your effectiveness. We are grateful for the work of your bombers. However, we prefer direct tactical support. We use Stormoviks, Aircobras and Yaks to clear the roads ahead of our troops."

All of these remarks were interspersed with flowery toasts. We drank to the T-34 and the Klim Voroshilov. The Katusha and the Allied Air Forces were also adequately toasted. By this time, the general had found a German camera which had come somehow into his possession. He passed it to me and asked to have his picture taken for the newspapers. I noticed that the camera was empty, but felt at that moment that it was not feasible to remind the general of this.

From the bed, the table top and the window sill, I snapped several candid shots—remembering with a dull feeling that there was no film in the box—of the general and his medals. Lieutenant Burke took notes as he continued to talk.

"At Stalingrad, the Germans killed little Russian children and drained their veins to provide blood for their wounded. They are cursed barbarians. When we first crossed onto German soil last winter, I told my soldiers, 'You have fought valiantly to save our homeland. Now we are invading the enemy's country. Germany is yours. Take what you wish.'"

(Following this there is a note: "A German in the hand is worth two in the bush," but neither Burke nor I remember whether it was the general or the vodka which prompted the statement.)

The general also had several diplomatic remarks to make of his chief, Marshal Konstantin K. Rokkasovsky, who commanded the Second White Russian Army. Borrisov, with all the enthusiasm of a fraternity brother, recommended his army and his chief as the best in the world.

After drinking to Marshal Rokkasovsky and watching the general kill imaginary Nazis with a German dress dagger which he had acquired, we realized that it was getting too late to leave that day and settled down to some hard drinking and long listening.

Despite all his exhibitionism and his acrobatics, Borrisov was clearly no fool. His dark squirrel eyes gleamed like the caviar, and the lines in his face proved his battles had not been fought on paper alone. His praise of the United States rang true—although he evidenced no great love for the British—and he seemed genuinely to approve of an enduring friendship.

Before we left, the general offered one more toast: "Barbarism must never again be permitted in the world. We have met in a great historic victory and we must always remain friends for the permanent peace of the world."

It would be wrong to attempt an analysis of the Russians we met during those seven wild days on the Baltic or to impart any too deep meaning to the scenes we witnessed while with them. Conditions were fantastically abnormal. The Red Army had just won the greatest victory in its history, and its soldiers were celebrating fully and without apparent restraint.

The Russians in Pomerania were certainly not inhibited by any policy of non-fraternization. Germany was truly theirs and they took what they wanted. There was an element of naiveté about them, a lack of sophistication and formality. If they liked you, and they did deeply like the Americans, they made sure you knew about it. If you were their enemy you did as you were told and kept out of the way.

Some Americans who celebrated with the Russians were guilty of hypocrisy, of feeling and behaving superior to these wild men from the east. There was sometimes too much back-slapping and wordy friendliness, after which the American would announce to a fellow, "These goddamn people are savages." Many of the Soviet soldiers were from the far corners of eastern Russia and their knowledge of European ways was limited to what they had picked up during the precious three months.

They had, however, an undeniable singleness of purpose. Their seeming lack of discipline and dignity was unimportant because they knew why they were fighting and so could dispense with parade-square formalities. Officers and men mixed freely together, I never saw a soldier salute an officer and only once saw a private standing at attention before his superior. But with their haphazard, apparently confused methods, they accomplished much. Eastern Pomerania was returning to order within a week of its conquest.

During seven days I saw not one example of army paper work. Soviet orders seemed all to be verbal, excepting those of policy from Moscow to Zone commanders.

Their energy and their enthusiasm were phenomenal. Their numbers were overwhelming. It seemed not so much an invasion as an immigration; it was difficult to believe that this horde of an army would ever be able to reassemble and move off again. Yet it had come from Stalingrad and its military prowess was irrefragable.

One inescapable impression was that these Russians were like the Americans of a hundred years ago, that the energy and vigor which had carried the United States to such great heights were now discovered to at least the same degree in another people. We should have to look to our laurels to compete with a nation of this physical caliber.

On May 10, nearly nine thousand liberated prisoners were evacuated by air in a division of Eighth Air Force B-17s. They were flown from the airfield at Barth to a vast tent city at St. Valerie, near Le Havre. There, gradually—as army red tape unraveled—they were shipped home to sixty-day furloughs which terminated just as the Pacific war was ending, and Stalag I's kriegies went back to the life of civilians.

On May 7, we embarked, without the Soviet pass, on a four-hundred-mile drive through the Russian, British and American lines toward our version of civilization. The trip was an effective antidote to lethargy nursed during long months in a prison camp. But it was stimulating to such a degree that a coherent report on observations is even now a difficult task.

Complete, indescribable chaos existed everywhere, along the roads, in the fields and the villages. Every European nationality was represented among the hordes of refugees who packed the highways in every type of transport and going in every direction. Hay ricks, fiacres, bicycles, carts and wheelbarrows were included in the vehicles. Crowds of walking refugees lined the fields and side roads. Milling masses of Russian soldiers and German prisoners dogged every junction.

Wildly driven jeeps, covered in oriental plush and tapestry, rushed Soviet officers through the traffic to their assignments. Efficient woman-MPs stood at the crossroads, trying to bring order to the flood tide of humanity. There was the sight of lend-lease trucks, speeding with supplies, and the sight of convoys of dog-drawn wagons which carried the knapsacks of Soviet infantrymen.

We passed burned-down forests, packed with half-melted German vehicles. Guns, machines and supplies littered the countryside. I had seen the wreckage of an army's defeat in France of 1940. This was not like that. This was a thousand times worse. We passed railroads where smashed armored trains still stood, their useless, shattered guns pointing like twisted fingers into the sky.

There were dead, nude bodies lying in ditches side by side with the bloated, decaying carcasses of horses and cows. The split barrels of German 88-millimeter guns jutted from behind hedgerows. Overturned tanks, cars and supply wagons littered the road's shoulder. Thousands of broken rifles, miles of camera film, boots, uniforms, helmets, medical supplies, smashed motorcycles, tin cans and reams of paper were scattered everywhere—this was the residue of a destroyed Wehrmacht and a vanquished nation.

The occasional crack of rifles, the stutter of machine guns, the screech of jeeps and trucks, and the rumbling and rattling of refugee wagons combined with cheers, songs and cries in a dozen languages to make a weird cacophony—a discordant theme for liberated, almost lawless Europe.

Our roundabout trip brought us to a road barrier at Wismar where Russian and British forces had met. There, I waved my red War Office License for Correspondents, and Bolton shouted something in Russian from the back seat. The Soviet major who guarded the gate ordered it raised and we passed through to a new world.

Neat British soldiers of the Sixth Airborne Division, shoes and rifle straps polished, faces clean and shoulders erect, patrolled the streets in pairs. Army vehicles were parked along the curbs. There was little evidence of damage. The city was quiet and there were almost no refugees on the streets. Looting here was on a more dignified, less individual basis.

We spent the night with headquarters' officers of the division, told them our story and drank their whisky ration. They offered us delousing powder and a bath, both of which we seriously needed. The next morning we pushed on in our two-cylinder car which, loaded down as it was, frequently stalled against a strong head wind.

Near Schwerin, we met the Eighteenth American Airborne Corps and traded our car for a truck ride to Hildesheim and Ninth Army Headquarters. Everywhere we were impressed by the quantities of motorized equipment and the comparative orderliness of occupation. The war was not yet officially ended, but whole German armies were surrendering along the roads to American lieutenants, and the end was at hand. We saw ice cream, soft drinks, Armed Forces editions of American magazines, clean, attractive American nurses and Red Cross workers—the transition was almost overwhelming.

I had last seen the American army in action in Tunisia, two and a half years previously. The difference between our neophyte battalions in Africa and our victorious armies along the Elbe was a throat-catching sensation. I witnessed there what our nation is capable of, what a magnificent, powerfully equipped force America had created in thirty months.

At Hildesheim—which had been wiped out by a twenty-minute air bombardment—we traded the truck for a plane ride to Münster. There we caught another plane to Magdeburg, zig-zagging across Germany to follow the traffic stream. Finally, we caught a plane to Le Havre in France. During that flight, we flew at low level across much of Germany, witnessing the smashed forests, the pockmarked fields, the jigsaw pattern of trenches and cists of bomb craters, the bombed cities and the tangled railroad yards—the route where our armies had battered their way into Germany. It seemed as if a holocaust had struck the country.

From Le Havre we flew to Paris, skimming the thatched roofs of Norman cottages and shadowing the lush fields of a region already beginning to forget the war and to produce for peace. We landed at Le Bourget airfield in Paris and jeeped to the Press Camp, the Hotel Scribe in the center of the city.

It was V-E night and we watched and were swept along with the bacchanal rejoicing. The capital of France was intoxicated that night with victory. The streets were flooded with millions of celebrants, civilians and soldiers of every nationality.

Flares and searchlights spangled the sky. Firecrackers, guns and whistles were drowned by the greater roar of jubilant crowds. Thousands danced in the streets. The Arc de Triomphe was floodlit. We went into a café where the band played the United Nations' national anthems over and over.

One old Frenchman, who had seen the defeat of 1871 and the seeming victory of 1918, was sobbing and laughing at the same time. "It doesn't matter what comes next," he said. "It's over at last, finished. There is peace again."

A few days later, I flew in an ocean-spanning C-54 Skymaster from Paris—via Scotland, Iceland and Newfoundland—to La Guardia airfield in New York. I came home for a vacation, and to see my second son for the first time.